The Complete Guide to Embroidery Stitches and Crewel

Jo Bucher

CHL CREATIVE HOME LIBRARY
In Association with Better Homes and Gardens
MEREDITH CORPORATION

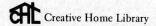 Creative Home Library

© 1971 by Meredith Corporation, Des Moines, Iowa
SBN 696-16500-7 Library of Congress Number 76-145622
All rights reserved
Printed in the United States of America

CONTENTS

ACKNOWLEDGMENTS

I should like to express my gratitude to Peg Campbell for the generous use of her extensive needlework library and for her encouragement. My thanks to Dorothy Davis, Mildred Davis, Mary Fry, and Nancy Rickert for the loan of their original works to help illustrate the various types of stitchery. And to those gals who took charge of my store so I could write the book, I shall always be grateful.

J.B.

DESIGN CREDITS

COVER: *Jo Bucher.*

PLATE 1: *Mildred Davis*—valence, lamp shade, boxes, book covers; *Jo Bucher*—picture in frame.

PLATE 2: *Nancy Rickert*—u.l. and l.l.; *Jo Bucher*—u.r.; *Dorothy Davis*—l.r.

PLATE 3: *Mary Fry.*

PLATE 4: *Mary Fry.*

PLATE 5: *Mary Fry.*

PLATE 6: *Dorothy Davis.*

PLATE 7: *Jo Bucher.*

PLATE 8: *Jo Bucher*—peace-symbol pillow; *Mildred Davis*—pillow and flat pocketbooks; *Nancy Rickert*—satin pocketbook; *Jo Bucher* and *Nancy Rickert*—doorstop.

ABOUT THE AUTHOR

Jo Bucher has been involved with needlecraft for many years. After receiving her certificate from the Embroiderers' Guild in New York City, she taught embroidery and crewel to adults in evening courses. Today Mrs. Bucher lectures to women's groups, but spends most of her time teaching classes in her own needlecraft shop, Stitch Witchery, in Denville, New Jersey. Mrs. Bucher has exhibited in national and international needlework shows, and has done a great deal of custom designing. She has drawn all the illustrations for *The Complete Guide to Embroidery Stitches and Crewel.*

Foreword

The pleasure of creating with one's own hands is being rediscovered in almost all the arts and crafts. The art of surface stitchery (crewel, free, or creative embroidery) is enjoying a renaissance unequaled since the advent of the machine age. Not only is it employed more and more widely in home crafts, but it has become a true art form, finding its way into the creation of well-known artists, interior decorators, and dress designers.

Many beautiful needlework projects have been created with only a few or even one stitch. However, as with speaking and writing, the larger the vocabulary, the greater the ease of expression.

An English teacher once told me, "Use a word three times, and it is yours." The same rule could be applied to stitches. Start with a few basic stitches, foundations for the more complicated ones that follow, and build a vocabulary, a repertoire of stitches, from which to choose for expression.

In modern needlework, as in all art forms today, many liberties are taken with traditional methods. It is necessary, however, to master the basic technique before embarking on variations for your masterpiece. The clown who falls off the horse at the circus becomes an expert horseman long before he attempts his first tumble.

The Cross Stitch and Lazy Daisy embroidery of my youth held no appeal for me, so I stuck to dressmaking, tailoring, knitting, and crocheting. It wasn't until my family was grown that I bought a crewel kit. Needless to say, in those days, the design and materials left a lot to be desired, but the stitch diagrams indicated that there was more to stitchery than I had thought. Following up, I found that an American branch of the Embroiderer's Guild of London had recently been established in New York and that instruction was available. I enrolled in a six weeks' course, and before it was half over, I was hooked. During the next few years, I made weekly trips to New York for instruction in many kinds of embroidery and design, and took a couple of summer sessions in Nantucket with British teachers.

Two things frustrated me during this period. To obtain threads and materials, I had to travel to Westchester County, New York, from my home in New Jersey, a tedious journey, or get them by mail order, which meant that I often could not see what I was getting. The second problem was books! I purchased every available book on the subject of surface stitchery, and even sent to England for more. I needed a book that included all embroidery stitches completely diagrammed and diagrammed well, as well as helpful hints for making my finished projects look professional. But none of the existing books contained the whole vocabulary of surface stitchery. The British books were best, but these assumed I had been embroidering for years (and rightfully so, because in England embroidery is taught in the schools). The American books were enjoyable, and each one explained *some* stitches, but even with a library that took up one entire wall of a room, I still did not own one adequate book.

I began volunteer teaching at a rehabilitation center near my home and found I loved teaching embroidery. There were other people in the area who wanted instruction, too, which led to my taking the Embroidery Guild Teacher's Examination.

There was still the problem of supplies and books. As my family was grown and away at college, I took over a room in my house and stocked up on some basic supplies (linen, Appleton crewel thread, needles, and hoops), but still had the book problem.

Here my engineering background came in handy. I designed a sampler as a teaching aid, then drew up some simple diagrams and wrote a bit of text for the students to use. These included thirty-five stitches and were merely a supplement to what was taught in the classes.

The needlework explosion had taken hold by then, and I was receiving all kinds of requests: lectures for women's groups, more classes including adult school, and one from my husband to relocate the supplies, which were rapidly taking over our home.

While hunting a place to set up shop, I found that the adult-school class I was going to teach was a good deal larger than the size I maintained in my own classes. I needed a good teaching text more than ever. I redid the booklet that I had been using in more detail, but it still wasn't the answer for those—and their numbers were growing—who wanted to continue on their own and didn't want to make a collection of books.

I opened Stitch Witchery, my retail shop and studio for classes. My aim was to stock everything the needlewoman would need for any kind of handwork, and I've nearly accomplished this ambition. The exception is, again, the books.

At last I decided I had to write my own, and the present volume is the result. I have chosen to cover surface embroidery rather than canvas, because, although public interest in the two is almost equal, surface stitchery covers more types of embroidery and stitches.

Besides the complete dictionary of surface stitches, I have tried to give the reader all the hints, basic steps, and supplies needed for pursuing this art. It is my sincere hope that students and teachers will consider this book as one of their basic tools, along with their threads, needles, and scissors, to be kept in their needlework bags.

The recent needlework explosion has brought, as might be expected, a deluge of commercial kits. Some of these items are inferior in both materials and design; the variety of stitches included is often limited, due to the lack of imagination or cost, and the designs are often trite. An unrewarding project could discourage a potential embroiderer. So, if you plan to buy a kit, be careful in your choice.

There seems to be at least one left-handed person in every class, and with young children even more. In most cases, the diagrams will make the needle-and-thread action clear when turned upside down. There are other times when the steps are reversed, usually in the line or border stitches. If reversing seems difficult, a hand mirror held upright next to the diagram will give a clear view. In any case, there will be a notation in the written description of each stitch directed to this long-neglected group, so that they too can experience the satisfaction that comes with mastering a stitch and discovering its possibilities.

The beginner should not be discouraged by the number of stitches. Start with the simple ones and build your vocabulary as you go. A number of fine books have been published in recent years, giving the history of embroidery, designing information, and a wealth of plates for inspiration. These should be used to the fullest, once you have mastered the basic stitch vocabulary.

It is my hope to bring this rich heritage of unfamiliar and foreign stitches to the potential or experienced embroiderer, and thus to stimulate interest and excitement in this splendid form of self-expression.

PLATE 1: Embroidery lends elegant, unusual touches to
many items for the home. A valance design can
be carried down edges of matching draperies.
White thread on white linen gives nice,
neutral look to lamp shade during day, looks
spectacular at night with light on. Covers are
easily embroidered for regular books,
phone books, and address books. Wooden boxes
covered with embroidery hold everything from
jewelry to matches. Pattern on
gold velvet frame consists of only
three stitches, was not pre-designed.

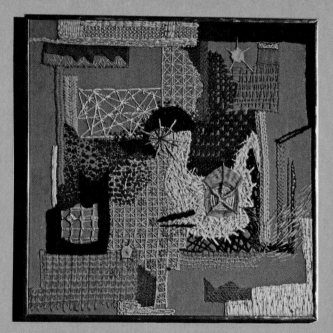

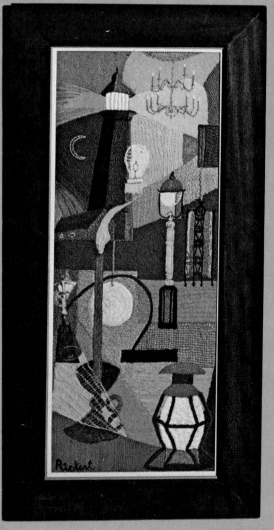

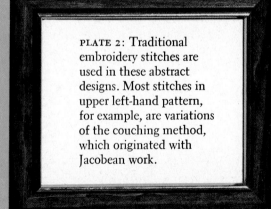

PLATE 2: Traditional embroidery stitches are used in these abstract designs. Most stitches in upper left-hand pattern, for example, are variations of the couching method, which originated with Jacobean work.

PLATE 3: In this grouping,
traditional stitches
and threads create
traditional floral designs.
All threads are wool;
the smaller pictures are
embroidered in crewel wool.
Each design could be
worked to blend with a
modern decor by changing
the kinds of stitches
and the colors of threads.

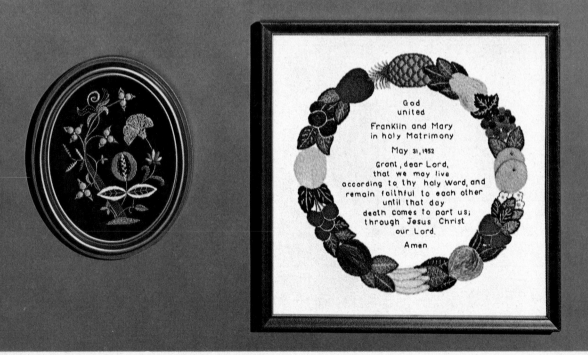

PLATE 4: Patriotic, sentimental, pretty—these
early American designs are a pleasure to stitch or own.
The eagle is entirely crewel wool. Marriage announcement
could also celebrate a birth. Flowers in oval frame show
effectiveness of working on velvet instead of linen.

Introduction

PARAPHERNALIA

Paraphernalia, an old-fashioned word found in some of the earlier stitchery books, is an apt description for the various equipment and supplies needed in embroidery. This book is basically a dictionary of the stitches for surface embroidery, with no effort being made to elaborate on color, design, and materials. However, I'm including some basic information on paraphernalia that will be of help to the uninitiated.

The best way to develop skill with paraphernalia, as well as with the stitches, is by using the time-tested sampler—not the painstaking Cross Stitch sampler of the nineteenth century, but the type worked earlier when the samplers were a true record of stitches and materials used. These samplers were so valued they were listed in wills.

New developments in both background fabrics and working threads give the needlewoman an almost limitless choice, but care must be taken in selecting suitable, effective materials.

If you are anxious to start experimenting with stitches, by all means do so with any material at hand, even string. For that permanent record, though, spend a little time choosing fabric, layout, and threads.

BACKGROUND MATERIALS

Which background fabric to choose is the first and most important decision you have to make, whether for a small sampler or a large room divider. The use to which the embroidered article is to be put should be the most important factor influencing your selection. For instance, burlap lends itself to wall hangings, and its texture and colors adapt to casual embroidery; but avoid burlap for anything that must take wear and tear—pillows, footstools, and pocketbooks, which require a tightly woven fabric like linen, linen twill, British satin, sailcloth, cotton twill (try mattress ticking), or certain synthetics. Fabrics for items which will need to be laundered should be test-washed before you begin.

The fabric should have a certain amount of body, but if you are

1

going to play with various threads, it shouldn't be too tightly woven. Looser weaves give the added advantage of a visible line to follow on linear stitches and make the actual working easier and faster. Linen is usually the most successful. It comes in a wide range of colors, so that the working threads can be all of one shade (even white), and in a variety of weights.

Most experienced needlewomen keep an extra piece of their fabric on hand, to play on as the work progresses. This enables them to test out how the selected stitch will look and to establish the "rhythm" for that particular stitch. This is an excellent habit to cultivate; mistakes can be avoided, thus eliminating unnecessary picking on the actual project, and in the long run your work will be speeded up.

Before you start on the project or on the practice piece, your fabric should be edged in some manner even if there is to be a hem of some type later. Unraveling threads can be a nuisance and will slow down your work if they get caught underneath in the working thread. You can machine-stitch the edges with zigzag or overcast by hand.

In laying out a sampler or design, be sure to leave an ample amount of material all around for blocking and mounting. I'll touch on design layout later, but for your sampler the design ought to be roughly outlined first on a piece of paper, because at this point you really don't have a visual picture of the stitches. In addition to line stitches, remember to include some areas that will allow for shapes. These need not be intricate—a simple leaf outline will do—and sometimes the stitch itself will suggest a design. Remember that you will seldom be working a straight line or square when in the process of embroidering.

THREADS

Threads should be compatible—in texture and color—with the background you are working. Certain threads are traditional for certain types of embroidery. I won't attempt to go into a discussion of them all as there are books on each specific type, but it should be brought to your attention that crewel is not a type of embroidery but a type of thread! It is a fine, two-ply wool traditionally worked on linen twill or British satin. Only a piece worked entirely in crewel thread can be classified as Crewelwork. To date there is no domestic crewel thread. The thread included in most commercial crewel kits is really Persian wool which is made up of a strand containing three two-ply threads of a rougher texture; it is not as tight a twist as crewel.

The thread best known in the United States is stranded cotton floss manufactured by a number of companies, both domestic and foreign. Other cotton threads, specifically for embroidery, range in size and gloss from pearl cotton, a mercerized twisted thread in several sizes, to soft cotton with a matte finish that resembles regular string. Other cottons in your collection should include string and crochet cottons. All these threads offer you a choice of colors.

Linen and silk threads also come in various weights, sheens and colors. Linen is a delightful thread to work with. Silk requires a little care, but it is well worth the effort.* If you are fortunate, there will be a shop near you that carries a selection of linen and silk threads. If not, they can be ordered by mail from suppliers for weavers. The drawback with weaving suppliers is that a large quantity must be purchased; however, many of these companies are now packaging stitchery yarn collections for handicrafters, which should give you a variety of types and colors to play with.

Wool threads run the gamut in weight and color. Fine imported crewel has over three hundred colors, with families of shades, as does Persian. Any kind of wool that is suitable for your project, including various knitting wools and heavy rug yarn for couching, should be given a try. If you are lucky enough to have a well-stocked shop in your community, it will have not only a wide selection of threads but also someone to give advice and guidance.

Usually the working thread for embroidery shouldn't be over twenty inches long. A longer thread is likely to tangle or knot. In the case of wool it can wear thin.

With wool, too, it's usually best to start with a fairly long tail and toward the end to keep moving the needle back and forth to a new position. Professionals, after every few stitches, twist the wool or silk between thumb and finger of left hand, to avoid untwisting.

COLOR

Color is a very elusive subject to tackle in print, and a browse through the book section in any art store will make you aware of the fact that it is an inexhaustible subject.

In embroidery you are aiming for an effect (as in brush strokes of

---

* If lightly waxed with beeswax, silk thread is a little easier to manage.

a painting) rather than reality, so you can take liberties with your selection. Don't hesitate to choose bold colors, because colors are never quite as bright when worked. The intensity of color also varies with the type of stitch.

A color wheel, which can be purchased at stationery or art stores, will give you basic color knowledge, but becoming conscious of colors around you is more important. Nature, printed fabrics, paintings, commerical advertisements—any number of things your eyes pass over daily—can be your inspiration.

To start your sampler, pick colors you like and will enjoy working on. If additional colors are needed, they'll probably suggest themselves. When laying out a project, actually place the threads on your design to get the best idea of how they will blend. Don't be discouraged if, after a stitch is completed, it needs to be picked out. In color selection, as with most aspects of embroidery, the actual doing is the best teacher.

NEEDLES

Needles, which were at one time so precious that the embroiderer had a special case to keep them in, are now so reasonably priced that you can have a good selection for a very small investment. A sharp needle is a must, for ease of working as well as accuracy. You should always be able to thread without difficulty, for too tight a fit will cause wear on the thread, particularly wool.

The four main types of needles—crewel, chenille, tapestry, and round-eye—come packaged in assorted sizes, so that you can pretty well cover your needs with one packet of each. Most commonly used is the crewel needle, which has a large eye and a sharp point. The assorted packages have two ranges, 1 through 5 and 3 through 9. The higher the number the finer the needle.

The chenille needle is slightly shorter, and the eye is a bit larger than in the crewel needle. As with other needles, the higher number indicates the smaller eye; however the number range varies so that the assortment goes from 18 to 22. These are good for use with the heavier novelty threads.

Tapestry needles, originally intended for Canvas Embroidery, are a must for some stitches. They are larger than other embroidery needles, and the point is rounded or blunt. The assorted package runs from 18 to 24.

Round-eye needles are not essential equipment but most useful for knotted stitches such as French and Bullion knots. They come in assorted sizes 3 to 9.

As mentioned before, your thread should enter the eye of the needle without a struggle, and this can usually be accomplished by moistening and flattening the end of the thread before inserting.

Wool thread has "direction" to the fibers. Before threading, the thread should be pulled through the thumb and forefinger to determine which way it feels smooth. The thread should always be pulled through your fabric in the smooth direction for appearance as well as ease of working. When a double thread is required, don't double over, or you will have one thread running smooth and one rough. Another disadvantage of folded thread is that you can't keep moving your needle along it (to avoid wear on one spot) or work near the end of your thread.

There is a special technique for wool. The needle is held in right hand between thumb and forefinger with the eye extended. Loop the thread tightly around the eye end of the needle, as shown in DIAGRAM 1. Next grasp the needle and looped thread between the left thumb and forefinger. The needle is then slipped out, and the thread is squeezed so that it almost disappears (DIAGRAM 2). Needle is then lowered over the thread (DIAGRAM 3), and when a tip of the thread appears, it can be easily pulled on through.

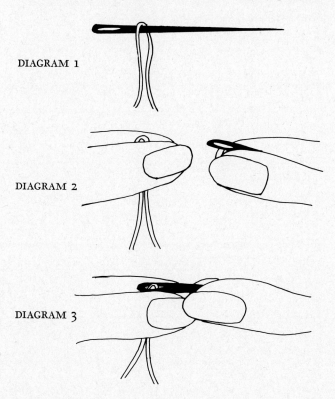

DIAGRAM 1

DIAGRAM 2

DIAGRAM 3

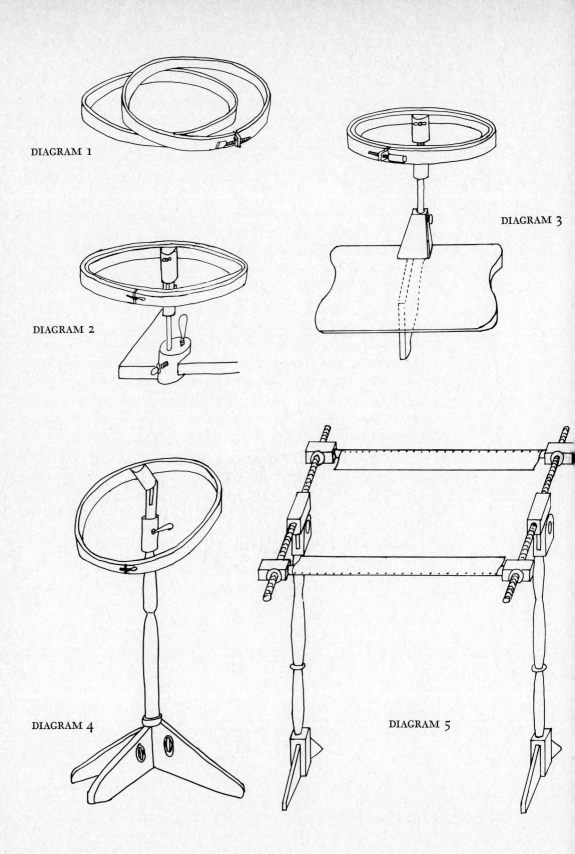

DIAGRAM 1

DIAGRAM 3

DIAGRAM 2

DIAGRAM 4

DIAGRAM 5

6

FRAMES

Frames are not considered as essential as they once were, but there are some stitches that do require them. *These stitches are marked with a small drawing of a frame under the title.*

There are several types of frames, the most common being the hoop (sometimes called the tambour frame). The hoop comes in varying materials, sizes, and shapes. Wooden hoops with the screw fastener (DIAGRAM 1) are the most satisfactory, because once the fabric is mounted, it stays in place.

Hoop frames are also available mounted on several types of bases. A base-mounted hoop is necessary if you plan to do your entire piece on a hoop because then both hands must be free.

The ring frame with a table clamp (DIAGRAM 2) can be useful if you have a particular spot for it, but not all tables are constructed to accommodate the clamp.

The lap and table hoop is probably the most adaptable (DIAGRAM 3).* There is an extra piece that can be held between the knees for stability (DIAGRAM 3) when the hoop is used on the lap. This piece is removable so that the base can sit squarely on a table. The height can be adjusted, and the ring moves freely.

The floor-stand hoop (DIAGRAM 4) has the same appointments as the previous two—adjustable height, detachable and movable hoop. It can be disassembled without too much effort, but if there's a corner to store it in the room where you work, it becomes a nice conversation piece.

The square or slate frame (DIAGRAM 5) comes in several sizes and does require a bit of room, but it's a great piece of equipment to own. It tilts to any angle and makes working large projects a joy. The piece being worked does not have to be as large as the frame as you'll see when we discuss mounting.

MOUNTING

For linen or any other sturdy fabric, the mounting on all types of round frames is the same. The material is laid over the inside

---

* The idea of a lap and table frame combination is certainly not new, but the one in the diagram was designed in 1969. It is supported by a single rod so you can work from any direction.

ring—easier to do on a table—then the screw is slightly tightened on the outside ring. Ease the outside ring over the fabric, making sure the grain of the fabric is true in both directions. When about halfway down, tighten the screw again and pull the material taut in every direction; tighten the screw again. A small screwdriver, like those that come with sewing machines, will help if you don't have strong hands. Finish fitting the outside ring over the fabric and the inside hoop so that the material will be taut enough to drum with your fingertips.

When working with more delicate fabrics, you need to protect fabric and thread. The inner ring may be wrapped with sewing tape, making sure the thickness is even all around, and finished off by a few stitches or surface glue on the inside. Another procedure: after the fabric has been laid over the inner ring, add a layer of either tissue paper or inexpensive lightweight fabric (organdy, sheer lining, etc.) before the outside ring is put on. This also prevents soiling. Proceed with mounting in the manner just described, then carefully cut back to within a quarter inch of the hoop all around, or expose only the immediate area to be worked.

Mounting on a square naturally calls for another procedure because of difference in construction of the frame. As can be seen in Diagram 5, both top and bottom rollers have a strip of webbing attached. These strips should be measured and the centers marked with a pencil. The fabric to be worked will also need to have the center of top and lower edge marked; a pin will do. The side edges will be finished for mounting with some sort of tape unless it is a heavy fabric with selvage on each side that will later be cut away. The tape or material attached should be of the same strength and weave as the fabric being worked so that the pull will be proper when mounted.

Starting at the center of the top roller, match the center of the fabric to be worked. With the raw edge folded back a quarter to a half inch, sew out to the edge in each direction, using a heavy carpet or buttonhole thread and either diagonal Overcast or Herringbone Stitch. Repeat on the bottom edge. If the piece measures longer than the depth of the frame, one end will have to be rolled up, depending on where the embroidery begins. On a delicate fabric, it's best to insert a thin, soft fabric between the working fabric and the roller as the roll-up begins.

Next, the inner rollers are attached to the side arms by whatever method is described in the directions you received with your frame. These are then tightened until the fabric is taut. The side edges of the piece should then be laced to the side arms of the frame with a strong thread; make sure the tension is kept equal on both sides.

When a design to be embroidered is smaller than the size of the fabric needed for the frame, first apply the smaller design to another, larger piece of fabric, such as muslin. Be careful to make sure the threads of the two fabrics lie in the same direction. Then proceed to mount in the regular manner and trim away excess muslin from the back of the fabric to be embroidered.

When your work is properly mounted, it should be almost impossible for the needle to enter and emerge from the fabric in one motion of the hand. The needle, whether going up or down, should always pierce the fabric in a vertical position. This action is done with more ease if both hands are free and requires a frame with some type of base. The work is then done with one hand above and the other underneath. A right-handed person keeps the right hand under, a left-handed person the left. This will feel awkward in the beginning, but with a little practice both speed and skill will improve rapidly.

OTHER EQUIPMENT

Scissors for embroidery have small, short, sharp blades; a good pair of scissors adds not only to neatness but the enjoyment of working. A larger pair is needed for regular cutting.

A thimble is not the must it once was. By all means, make sure you have a proper fit.

I also keep a pair of tweezers in my bag for any picking that might occur.

Not necessary to have in your bag but helpful for special types of work is a stiletto. Similar in shape to an ice pick, it's a small, sharp instrument originally used for Broderie Anglaise (a type of openwork similar to eyelet) and Gold Embroidery, which is done with heavy metal cords. The ends of these cords are put through a hole made with the stiletto and then couched down with a fine silk thread. Both these methods are effective in contemporary stitchery.

A magnifying glass can be of great assistance in doing any kind of fine work. There are several types (mounted on lights, etc.), but for most needs the one that comes with the adjustable neck cord, leaving hands free to work, is more than adequate.

For storage of various materials when not in use, the clear plastic boxes of various sizes are best. Dust is kept out, and the type and color of either threads or fabrics can be seen at a glance.

For work in progress, unless it's a large piece mounted on a frame, a work bag can be either purchased or made. With two zippers around three sides (meeting in the middle) and with handles, it transports all the paraphernalia with ease but can be laid out flat exposing everything for convenience in working.

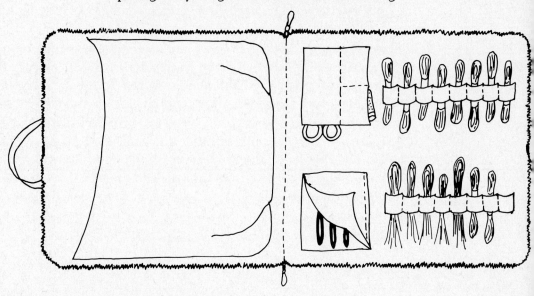

DESIGNS

The easiest method of getting a design on material—especially for those who are timid about adapting or sketching their own—is the printed transfer. They are sold in several colors, yellow transfers for dark and blue transfers for light backgrounds. There is a large variety in both traditional and contemporary designs available to members of the Embroiderer's Guild and to be ordered by mail from the American Crewel Studio. They are easily applied. Spread out the fabric smoothly on an ironing board with the right side up; then carefully center the transfer over it, shiny side down. The iron should be medium hot and placed in one area for a few seconds, then lifted and moved to next spot. Don't wiggle it around.

When transferring to a fabric with rough texture, it is wise to go over the surface first with a steam iron, which will temporarily flatten the weave. Then apply the transfer quickly before the weave has a chance to rise again. For pile fabrics (velvet or corduroy) you'll need the help of a friend. After the transfer is attached to the fabric, have the other person hold the fabric taut while you go over the lines of the pattern with the tip of the iron. Flattened areas will come up with a bit of steaming.

Designs for adapting can be found in many places: china, nature books, fabrics, even children's coloring books. Look for nice simple shapes, without too much detail. Most of these can be easily lifted from the original item. Place a piece of good heavy tracing paper (vellum) over the design and trace with a medium-soft pencil. The heavy paper is sturdy enough to use more than once, so save it for future projects.

If your design needs to be enlarged or reduced in size, there are simple ways to handle this problem. You can purchase clear plastic sheets marked with various numbers of squares per inch (grids). After you have decided how much larger the new design is to be, place the grid sheet with the smaller squares over the design and put the sheet with the larger squares under a sheet of tracing paper. (Remember, if you want the design twice as large as the original, you only enlarge half again in each direction.) If the squares are relatively small, the transposing can be fairly accurate by repeating the same proportions square by square.

An alternate method takes a little more time but doesn't require the extra supplies. If you have no further use for your original design, you can start the process right from there, but if you want to preserve it, trace the outline needed onto a rectangle of tracing paper. Fold this in half in each direction. You now have the center established. Then either fold or mark off equal squares over the entire area to be enlarged. Another sheet of vellum, large enough to accommodate the size you desire, is marked off in like manner, with the squares proportionately larger. Enlarge by the same method as the above.

TRANSFERRING ORIGINAL DESIGNS

There are several techniques for transferring your original design to the material. The prick-and-pounce method is not much in use now except by professionals. The easiest and fastest for the typical fabric is the use of dressmakers' carbon. (Regular carbon will smudge.) The fabric is first stretched taut on a smooth surface and held in place with either pushpins or masking tape. The design on vellum is centered over the material and then attached to the board so there'll be no shifting. Slip the carbon between the two, with the wax side facing the fabric. With a ballpoint pen or stylus and fairly heavy pressure, trace around the design on vellum.

On heavily textured or pile fabric a design without too much detail can be put on by another system. The design will first need to be drawn on tissue paper. The outlines are then gone over either by hand or machine basting stitch. The tissue is then torn away, and if need be, the threads can be pulled out after the embroidery is finished.

Never use a ballpoint pen directly on fabric. It will run when moist. There are times when a hard pencil will be a help for stitch direction, but use it with care, for the carbon in the lead can get on thread and doesn't wash out.

STITCHING

When the actual stitching begins, there are a few tricks of the trade that can give a more professional look to your project. So let's start at the beginning—NO KNOTS! Knots can make an unsightly bump when work is mounted and, on a piece that is subject to any wear, can come undone. As a rule there is no way to correct this without taking the stitches apart and redoing an entire area.

The following diagrams show the best method for avoiding knots when working without a frame. First a spot is found either inside an outlined shape or a short distance away from the starting end of the line to be worked. The needle is passed under as few threads as possible and pulled on through so that there is only a short end of thread left (DIAGRAM 1). The needle picks up the same amount of fabric at the same spot in the right-angle direction (DIAGRAM 2). When the thread has been pulled up snugly, it's almost impossible to work loose. Finish off in the same manner and clip thread closely.

DIAGRAM 1   DIAGRAM 2

On a frame with the material taut, you may (and should) have difficulty in anchoring the thread as just described. Again select an area that is to be covered with embroidery. Take two or three running stitches, remembering that the needle will be stuck straight up and then vertically down when making any stitch, then return to split the last stitch as illustrated.

When you begin to embroider, the shapes that lie underneath should be worked first. For example, if a stem or leaf is overlapped on the design by a flower petal, they should be completed before work is started on the flower. It is much easier to cover the edge of a piece already embroidered than to slip the needle out from underneath. If a shape is to be outlined in any manner, particularly in Laid Work, do the inside area first for the same reason.

Whether doing a line or a shape, be sure that your stitches completely cover. Exaggerate the stitches at points, corners, and curves. You will notice that material, even tightly woven fabric taut on a frame, will give a bit when the working thread is pulled against it. Work beyond the outline if you have any doubt.

When filling a shape with a particular stitch, you will often find that you don't come out even, and you have to adjust the stitch to give a finished or complete appearance. The idea is to give the feeling that the stitch being worked flows right on to the very outline of the shape. Suppose you are working the Fishbone Stitch on a leaf shape; you will reach the bottom before the areas on either side are filled in. Keeping the same angle, take a few straight (uncrossed) stitches until the shape is completely covered on one side (as in DIAGRAM 3) and then fill in the rest the same way.

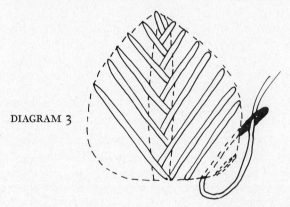

DIAGRAM 3

There will be times when you'll have to take a half stitch or come back to do a little extra tie-down stitch for the proper effect. Usually it only takes a try or two to discover what will best suit the need.

The back of your work is a really personal thing. I don't make a practice of checking on the back of my students' work. However, I feel that it is much easier to work without extra threads getting in my way, catching in my working thread and possibly being pulled to the front of the work. Of course the more comfortable your working conditions, the more professional the result. Nevertheless, I've seen a couple of beautiful projects that were a mass of thread on the back.

As for carrying a working thread from one area to another when using the same color, it is best to keep it to a fairly short distance. Even a slight strain can leave a permanent pucker that no amount of blocking will take out. Wool especially will stretch but later pop back to its original size. Anchoring and finishing off doesn't really take much time and certainly is better than having to go back and redo.

The stitches should always be firm but not tight. There is no way to describe this regulation of tension or even show it by demonstration. Establishing the rhythm for each stitch on practice cloth will help, and keep your work flowing smoothly. When working with wool, remember it has an elasticity that other threads do not have.

Stitchery should be done with good lighting. Today the high-intensity lights are so reasonably priced that those who can't work during daylight can still have proper lighting.

One other thing to consider is your physical condition. I must admit that I was rather inclined to take this advice with a grain of salt when it was first given to me, but I have found that it is worth remembering. Don't embroider when your hands are cold or when you are tired. When you go back and take a fresh look at your work, you'll probably be dissatisfied and end up by picking out.

STITCHES

So that the action of the needle and working thread can be clearly seen, the diagrams in this book are enlarged. Read the text before trying out a new stitch, because usually there is a suggested size and type of thread.

Even on the stitches which have been marked as being done on a frame, the needle is shown entering and emerging from the fabric as in sewing—that is, horizontally. If the needle were shown as it is actually worked—that is, vertically—only a dot would appear. Follow the alphabetical letters in order. Pierce fabric with an upright needle in either direction for crisp, well-defined embroidery.

As this book is essentially a dictionary, the stitches appear in alphabetical order with the name currently in use. An effort has been made to include all of the alternate names for a stitch; some stitches have several. Many of the names are descriptive or carry a regional name where the stitch has often been used. During the Victorian era, when a lot of needlework was busywork, a number of elaborate names were attached, so that during my research the out-of-use stitch that I hoped to revive turned out to be another Old Faithful with a fancy title.

Some stitches, which have a common base but are altered somewhat by a slight change in the working, are grouped together and the variations listed in alphabetical order. The Buttonhole stitch has Alternating, Blanket, Closed, Crossed, etc., directly under the main listing.

SIGNATURE

The old custom of signing and dating an original piece of embroidery has been somewhat revived recently and really adds a nice personal touch if it doesn't overpower or detract from the design of the piece itself.

Although most of us find it hard to visualize our work eventually ending in museums, many modern museums do maintain textile departments, which have a strong interest in embroidery. One of the most time-consuming parts of the curator's job is tracing just the approximate date of an embroidery piece, to say nothing of the needlewoman's name. So naming and dating your work can be important.

BLOCKING

When all embroidery has been completed and removed from the frame, it will be obvious in most cases that some cleaning and blocking is needed. Most fabrics and threads today are washable with a mild detergent; in the case of wools, a soap specifically made for wool is fine. Don't rub. Let the article soak a few minutes, rinse well and roll up in a towel just as you would a fine sweater.

When the moisture has been mostly absorbed—and it doesn't take long—smooth out on a flat, clean surface to dry.

For blocking, a board of some type is needed. A drawing board or piece of wallboard (not Masonite) works well. It needs to be firm but soft enough for pins to be put in by hand. You can speed up the drying if aluminum foil is spread over the surface of the board. Before the embroidery is put down, place on the board a piece of brown paper with the outline of the work.

With pushpins handy, start at opposite corners, stretching to the outline on the paper. If you want a smooth surface to the work, put the embroidery face down; if the stitches are eventually to stand out, put the right side up. Now pin the other corners and then pin the middle of each side. Keep placing the pins all around the edge until they are an inch or less apart; keep the fabric tightly stretched. With a sponge or towel soak fabric until stitching is thoroughly wet. Blot up excess liquid. Keep board flat until piece is thoroughly dry.

If the work is not going to be framed right away, it should be rolled around a cardboard tube with the embroidery kept outside to prevent crushing the stitches.

If the work is destined for a pillow, or anything other than a picture, it is now ready to be made up.

To prepare a work for framing, the piece should first be mounted on heavy cardboard. Cardboard should be cut slightly smaller than the inside of the frame, to allow for the thickness of the material. An adequate amount of fabric must be left around all the edges.

The corners of the fabric will need to be mitered for a smooth fit. Fold and press one quarter to one half inch around all four edges. Then cut from each corner a triangle that will still leave enough fabric to cover the corner of cardboard. Get the design centered and hold it in place by taping the folded-over fabric to the cardboard in the middle of each side of the back.

Fold fabric over at the corners so that one edge overlaps the other and whip together with a heavy carpet thread. When all four corners are completed, take long stitches from side to side and pull up tightly, like lacings. Do the same between top and bottom edge. At this point I usually give pictures several coats of a silicone spray, letting the fabric dry thoroughly between each coat. I don't advise glass; it will flatten and make the stitches lose their depth. (Dust can be vacuumed off every few months.)

The mounted piece is then placed in the frame and secured in place. Cut a piece of brown wrapping paper slightly smaller than the frame. Lay it across the back of the frame and attach on all four edges with strips of masking tape. Then wet down the brown paper. It will shrink as it dries and give a neat dust-proof backing to the entire piece.

A Dictionary of Stitches

1 · ALGERIAN EYE STITCH

The Algerian Eye Stitch is entirely made up of a combination of straight stitches; this is true of most of the earliest known stitches because of crude needles, threads, and techniques. It is most effective if done on evenweave fabric, and therefore is often used as a canvas stitch.

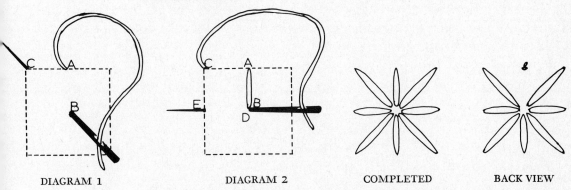

DIAGRAM 1   DIAGRAM 2   COMPLETED   BACK VIEW

The needle first emerges on the outline of the square at A, DIAGRAM 1, halfway between the corners. The needle is then inserted in the center B and brought out at the left-hand corner C. First stitch is then completed, and the thread is in position for the second stitch.

For this stitch and the other seven (DIAGRAM 2), the needle always enters the fabric in the same hole at center B and emerges on the outside edge of the shape. A slight pull when working the thread at the completion of each stitch will produce a small opening in the center which enhances the overall appearance.

Left-handed stitchers will probably be more comfortable working in the opposite direction.

This attractive open filling is usually worked diagonally as shown in FIGURE 1. Algerian Eye is also very effective when used as a solid filling (FIGURE 2) or as a border (FIGURES 3 and 4).

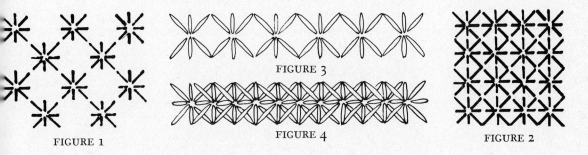

FIGURE 3

FIGURE 4

FIGURE 1   FIGURE 2

2 · ARROWHEAD STITCH

The Arrowhead Stitch is another interesting variation of the straight stitch and is found in many of the early embroideries from the Near and Far East.

In reality the Arrowhead Stitch is a type of Back Stitch, and there are several methods of working it. The detached stitch is effective as powdering, while groups may be used as a line or filler.

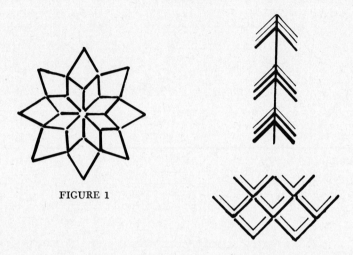

FIGURE 1

An entire motif can be built up by arrangement (FIGURE 1). Varying the weight or color can produce a variety of results with a basically simple stitch. The most common method of working the Arrowhead Stitch is shown in DIAGRAMS 1 and 2. The needle is brought out at A, goes back into the fabric at B and emerges at C. The needle is then inserted at B and comes through the fabric at D. This step completes the stitch and puts the thread in position for the next stitch which is worked vertically below.

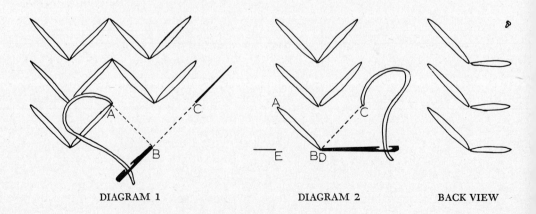

DIAGRAM 1   DIAGRAM 2   BACK VIEW

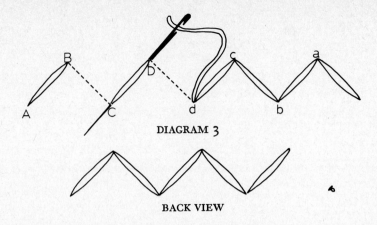

DIAGRAM 3

BACK VIEW

DIAGRAM 3 shows another way of doing the Arrowhead Stitch, which is horizontally rather than vertically. The stitch is not completed, but half of each stitch is worked in the first movement (DIAGRAM 3 A, B, C, D) and then is completed on the return trip (DIAGRAM 3 a, b, c, d). This method is seen in old embroidery, especially Yugoslavian, as a border stitch.

DIAGRAM 4 illustrates the third method which is worked as shown.

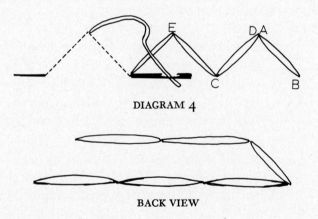

DIAGRAM 4

BACK VIEW

Left-handers reverse the action. The thread is at C (DIAGRAM 1) to start. The needle goes in at B and emerges at A. Next put needle in again at B and out horizontally, directly below C.

3 · BACK STITCH

Though perhaps most often thought of in connection with clothing construction (seaming dresses or knitted garments), the Back Stitch can also be very decorative. It can be worked by itself as an outline, in various geometric arrangements, quilting designs, or as a base for some more elaborate stitchery. When you start to experiment, you will find you can achieve various effects by spacing stitches and changing line arrangements.

The actual execution is quite simple either in the hand or on a frame; however, to achieve the regularity which is part of its beauty takes a little practice. An evenweave fabric with fairly coarse texture is best for practice, as the threads can be easily counted.

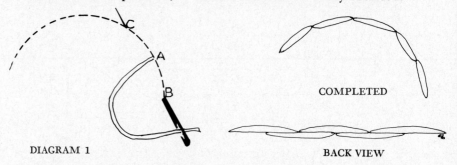

DIAGRAM 1

COMPLETED

BACK VIEW

Right-handers start at the right end of the line and bring the needle out first a few threads to the left at A (DIAGRAM 1). The needle then goes in at B which is to the right, a few threads from the spot where the working thread has come through the fabric. The needle emerges to the left of A at C, the same distance (or number of threads) covered between A and B. Continue with this needle action, going back and putting the needle in the same hole at the left end of the previous stitch and bringing it out beyond the working thread the same distance as the stitch first made. This will make a neat outline without the worry of flop as in the Stem Stitch.

Left-handers turn the diagram upside down and start work from the left end of the line to be covered.

Diagrams 2 and 3 are really just variations of the basic stitch, as are all the Back Stitches described.

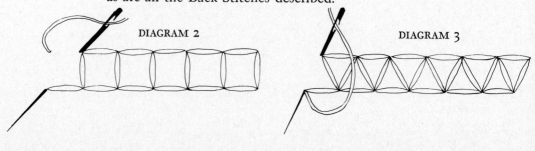

DIAGRAM 2

DIAGRAM 3

4 · BACK STITCH—THREADED

This is a speedy way to get an outline with a little texture. Another color can be introduced for interest or a heavier weight of yarn that might not be taken successfully through the fabric.

The Back Stitch (Number 3) is first worked along the line; the needle is then brought out again at the end of the work. It doesn't really matter which direction this second step goes as long as you are working comfortably and can keep an even tension.

The blunt needle slides under each Back Stitch, without going through the background, alternately up and down as shown in the diagram. The black stitches are the Back Stitches.

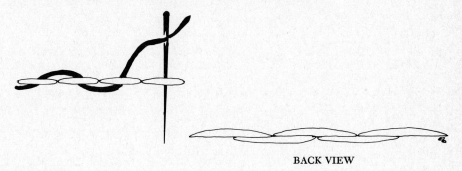

BACK VIEW

5 · BACK STITCH—THREADED, DOUBLE

Useful as an outline for various shapes, this stitch can be decorative as a border, especially with varying weights and colors of threads combined.

The working is the same as 4, but the second thread (shaded thread in the diagram) fills in the spaces left by the first journey.

6 · BACK STITCH—TRELLIS

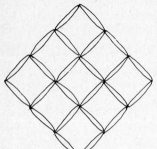

Actually this is an arrangement of Back Stitches (Number 3) in parallel lines at right angles to each other. They can be arranged running vertically and horizontally or diagonally as shown in the diagram. Spaces formed can be further decorated by French Knots, small Cross Stitches, or Detached Chain. Often used in Jacobean work or any light filling.

You can work most quickly by stitching all parallel lines in one direction, going up one row and down the next.

7 · BACK STITCH—TRIPLE
(HUNGARIAN)

This attractive variation on the basic Back Stitch gives a completely different appearance from the original, for you are working three lines simultaneously. The result can vary with spacing either between stitches or rows (FIGURE 1).

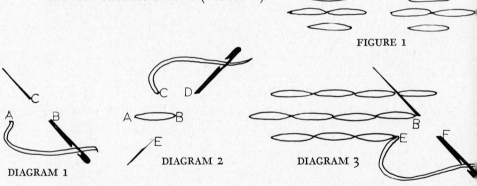

FIGURE 1

DIAGRAM 1

DIAGRAM 2

DIAGRAM 3

This stitch is begun at the left-hand end of line, and the needle is brought out on the middle one at A. It is inserted at B and emerges at C on upper row, which is above and halfway between A and B (DIAGRAM 1). Put the needle at D, same row as C, and bring it out at E on the lower row, halfway between A and B (DIAGRAM 2). For the last stitch in the series, the needle goes in at F on the lower row and comes out at B on the middle row (DIAGRAM 3). Your thread and needle are then in position to start the next series.

Left-handers turn the book upside down and begin working on the right end.

BACK VIEW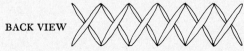

8 · BACK STITCH—TRIPLE, CLOSED

As the name implies, this is a tightly worked stitch with no fabric showing. Generally worked as a linear border, it is a very effective solid filling when one or more colors or weights of thread are used.

The actual working of the stitch is exactly the same as 7; however, the lines are closely packed as can be seen in FIGURES 1 and 2.

FIGURE 1
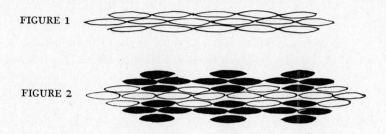
FIGURE 2

9 · BACK STITCH—WHIPPED

A nice firm line can be formed with this stitch, and on curved lines it is really more accurate than the Stem Stitch. An interesting raised effect is created, giving a line dimension.

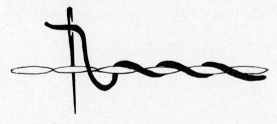

The basic Back Stitch (Number 3) is worked first, and then a second thread is brought out at the end of the line. This can be worked in either direction, but I find it most comfortable to work from right to left. Using the most comfortable position is important with this stitch, for it should be worked smoothly and not pulled too tightly. The needle is passed under each stitch always in the same direction.

25

10 · BASKET STITCH

The Basket Stitch forms an effective border whether it is worked open or closed. At first glance the working looks very complicated, but actually it is quite simple when you follow each step of the diagrammed method with care. Once your rhythm is established, it is a matter of two simple steps. On the first step, forward one stitch; on the second, back two stitches. To see the complete action of the needle and thread in working this stitch, I would suggest working on an evenweave fabric. If you are covering a large area, try using a frame even when practicing for the first time. Care should be exercised with the tension on this stitch, for it has a tendency to draw the fabric together. It is best to think in terms of squares between two parallel lines. Start at the left-hand end of the line. Your work will look as illustrated in DIAGRAM 1.

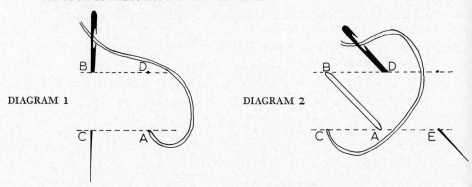

DIAGRAM 1

DIAGRAM 2

The needle is brought out at A on the lower line, a few threads in from the left end of the area to be worked. The needle is then inserted at B on the upper line, going back to the left and brought vertically down and out at C. The working thread is then carried across to the right and the needle inserted at D, making a square cross. The needle emerges at E as in DIAGRAM 2, an entire square section beyond A. Next the needle is carried back and inserted in the fabric midway between B and D on the upper line at F and

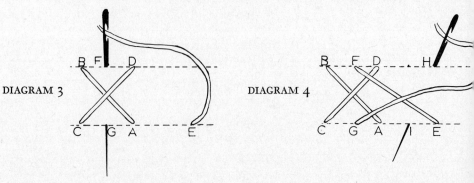

DIAGRAM 3

DIAGRAM 4

brought out vertically again directly below at G. DIAGRAM 4 shows the thread that has come through the fabric at G and the needle drawn forward again and inserted in the upper line a full square beyond D at H. Slanting backward under the fabric, it is brought out on the lower line, midway between A and E, emerging at I.

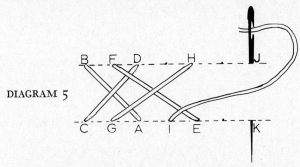

DIAGRAM 5

DIAGRAM 5 shows the needle being carried forward the one full space beyond H and inserted in the upper line at J and brought out directly below on the lower line at K. The second step carries the needle up and back two stitches on the upper line, the needle inserted midway between D and H at L. The needle slants forward on the back of fabric, and is brought out on the lower line at M, midway between E and K.

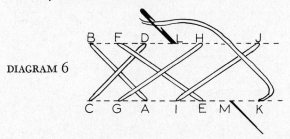

DIAGRAM 6

This establishes your pattern. You now go ahead a full square, the needle entering the fabric from top to bottom. Then back two stitches on upper line and forward to the lower line again.

DIAGRAM 7 shows the second step of this action, with the stitches being worked a little closer together. Note: dotted lines indicate where extra stitches may be inserted to give the band a finished appearance. As you close up your spaces, you can see the tighter border emerging.

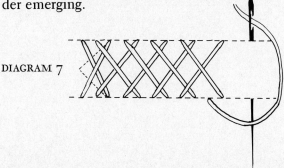

DIAGRAM 7

Going on to DIAGRAM 8 you will see a tight solid line, which gives a heavy, padded effect. The Basket Stitch somewhat resembles both the Closed and the Plaited Herringbone Stitches. The difference can easily be told by the back of the fabric. As shown, the back view of Basket Stitch will have a combination of slanting stitch and straight stitch across the back, but the Closed Herringbone has overlapping, horizontal straight stitches on parallel lines, and the Plaited Herringbone would show a row of double, vertical straight stitches.

Try doing this stitch with a nice heavy thread such as a Number 3 pearl cotton or Number 8 linen.

DIAGRAM 8

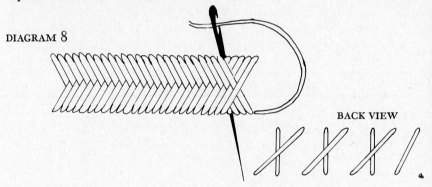

BACK VIEW

11 · BASQUE KNOT

The Basque Knot is another of the pretty knot stitches that can be used for either line work or solid filling. It's very effective when worked with some of the heavier threads such as heavy pearl or soft cotton. The stitch is worked from right to left and is similar in appearance to the Palestrina Knot, but the procedure varies.

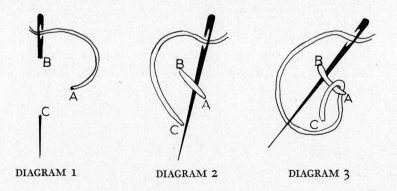

DIAGRAM 1   DIAGRAM 2   DIAGRAM 3

28

The work begins at the right-hand end of the line. Looking at DIAGRAM 1, you will see that the thread is first brought out at A, then the needle is put in at B and brought vertically down and out at C. These spaces should be about equal in size. In DIAGRAM 2, the needle is slipped under the thread laid between A and B, but not passed through the fabric, and pulled right on through. A small loop is formed over the thread, and it is again slipped under the same thread just above the first loop, but this time the working thread is held down below with the left thumb, so that after the needle has gone under the stitch AB, it slips over the working thread.

FIGURE 1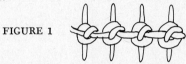

As can be seen in FIGURE 1, you will be forming a series of little knots with legs on either side. As in most of your stitches, variations can be obtained by changing the weight of the thread or the size of the stitches or even the distance between the knots. The back of the work is simply a series of straight lines, because most of the work on this stitch is done on the surface.

BACK VIEW

12 · BASQUE STITCH

The Basque Stitch is not to be confused with the Basque Knot. In fact, it more resembles in actual appearance the Petal Stitch. Although the Basque Knot is completely different from the Basque Stitch, they are often used together in the traditional work and are particularly effective when worked with white thread on a colored background. Because of the appearance of the line with the little petals flowing away from it, it lends itself to scrolls and outline designs and floral shapes very nicely. This stitch is often found on old embroideries of Spain, Portugal, and southern France.

It might be well to draw yourself two parallel lines for practicing this stitch. The needle would then be brought out on the top line at the left-hand end as in A (DIAGRAM 1). The stitch is being worked from left to right, and the thread is carried on over to the right before the needle is inserted again. The needle then goes into the fabric at B, in front of the thread emerging at A, and is brought out directly below at C. With normal thread, the distance between B and C should not be more than about one-eighth inch long. The needle is not pulled through until the thread is (1) brought around in front from behind the needle, (2) crossed over on the front of the fabric, and (3) carried under the needle again at the lower edge (C) from left to right, forming a little loop (DIAGRAM 2). Firm the loop up a bit and pull needle on through.

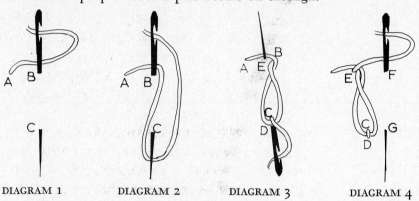

DIAGRAM 1   DIAGRAM 2   DIAGRAM 3   DIAGRAM 4

Then the needle is inserted just the other side of the thread, forming a small tie-down stitch at D as in DIAGRAM 3. Carry the needle back up to the top line and bring it out just to the left of B, at E, going in front of the thread at the top between A and B. This makes a complete stitch.

The needle is then carried on to the right and inserted at F and brought out at G to begin the working of a new stitch as in DIAGRAM 4. FIGURE 1 will show you several completed stitches.

FIGURE 1  BACK VIEW

For left-handers, this stitch is probably best worked by reversing the procedure, rather than by turning the diagram upside down. Start at the right-hand end of your parallel lines. Bring the needle out and insert in front of the working thread, as in DIAGRAM 1, with the thread to the right of the needle rather than to the left. Cross over in front of the needle and then under the point from right to left, etc.

30

13 · BLANKET STITCH

The Blanket Stitch is actually one of the many variations of the Buttonhole Stitch and not in as common use as it once was. The main difference between it and the Buttonhole Stitch is the spacing allowed between the upright stitches, which will vary with the length of the uprights and the size of thread used. It is called the Blanket Stitch because it was used on the edges of blankets to keep material from fraying. This is another of the loop stitches and the basis for many of the variations to follow.

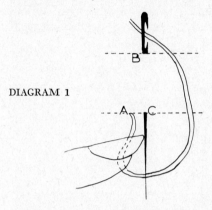

DIAGRAM 1

If you have not worked this stitch before, draw two parallel lines first. Work with heavy thread and with stitches about a half an inch long, so that you can easily see the action of the needle and thread. Starting with DIAGRAM 1, bring the needle out on the lower line at A. Thread is held in place with the thumb while the needle is carried to the upper line, where it goes in at B and emerges at C. Be sure that it goes over the thread held by the thumb. Pull on through and proceed to do the next stitch in exactly the same manner.

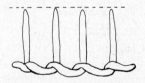

Since the Blanket Stitch is generally used for an edging stitch, you would start at the left-hand end of the line. This stitch is easily worked in both directions, but the left-hander will probably feel more comfortable starting on the right end and reversing directions.

14 · BOKHARA COUCHING

For Bokhara Couching, as opposed to regular Couching, the same continuous thread is used for both the laid thread and the tying-down stitches. This stitch was originally used in the Near East to embroider rugs and wall hangings, and has developed into an interesting embroidery stitch that can be used in several ways—as a solid filling with rows locked together and no fabric showing (FIGURE 1), or the tied-down stitches spaced so that another stitch can be worked in between the couch stitches as in FIGURE 2. Bokhara Couching is similar in needle action to Romanian Couching, but the end results differ. In the first the tying-down stitches are short on the surface and long underneath, while the reverse is true for the second.

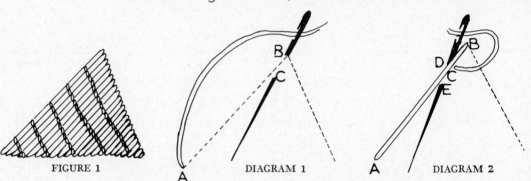

FIGURE 1 · DIAGRAM 1 · DIAGRAM 2

The thread is brought out at one edge of the area to be worked and carried completely across to the other edge as in A to B (DIAGRAM 1). The needle is then brought back to the left, and the working thread emerges just barely below laid thread at C. The next step is a small tie-down stitch, which carries the working thread over the laid thread as in CD (DIAGRAM 2). Needle is then brought out a little further along at E. These tie-down stitches should be quite near together and pulled tight, leaving the longer threads just a little loose in between. The back of the work will look like a series of darning stitches, and the spacing will depend on how close together your couch stitches are laid.

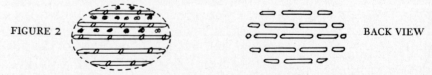

FIGURE 2 · BACK VIEW

For left-handers, the procedure is exactly reversed. The thread is brought out at the right-hand edge of the shape and carried across to the left and followed with tie-down stitches.

The Bosnia Stitch, often used in Yugoslavia as a solid filling, also makes interesting border. The French call it Fence Stitch, and it is worked with a slight variation which will be shown in the diagram. It is actually a series of straight stitches worked in different journeys. Since this is a geometric stitch, you would be wise to start your practice piece with parallel guidelines, either by counting threads or marking them off on your fabric. The same holds true for spacing the stitches on the first journey.

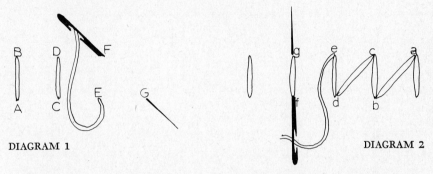

DIAGRAM 1   DIAGRAM 2

Beginning at A, Diagram 1, go up to B with a vertical stitch, carry the thread diagonally across the back down to C. This pattern will give you a series of vertical straight lines right across your line. When the first journey is completed, you make a return journey, starting at the end where you have just finished off unless you are changing threads. Starting with a, Diagram 2, carry your needle diagonally down across the front of your work to b and bring it out directly above at c, proceeding across. This will give you a series of diagonal lines between your upright stitches that connect the work as a whole.

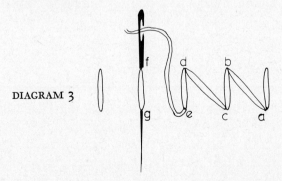

DIAGRAM 3

Diagram 3 shows the French Stitch, which is merely a change in the direction of the diagonal stitch. It is started at the bottom line and carried up to the top line. FIGURE 1 shows the stitch done with a heavy thread and a fine thread in the same color, and FIGURE 2 shows the same weight of thread in two different colors. These are only two of the many variations that can be applied to this stitch. Your back view shows that the stitch looks almost the same on the back as it does in the front except that your diagonal stitches will be reversed.

FIGURE 1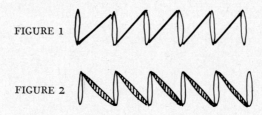

FIGURE 2

Left-handers need not change procedures for this stitch, because you are working back and forth in two directions on the same stitch.

BACK VIEW

16 · BRAID STITCH

(GORDIAN KNOT STITCH)

As the name implies, this stitch makes a rich braided look, nice for borders, and unless it is worked on fabric that is not to be laundered, the stitches should be kept quite small and worked closely together to get the proper effect. A coarse thread, particularly of the pearl type, works best on this stitch, for it gives you a nice twisted effect. Before you start to work, it might be a good idea (if you are working on a fabric that will lend itself to it) to pull a couple of threads, about an eighth of an inch apart. This will define the lines you should work between and also give a lacy effect to the completed stitch.

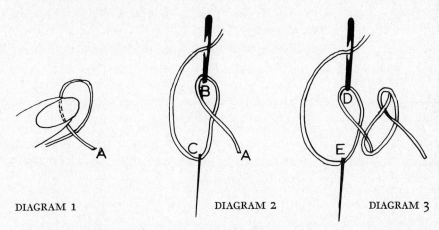

DIAGRAM 1   DIAGRAM 2   DIAGRAM 3

Working from right to left, bring the needle out on the lower line at A. Then form a loop, using the left thumb, which can be done either of two ways. You can loop it by hand by folding the far end of the working thread under the thread coming from A, or hold your working thread coming out from A and, slanting it to the left and up with your left thumb, slip the needle under (without going through the fabric) to form the loop as shown in DIAGRAM 1. The needle is then inserted in the fabric on the top line inside the loop you have just formed at B (DIAGRAM 2).

Again hold the working thread with your left thumb so that it forms a loop below the area to be worked. Then bring out the needle on a lower line, over the working thread at C (DIAGRAM 2). Before pulling the needle on through, tighten up the loop just made. Then pull the needle through, and you have completed your stitch. Proceed on to the left by forming another loop first before inserting the needle in the fabric as shown in DIAGRAM 3. This border will curve easily, but you must remember to keep the stitches small and close together to get the proper effect.

BACK VIEW

Your back view will show a single series of parallel straight lines. Left-handers should turn the diagrams upside down or reverse the direction by starting at the left end and make the beginning loop to the right.

17 · BRAID STITCH—PLAITED

This is one stitch that is *not* easier to work than it looks. Mastering it does take a little practice, but it is well worth the effort. Often found on old work in a heavy gold thread, Plaited Braid Stitch has a very rich effect as a border and lends itself well to metallic thread, for it is both decorative and economical of back thread, since most of the work is done on the surface. Whatever thread you use, it should be coarse and stiff, or the stitches will lie flat and droop.

First, study the diagram before starting right in. You will note that, once you have established your pattern, it is merely a repeat of a series of steps.

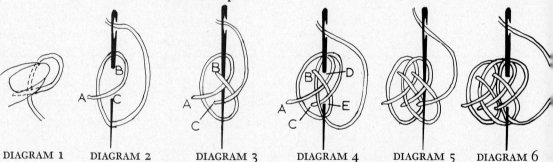

DIAGRAM 1   DIAGRAM 2   DIAGRAM 3   DIAGRAM 4   DIAGRAM 5   DIAGRAM 6

The border is worked from left to right, and if you notice the dotted line under the thumb in DIAGRAM 1, you will see that the first stitch is formed by laying the working thread under itself and forming a loop, which you hold in place with your left thumb. Insert the needle inside this loop at B while holding a new loop with the left thumb in position, and bring the needle on through to the outside of it. Pull the thread over the working thread as in DIAGRAM 2. For the next step, the needle is passed under the two threads that cross on the surface without entering the fabric at all, as in DIAGRAM 3.

For the fourth process in this stitch, the needle enters the fabric and comes out in the center of the loops illustrated in DIAGRAM 4. In the fifth step, as the diagram shows, the thread is slipped under the crossed threads to the right but over the working thread and the previous loop. The sixth step is actually a repeat of DIAGRAM 4, with the needle entering and coming out of the fabric again and over the working thread, through the previous loop.

The last two steps are repeated alternately as you work along toward the right. It is absolutely essential in this stitch that the points where the needle enters and emerges should lie directly above and below each other.

I found that I could make an exciting border with this stitch, using some of our new threads on an old type of fabric: a heavy rug warp weave, which was loose enough for the thread to enter and come out, and a nylon cording braid. This produced a white-on-white effect, in which the sheen of the nylon complemented the matte finish of the rug warp, to produce an unusual border. This is a good time to see how raffia works up on a conventional stitch.

Left-handers should reverse the procedure. Then A would be to your right, and you would start your work by forming your first loop to the left of the starting point.

18 · BRETON STITCH

This little-known stitch is simple to work but very effective, particularly when you use a heavy twisted thread on a colored background. The stitch is worked best between parallel lines, and I suggest that a hoop be used to keep the lines from drawing together as you work. The distance between the lines can be varied, but remember, the greater the distance, the heavier the thread you need for proper effect. When doing stitches like this, which requires a great deal of passing the thread under another thread and not going through the fabric, it's usually a good idea to use your tapestry or blunt needle.

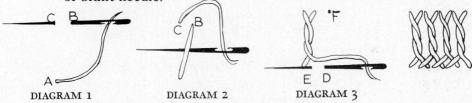

DIAGRAM 1   DIAGRAM 2   DIAGRAM 3

The needle is brought out at A on the lower line and inserted on the upper line at B, making a stitch which will be slightly on the slant. Then the needle is brought back to the left and out at C. C will be exactly above A. Your needle is then brought out and taken under the stitch AB, but not passing through the fabric, going right to left and forming a slight twisted effect. After your stitch has been firmed up, the needle is then inserted at D on the lower line as in DIAGRAM 3, just a bit to the right of B on the upper line, and brought out again to the left, midway between the space CB. Pull your needle on through and proceed as in DIAGRAM 1 back up to the top, insert needle at F, bring it to the left again, coming out in the same hole as B, and pull the needle through gently. This starts another base stitch; put your twist under and repeat on across the border.

An interesting effect can be achieved by making the stitches a bit longer and doing two twists under the thread before inserting the needle on the lower level. This stitch gives you a nice spindle effect across, and it can be worked in curves as well as straight lines. The back view will show a series of little stitches side by side in horizontal lines both top and bottom.

This is a simple stitch for the left-hander if the diagram is turned completely upside down, which means that your thread will be coming out on the top line facing you on the right-hand end while you work across your area.

BACK VIEW

19 · BRICK STITCH

When Brick Stitch is completed, it will show a nice solid filling as in FIGURE 1. It can also be used as a shading stitch, the colors graduating from light to dark, the overlapping stitches helping the tints merge smoothly into each other.

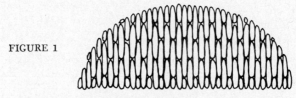

FIGURE 1

Because the stitches should be of uniform size, your spaces need to be marked off in some manner before you start. You can use a hard lead pencil for this, but you must mark it lightly so that the carbon does not rub off on the working thread. The row that establishes the size of stitches can be worked either of two ways: by leaving spaces on the first row across (DIAGRAM 1) or by doing a double set of stitches in one row (DIAGRAM 2). I prefer to leave the open spaces.

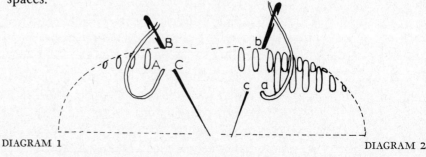

DIAGRAM 1

DIAGRAM 2

The first row is worked as a series of straight stitches, from the lower line up to the top line, then over and back down, bringing the needle out again on the lower line. Then on to the next stitch. As a rule, one leaves the width of a working thread between each of these vertical stitches. On the return journey, the stitches will go all the way to the top of the design again but be twice as long as the largest stitch in the edge row, as in Diagram 2. The upper half of the stitch covers the space between the vertical lines on the original row.

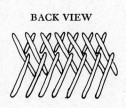

BACK VIEW

If you prefer, you can make two rows in one by taking alternately long and short stitches. All the succeeding rows are worked with stitches that are exactly the same size.

On the Brick Stitch it does not matter if you are right or left-handed, because you work in alternate rows from right to left and left to right.

20 · BULLION STITCH
(CATERPILLAR STITCH, COIL STITCH, KNOT STITCH, POST STITCH, PUERTO RICO STITCH, ROLL STITCH, ROSE STITCH, WORM STITCH)

As can be seen by the number of alternate names, all of which it has carried at one time or another, this stitch suggests many types of things to many people. A little practicing and you can do this stitch with ease. To make it go more smoothly, I suggest you use a needle with a round eye and no bulge, so that it will slip easily through the twisted thread. Doing the twist near the heaviest part of the needle also helps to make the needle go through without too much difficulty.

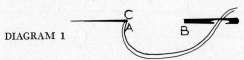

DIAGRAM 1

Your needle is brought out at A, and inserted at B (the distance between these two establishes the length of your knot), then brought out again at A which will now be C, in the working diagrams. Do not pull your needle through.

The next few diagrams, starting with DIAGRAM 2, shows the method I have found the easiest to hold the twist firm and get the needle through without too much pull on it or losing the twists. You might want to try putting your fingers in the position to be used, before you actually attempt working with the fabric. The forefinger of the left hand is folded at the second joint back toward the palm of the hand, and the thumb rests on top of this. When you are actually working this stitch, your fabric will be between the two fingers and your needle wedged in an upright position against them, as in DIAGRAM 2.

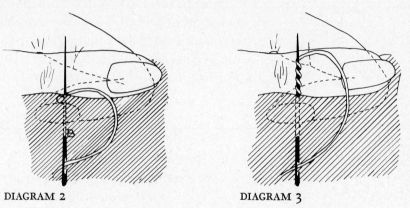

DIAGRAM 2   DIAGRAM 3

With your finger and thumb pushing against the needle so that it is held firm, your thread is taken in the right hand and wound around the needle. The number of twists will be determined by the length of the stitch and the thickness of the thread. As a rule, five or six twists will take care of the area to be covered. Note DIAGRAM 3. Still holding the working thread so that the loose end is at the top of the twist and held fairly taut with the right hand, bring your left hand out from under the fabric and place the thumb and forefinger around the twist just made (DIAGRAM 4).

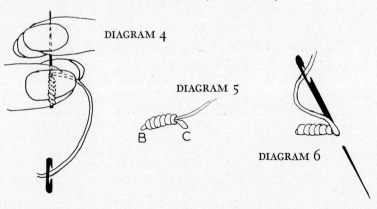

DIAGRAM 4

DIAGRAM 5

B   C

DIAGRAM 6

The needle is then eased up through the twist, with the right hand being careful not to let the top thread slip down onto the twist. Do not release your hold when the needle goes through. Pull the remainder of the thread on up through the twist, still holding it between thumb and forefinger. You can feel the stitch starting to flatten out as you get toward the end of the thread. At this point I find it easier to lay the fabric flat on the working table and put my left forefinger only on the twist, then pull the thread down until it is absolutely flat. By now you should have a series of smooth little twists lying on the thread.

Your needle then goes in at B, at the end of the stitch in the same hole, and the stitch is completed. You can carry the needle under the fabric right on to the spot where you intend to make the next stitch, as in petals of a flower (FIGURE 1).

FIGURE 1   BACK VIEW

If your work looks skimpy, you have probably not put enough twists on your thread. If it's inclined to bulge, you have put on more than is needed. (On some occasions, of course, you want a rounded effect.) If your twists don't look even, it means you have not used a good tension either in winding or pulling your needle through. However this can be corrected by using the large end of your needle and sort of straightening them back into place. It is best to do this before your needle is inserted at the end of the stitch. To get a smooth-looking result each time does take a little practice.

FIGURE 2

Note FIGURE 2. You can obtain a bud or a rose effect with a series of curving bullion knots placed around each other, which can be shaded out from the center. This little floral effect is often used on children's smocked dresses. The Bullion Stitch can also be used to make little leaves, petals, or even wheat sprays for the relief-effect stitch.

The left-hander works just the reverse when doing this stitch. The working needle is held in the right hand and the twist made with the left, but otherwise each of the steps is worked exactly the same.

This version of the Burden Stitch has come into popularity in recent years, and if you inspect the diagrams you'll see that it's a combination of Laid Work and Brick Stitch. This stitch can be used very nicely in shading, and the spacing of both overstitching and Laid Work can give you some unique effects. By using a different color of thread for Laid Work than for the surface stitchery and working with stitches close together, you can obtain an effect of weaving. You can add an interesting texture by spacing out your top stitching and having the background part of the overall effect. This works very well in shading a petal and is equally effective on the breast of a bird, where roughness is indicated without heaviness. Wool lends itself to this stitch very well.

Working of the stitch begins with the Laid Work. Start at one end, carry your thread across the space to be covered, and insert the needle. Bring it out directly below on the same side of the area and then carry the thread back in the other direction for the next laid thread as in DIAGRAM 1.

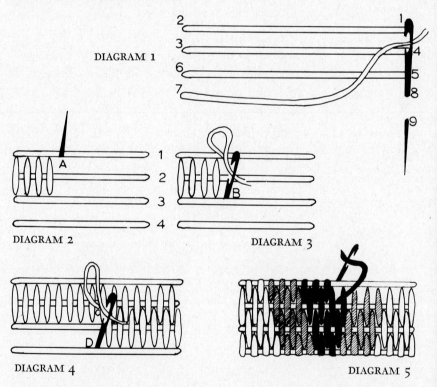

DIAGRAM 1

DIAGRAM 2

DIAGRAM 3

DIAGRAM 4

DIAGRAM 5

DIAGRAM 2 shows the first top-stitch row being established. Your needle is originally brought out at the left-hand end, as close under the first laid stitch as possible without piercing the thread. It is then carried over the second laid thread and inserted as close to the third as possible at B, as in DIAGRAM 3. There should be at least the width of your working thread between each of these vertical stitches that form your first row of surface stitching. On the return journey the needle follows the same action, except that it comes up between stitches already worked. The needle is again brought out as close to the top thread as possible, in this case the second laid thread, over the third laid thread, and as near the fourth one as possible, and continued across the row in the same manner.

DIAGRAM 5 shows the final row which will match the bottom row of the diagram. You are actually making only a partial stitch, just over the outside laid thread, and putting your needle in directly beside it to give a nice finished edge to the shape.

DIAGRAM 5 also shows several colors being used. When working with more than one color in the Burden Stitch, it is well to have a needle threaded with each one of the colors. Do the number of stitches for that color on the first row; do not finish off the thread but pull it tightly out to the outer edge of your hoop, anchoring it down and away from the direction you will be working. Then start with your next color. Complete the number of stitches that are needed in that color and again anchor your thread off to the left in the first row of your work, so that it will not interfere in your next series. Your third color is then brought to the surface and the required number of stitches worked. Then continue on across the line. Don't try to work all of one color at once; each row should be completed before the next one is started. If all of one color is worked first, it's very likely that uneven spacing would be left for the filling in of the other colors, causing an irregular appearance.

Generally Burden Stitch is done best with very heavy, perhaps even double wool thread, using the darkest color underneath. You will also find that you need to outline the shape in some manner afterward.

Both the Laid Work and the overstitching are done in both directions, so left-handers need no special instructions.

22 · BURDEN STITCH—TRADITIONAL

This stitch is named for a certain Miss Burden at the Royal School of Needlework, London. If you look at the diagram, you will see that it is really a form of Darning Stitch, with alternate spacing. This can be used very effectively for covering various areas, and any number of effects can be achieved with it by varying the weight of the thread and the spacing between the stitches or rows. Do experiment with several types. It makes a very interesting solid filling for almost any kind of shape.

It can be worked from either right or left, so there are no special directions for the left-hander.

23 · BUTTONHOLE STITCH

As the name implies, this stitch has been used for generations for edging buttonholes, to prevent fraying when the button is being passed through. I suggest you take a look at the Tailor's Buttonhole Stitch before starting your first buttonhole. It's a wonderful edging stitch also and has been used for years on special types of ornamental embroidery such as Richelieu, Hedebo, etc. In this fancy openwork, the stitching is done and then the fabric cut away later. The Buttonhole Stitch was frequently used in traditional Jacobean embroidery to soften the edges of large leaves. It is also used to edge linens of all types, and you may want to try other interesting variations, which are illustrated here. As a purely decorative stitch, its varieties are endless.

DIAGRAM 1

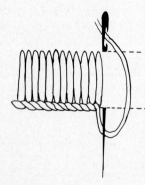

Like the Chain Stitch, the Buttonhole Stitch is the basis for many of the other loop stitches, and like all loop stitches, it requires constant use of the thumb. When using the Buttonhole Stitch as an edging on regular fabric, make sure that the width of your stitch will embrace the folded edge of your material. Always space the stitches just far enough apart to allow the loops on the edge to lie smoothly side by side.

The actual working is the same action exactly as the Blanket Stitch, 13. DIAGRAM 1 shows the needle entering and emerging over the loops held by the left thumb.

There's no difficulty in working both directions if procedure is reversed for the left-hander.

The Alternating Buttonhole Stitch is started in the same manner as the regular Buttonhole and with spacing similar to the Blanket Stitch. If you are doing this for the first time, draw a series of three parallel lines. For the first step, the needle is brought out at A on the middle line, and the Buttonhole Stitch is made. The second step reverses the procedure, carrying the needle down below the first stitch. Using your thumb again, hold the loop on top and put the needle in at D and bring it out at E. This gives you a little arm in the opposite direction (Step 2, DIAGRAM 1). Then go back and repeat the first step again, with the same spacing.

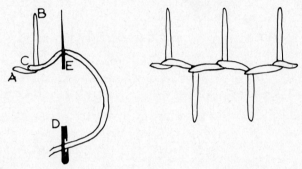

DIAGRAM 1

FIGURE 1 shows stitch variations. You can have two stitches close together, two side by side going up and two side by side going down. On the upper row you'll note that there are French Knots between stitches and on the lower row a small detached chain. Toward the end of the row the size of the stitches are varied. These suggest only a few of the variations possible with this stitch. Do experiment, especially with the effect of different threads.

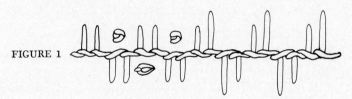

FIGURE 1

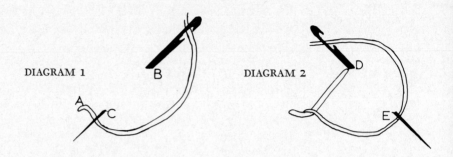

DIAGRAM 1

DIAGRAM 2

The term "closed" in this stitch refers to the upper-line closed sections. On the first stitch, after the thread has been brought to the front of the fabric, the needle is put in at the upper-line B, much farther to the right than for the Buttonhole Stitch. You want the needle to slant back toward A at a 45-degree angle, so that it will come out at C at the same distance it would with the regular Buttonhole Stitch (DIAGRAM 1). This will give you a sloppy-looking slanting stitch. The needle is then inserted in the same hole on the top line at D and, with the thread held below as for a loop, emerges at E. When your needle is pulled on through, you will have a teepee effect. Continue on across the row in this manner.

FIGURE 1

This stitch need not consist of only two slanting stitches. The right-hand end in FIGURE 1 shows a series of three worked into the same hole on the upper line. The middle stitch would be a regular Buttonhole Stitch.

This stitch isn't often worked in both directions so it would probably be easier for a left-hander to start at the right-hand end.

26 · BUTTONHOLE STITCH—CROSSED

In this variation of the Buttonhole Stitch, it is essential to achieve even spacing and regularity of the crossings. The work is started in the same manner as the Closed Buttonhole with the initial needle insertion slanting sharply to the left as in DIAGRAM 1.

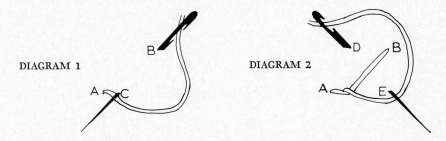

DIAGRAM 1

DIAGRAM 2

For the second step, the needle is put in on the top line above A, slanted sharply to the right, and brought out directly under B, which gives you a square cross (DIAGRAM 2). You will note that the first half of FIGURE 1 shows the squared-off crosses, the second half a variation achieved by making your top-row insertions not directly above your lower-row insertions.

FIGURE 1

27 · BUTTONHOLE STITCH—DETACHED

The Detached Buttonhole is useful for any sort of shape. Its chief technical difficulty lies in keeping the extremities of the line neat and firm, at the point where you turn to come back along the row. These successive turning stitches eventually form the side edges of your design, and if the working is loose, an irregular line is built up, and the result is most unsatisfactory. The whole stitch is quite detached from the material, so I suggest you use a blunt needle and a stiff, firm, perhaps linen, thread.

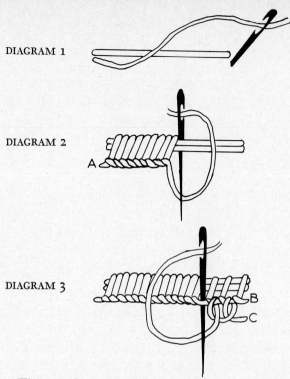

DIAGRAM 1

DIAGRAM 2

A

DIAGRAM 3

B
C

This stitch requires more than one process in working, so you begin by laying two long stitches right across the fabric (DIAGRAM 1). Then go back to the beginning to start the work. Beginning at A, work the regular Buttonhole Stitch over the two threads just laid but do not let the needle pierce the fabric (DIAGRAM 2). DIAGRAM 3 shows the return journey of the work, with the needle going into the bottom edge of the row above. You will note that, at the end of the row, the threads go in and out of the fabric and get into position to start back.

In the diagram, for demonstration purposes, the stitches are shown spaced out, but in actual execution they must be packed closely together, or you will lose the entire effect of this stitch. The work should not lie flat when completed. If you want to make your design larger, the extra stitches should be added at the edge. The lower right-hand edge in FIGURE 1 shows the doubling up of stitches to give the effect of a ruffled edge. Do try it.

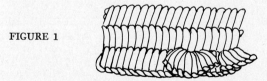

FIGURE 1

The Detached Buttonhole is normally begun from left to right, but left-handers could start on the right-hand edge, using the same action as in the regular Buttonhole Stitch.

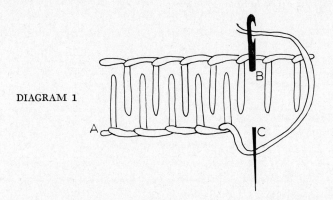

DIAGRAM 1

This stitch is worked in the ordinary Blanket Stitch manner on the first journey. Starting at A, work a row of Blanket Stitches equally spaced across the area to be covered. When the row is completed, turn your work around and do the same sort of stitch back in the other direction, filling in the spaces of the first row with the arms of the second row.

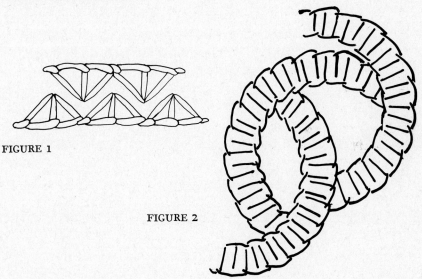

FIGURE 1

FIGURE 2

This will form a simple decorative border that can be worked in curves and rows very nicely. Depending on the weight of your thread and the size of your stitch, this stitch can be used for anything from a delicate line in a monogram to a heavy ornate border. FIGURE 1 shows the Closed Buttonhole worked in alternate rows in the same manner.

A left-hander would work the stitch in the usual manner for the Buttonhole Stitch.

29 · BUTTONHOLE STITCH—EGYPTIAN

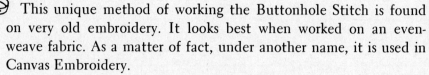

This unique method of working the Buttonhole Stitch is found on very old embroidery. It looks best when worked on an even-weave fabric. As a matter of fact, under another name, it is used in Canvas Embroidery.

Make one straight stitch from A to B on the upper level of the area to be worked and another one from C back to A. It is very important to make the cross on the back of this stitch, to hold the surface in the proper shape. After the needle is inserted at A, bring it out diagonally across the back of the fabric at D, and then work a Buttonhole Stitch without going through the fabric over the line AB (DIAGRAM 3). DIAGRAM 4 shows the direction of the Buttonhole Stitch made over line AC. This completes one square of your work. After the last Buttonhole Stitch, the needle is inserted at D and brought out on the upper line at E, which is the same hole as B. You commence another stitch by making your first straight stitch from E to F and bringing the needle across the back and out again at D.

This unusual textured stitch can be used in filling squared-off areas and is most attractive. Note that the second row is worked in reverse (FIGURE 1) so the left-hander might want to start from right and reverse procedures.

DIAGRAM 1

DIAGRAM 2

DIAGRAM 3   DIAGRAM 4   DIAGRAM 5   DIAGRAM 6

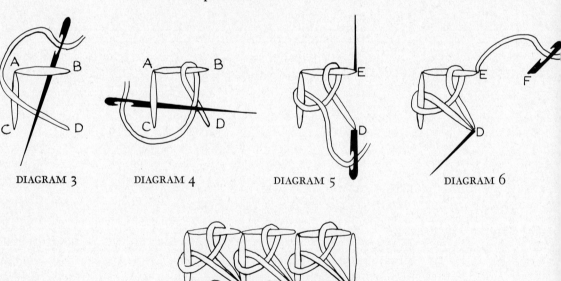

FIGURE 1

First, your design must be outlined, with either the Back Stitch or the Chain Stitch. Thereafter, at no time does your needle enter the fabric again. For this reason it is suggested that you use a blunt needle.

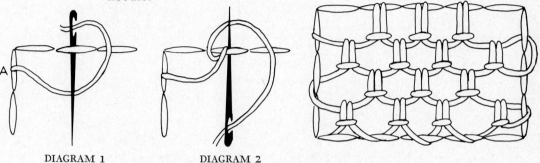

DIAGRAM 1   DIAGRAM 2

The working thread is brought out at A, outside the Back Stitch line or in the middle of a Chain Stitch line, and carried over, skipping the first stitch, to the second stitch on the top of your outline. Work a Buttonhole Stitch without going through the fabric, under the surface stitch as shown in DIAGRAM 1. The second step in this stitch is actually a reversed Buttonhole. The thread is held above the stitch just formed, and the needle is passed from the bottom up under the same stitch and pulled on through. The working thread is then pulled sharply downward, to bring the two parts of the stitch close together and into position.

The work continues on to the next outline stitch, leaving a tiny space between the stitch just worked and the one being started, and on across the row. The needle is then passed under the outside stitch at the end of the row and carried around into position to start the second row of work. The second row is worked in the opposite direction so that the Buttonhole Stitches are reversed.

After the first row has been worked the second row and all the following rows are worked into the little loops which lie between the pairs of stitches. When the bottom row is reached, either take the loop through a lower line of Back Stitch, to secure the whole filling, or (depending on the shape) pick up a few threads of fabric.

Since all the work is done on the surface, the back view of this stitch shows only the lines along the outside edge of your design. If you prefer, the fabric can be cut away from the back of your design, leaving only the Buttonhole Fillings.

Because the work is done back and forth in two directions, the left-hander needs no special instructions.

First, outline the shape of the area to be worked with either the Back Stitch or the Chain Stitch. This is the only time the needle goes through the fabric; the rest of the stitches are worked entirely on the surface, using the border stitches to anchor the thread. This stitch forms a knotty irregular surface, which looks good worked in a coarse thread.

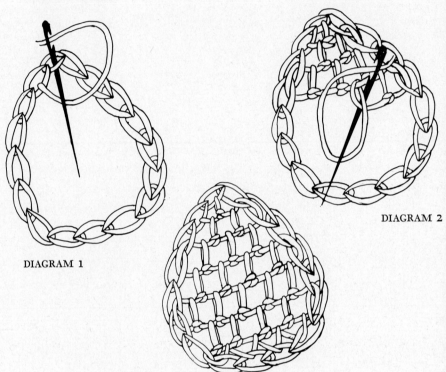

DIAGRAM 1

DIAGRAM 2

At the beginning of the work, the needle is brought out on the upper left-hand corner, either through a Chain Stitch as in the diagram or on the outside of a Back Stitch. The needle is then passed through the first outline stitch to the right, and the Buttonhole Stitch is formed by passing the needle under the surface stitches. The second stitch, or knot, is done over the one just worked, forming a slanting Buttonhole Stitch through the loop as in DIAGRAM 2. At the end of each row, carry the threads outside the outline stitches. The thread is either slipped under your outline stitches, or a few threads of fabric are picked up at the very end to finish off.

DIAGRAM 2 also shows the work being done on a row coming from left to right. The rows are worked back and forth so that left-handers don't need special directions for this stitch.

The Open Buttonhole Filling gives you an interesting lacy texture. The only times the needle enters the fabric are on the beginning row and at the end of each row as you work back and forth. This stitch needs some type of outline when completed.

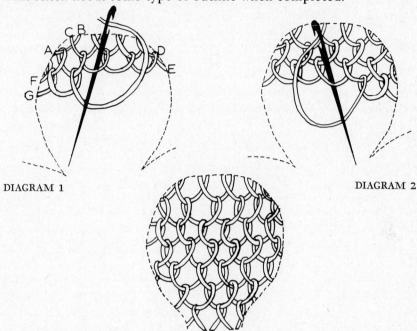

DIAGRAM 1   DIAGRAM 2

Start work by bringing the needle out at A (DIAGRAM 1). Carry the thread up to the top of your shape and take a small Back Stitch, picking up only a few threads of fabric. Leaving a little space and the thread slack, go on to the right and do the same thing again, forming a series of loops across the top edge of your shape. The needle is then passed into the fabric and brought down the space desired between the rows, as in DE, to start the second row. Across this row the needle no longer enters the fabric. It goes up and is passed under the loops in the row above, working a Buttonhole Stitch in each loop. Go on across the row and insert the needle in the fabric at F, bringing it out at G. When you reach the bottom edge of your design, the needle is passed under a few threads of the fabric in between each two loops.

It requires a little practice to obtain an even tension in working this filling stitch. Some interesting results can be obtained by slightly varying the tension for different geometric patterns.

Because this stitch is worked in both directions, the left-hander needs no special directions.

This is a simple yet very attractive filling, consisting of rows of buttonhole stitches worked in groups. The diagrams show two stitches together and then a space, but this stitch can be equally effective worked in groups of three or even four.

The variations are endless. If your stitch spaces are equal, you can get a checkered effect. By using a fine crewel wool and making small stitches, you get a very lacy appearance with this stitch. You will provide yourself with a very useful reference for the future if you work a number of these variations on your sampler, changing weight of thread and spacing.

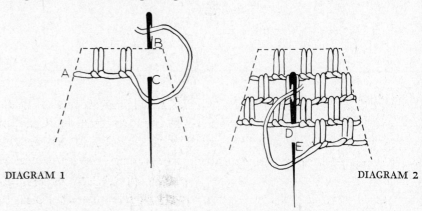

DIAGRAM 1   DIAGRAM 2

To start the actual work, the thread is brought out on the upper outline of your design at A. The stitches are worked in the regular Buttonhole Stitch on across the row. The needle is inserted at the end of the row and brought out at the space desired between rows, for the return journey in the opposite direction (DIAGRAM 2). FIGURE 1 shows a number of groupings and variations that can be tried, including three successive rows on top of each other. Try these rows in three different shades of the same color.

The working is done from left to right and then from right to left, so both left- and right-handers work the same.

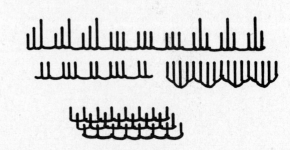

FIGURE 1

Technically this stitch could be listed under the knotted stitches, for it is actually a French Knot on the top edge of a Buttonhole Stitch. As the basic working does include buttonholing, I'm going to leave it here.

It can be used as a line or border stitch or, if worked in a circle, to form a flower shape. To form a leaf, work two rows back to back.

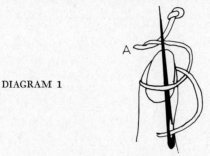

DIAGRAM 1

The thread is brought out from the background and wound around your left thumb, forming a loop. The working thread goes over the front of the thumb and around the back, and is carried above the thread, which has emerged from the fabric as shown in DIAGRAM 1. The needle is then inserted under the loop and the loop slipped off the thumb and onto the needle. At the same time, the needle is carried on up and inserted in the fabric and brought out below as for a Buttonhole Stitch. The left thumb holds the loop underneath in the usual manner. The thread is tightened up on the needle so it can be pulled on through, leaving a tight little knot at the top. Don't lose the desired effect by letting the knot slip off the end of the needle. DIAGRAM 2 shows the needle in position to be pulled through the stitch.

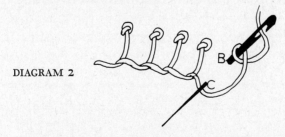

DIAGRAM 2

A left-hander reverses the direction—that is, starts the process on the right-hand end of line. Loop the thread around the right thumb and follow the letters as indicated in DIAGRAMS 1 and 2.

35 · BUTTONHOLE STITCH—RAISED BAND

This stitch gives a nice three-dimensional effect in the proper place. The work is begun as in other raised-band-type stitches—that is, with laid thread. DIAGRAM 1 shows the threads being laid to form the foundation for this stitch. Because this is a band, the stitches won't be very long and should be quite close together. The size of your thread will determine what would be considered close; for example, with Number 5 pearl cotton, about one-sixteenth inch would give the desired effect.

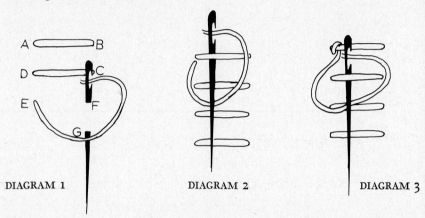

DIAGRAM 1   DIAGRAM 2   DIAGRAM 3

The needle is brought out at the top, just under the first laid thread. From here on, the work should proceed with a blunt needle, as you are not working through the fabric. The needle is passed under the first laid thread at the top. As usual with the Buttonhole Stitch, the loop is held with the left thumb so that the needle passes above the loop over the first laid thread. DIAGRAM 3 shows the work proceeding in the same manner as in DIAGRAM 2, dropping down one laid thread at a time to the bottom of the design. On the last laid thread, the working thread is carried over, and the needle is passed through in the same manner except that it is inserted in the fabric directly below the last laid thread (DIAGRAM 4). The work is started again at the top of the row just under the first laid thread. Work several lines close together but do not pack too tight, or the proper effect will be lost.

DIAGRAM 4

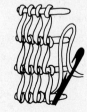

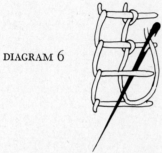

DIAGRAM 5

DIAGRAM 5 shows an interesting variation on this stitch. Work as in the Raised Buttonhole Band, but at the end of each stitch enrich with a tiny Chain, which gives a knotted effect when pulled up tightly. When working this variation, finish it off at the top with another row of Knotted Buttonhole Stitches along the upper edge.

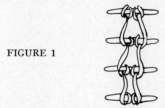

DIAGRAM 6

DIAGRAM 6 shows a different way of laying the foundation, simply a line of Buttonhole Stitches worked over. This can give a nice finished edge to your stitch even before you start work. The buttonhole method of laying a foundation is good to keep in mind for other raised-band stitches.

FIGURE 1

Left-handers should start from the right-hand edge of the laid threads and work the buttonholes in the usual manner. FIGURE 1 shows the Buttonhole Stitch worked with one row in the right-hand manner and one in the left-hand manner, which gives you an interesting appearance and makes use of the fabric background.

This is a stitch that is seldom used nowadays, and yet it can be most useful. When it is worked closely in the ordinary manner, it gives a slightly raised edge for a border. It also curves well and can follow almost any line. It can be used with freehand stitches and varied somewhat. The arms can be on the slant as well as perpendicular and can vary in length. The stitch looks equally good when the arms are worked closely together, or slightly apart, the choice depending on the weight and type of your thread. Once you get used to the technique of working this stitch, you'll find it an interesting addition to your stitch vocabulary.

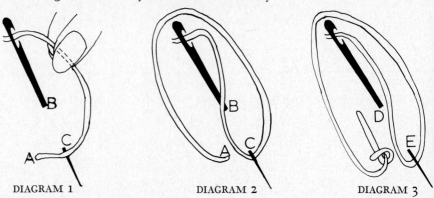

DIAGRAM 1   DIAGRAM 2   DIAGRAM 3

As a rule it will be worked from left to right. Starting with DIAGRAM 1, the thread is brought out at A. The needle is inserted in the ordinary buttonhole manner except that the loop is not under the needle. With your left thumb hold the thread from A *up* instead of *down*, as in the normal Buttonhole Stitch. The thread is then grasped with your right hand as shown in the diagram, brought around and slipped under the needle, forming a loop that runs counter clockwise from left to right. Now the needle is pulled on through, and the knot is tightened up at the base of the stitch. On the second stitch, the needle is inserted to the right a short distance at D, and comes out at E. Then the twist is again made, and the reverse loop formed under the tip of your needle.

FIGURE 1 shows a rich, textured outline that is produced in working a row of these stitches, particularly on the edge of a fabric.

Left-handers might want to use a mirror to help work in reverse.

FIGURE 1

This is a useful shading stitch where regularity is required. The actual stitching is done the same as for the ordinary Buttonhole Stitch, as shown in the diagram, but each row is worked into the looped edge of the row above. The shading is supplied by working each row or pair of rows with different colors or shades. The stitches can be close together or spaced a little apart to show the fabric underneath. This stitch often has under-thread, as can be seen in the unfinished portion of the diagram. This underlay can be of the same color as the working thread or of a contrasting color.

The work is generally done only from left to right, for right-handers, and at the end of a line the working thread is taken in and carried back to the left-hand side, putting the thread in position to start work on the next row. Sometimes, when the Open Buttonhole is used, the shading is done with the under threads. The top stitching can be of single color and the shading varied with the threads that are laid under. This makes interesting rows of shading in a regular shape, but you can also follow the direction of curves with a little bit of care, particularly if you are having the under threads show through.

When the stitch is employed as a filling, whether Open or Closed, each succeeding row of stitching is worked into the lower loops of the previous row. For certain effects in a solid filling, a line of thread is laid across and the stitch worked over this, as well as into the heading of the row before. This would suggest another use for these stitches, which is to couch down various forms of laid threads, perhaps spirally from the center to the outside of a circular design. (See the section on Couching.) You can achieve a pretty ribbed effect by working a narrow band of your closed Shaded Buttonhole over a heading of your last row.

Left-handers simply start from the other side and work in the manner prescribed for the left-hander under the Buttonhole Stitch.

This stitch is worked similarly to the Double Buttonhole. However, the stitches are taken at a slant. It lends itself to curves very nicely, as illustrated in FIGURE 1.

FIGURE 1

Stitches are spaced as in the Blanket Stitch. Work the first row with a sharply slanted angle resembling the Feather Stitch. The work is then turned over and worked in the opposite direction, the needle inserted in the spaces left by the original row at the same slant.

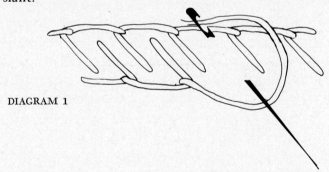

DIAGRAM 1

When done with heavy thread, the Spiral Buttonhole gives a rich bold effect; with fine thread, a delicate lacy one.

This variation is similar to the ordinary Buttonhole Stitch, except that it has an extra little twist in it. It is useful in both plain and fancy needlework. The firm edge makes it useful for garment buttonholes that must take heavy wear, and at the same time its ornamental appearance enables you to use it decoratively to obtain a rich-looking effect with heavy thread.

The Tailor's Buttonhole cannot be worked with spaces between stitches as in the Blanket Stitch, because it needs the support of the stitches on either side to keep it rigid. Any variation that you might want to use would have to be in the width of the stitches.

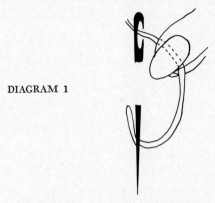

DIAGRAM 1

The needle is inserted in the fabric as for the regular Buttonhole Stitch, and then the working thread is grasped near the eye of the needle as illustrated in Diagram 1. Pass it under the point from right to left so that it takes the position of the thread in Diagram 2. Pull the needle through and bring the thread up tightly to form a little double knot, and proceed on to the next stitch.

Left-handers work a Buttonhole Stitch in their usual manner, and the working thread is passed from left to the right before being pulled through.

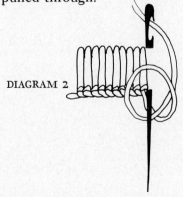

DIAGRAM 2

In the Threaded Buttonhole Stitch, two rows of regular Buttonhole Stitches are worked facing each other, and an ornamental effect is achieved with a second thread woven between them. The action of the needle is not shown in the accompanying figures. The base rows and the stitch arms may be spaced in any way you desire to give different results. The thread does not go through the fabric once the initial buttonhole rows have been worked.

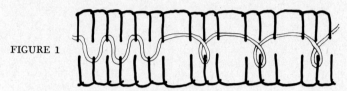

FIGURE 1

Note the left end of FIGURE 1, where the thread is simply slipped in and out under the top of the stitches already worked, which forms a snakelike design. The results can be varied by the weight and color of the thread. A heavy thread gives a rich braid effect. At the other end of FIGURE 1, the Buttonhole Stitch has been spaced differently, and the center stitches are twisted for a more decorative effect. FIGURE 2 shows a more involved stitch. The arrows indicate the direction in which the thread is worked.

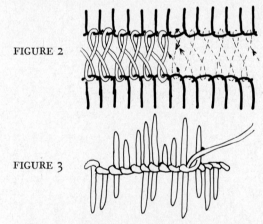

FIGURE 2

FIGURE 3

FIGURE 3 shows another decorative use for the Threaded Buttonhole. It is not truly a threaded stitch, nor is it a whipped stitch, but something in between. Make a base row of Buttonhole Stitches of varying lengths and spacing in one direction. The work is then turned around, and the Buttonhole Stitch is worked in the other direction, again with varying lengths of stitches and spacing. This second row does not go through the fabric but only uses the base of the previous row to work the stitches. This can give some most interesting results, particularly in contemporary work.

41 · BUTTONHOLE STITCH—WHEEL
(WHEEL STITCH)

The action of the needle in this stitch is the same as in the ordinary Buttonhole Stitch. However, the needle is inserted each time in the same spot in the center of a circle, as shown in the diagram, and emerges on the edge of the outline. If a slight tug is given to the thread, a little hole will be formed in the center, even on tightly woven fabric. This is a useful stitch for tiny flowers as suggested by the diagram.

It is often used in Drawn Fabric Work. When doing this drawnwork, leave an intersection of thread in the center of the center hole, and as the thread is pulled away, a little cross bar appears in the center of your design. Choose a fairly loose-weave fabric for best results with this technique.

42 · BUTTONHOLE STITCH—WHIPPED

A single edge of Buttonhole Stitch can be whipped with a contrasting color or weight of thread as shown in DIAGRAM 1. The buttonhole is worked in the usual manner. Then the whipping thread is entered at one end, carried over the base thread without the needles entering the fabric, and passed under the bar across the lower edge of the Buttonhole Stitches. A slightly different effect can be obtained, by working it in the opposite direction.

DIAGRAM 1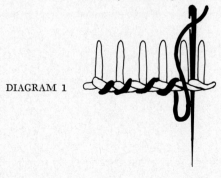

63

FIGURE 1

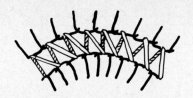

This could also be considered a threading stitch if it is worked between two rows. When the two rows are edgings on two separate pieces of fabric, it becomes a joining stitch for insertion work on a garment. In such work the Buttonhole Stitch is in effect a hem. Be sure that the stitches completely embrace the fold. FIGURE 1 shows the whipped stitch used in this manner.

43 · BUTTONHOLE STITCH—WOVEN

This stitch, as the name implies, has a contrasting thread woven in and out of the space made in the Buttonhole Stitch and allows you several interesting variations. If you are doing a circle with this method, you must remember to make an *uneven* number of arms, so that as you weave around and around, you will automatically come out right with your alternate unders and overs.

The Woven Buttonhole Stitch works up well in a band, and when made with a fairly heavy thread and packed quite tight, it gives a woven appearance. Try making it as shown, with a little edging in light-colored threads and the dark-colored ones woven through them. When doing this from one side to the other, instead of around and around, simply put your thread through the fabric at one end and bring it up at the same end and start back in the opposite direction.

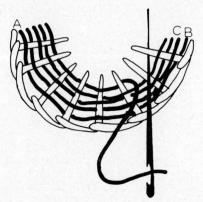

The Zigzag Buttonhole Stitch is actually a combination of two of the stitches already discussed: the Alternating Buttonhole Stitch and the Fancy Buttonhole Filling Stitch, which when worked through the fabric, is sometimes called the Up-and-Down Stitch.

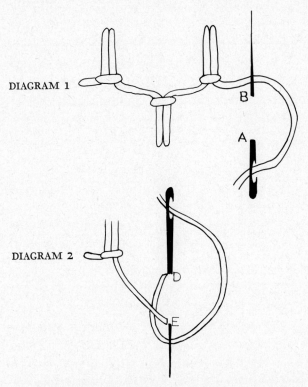

DIAGRAM 1

DIAGRAM 2

Start at the left-hand end of the row by working a regular Buttonhole Stitch. Then in the opposite direction, with the needle coming down from the top and the loop held up behind the needle at that point, bring the needle out on a level with the stitch just worked and right next to it. After drawing the needle through, pull the working thread down sharply so that the two stitches are linked together with a little base stitch. Now the process is reversed, and your first stitch is taken on the lower level, with the needle coming from the bottom up, the loop held above. The needle is pulled through and then brought from the top down, for the second step in this action, in which the thread is pulled up sharply to form another little tie-down. With a little playing around, changing the distance between the upright parts of the stitches to exaggerate the zigzag, you can make a good filling. This stitch admits of many variations.

This is a very useful filling stitch, which can be worked either close together or spaced out in horizontal lines of varying colors, and can be used to fill a small area as in our diagram or a long, wide space.

A thread is brought out on the outline at A and carried across. The needle is then put in at B on the opposite side of the outline, carried completely across the back of the work and brought out a short distance below A at C, on the left-hand outline (DIAGRAM 1). Next, the needle is slipped under that first laid thread from top to bottom, with the thumb holding the working thread below to form a loop, as in a Buttonhole Stitch. Pull on through, forming a loose loop.

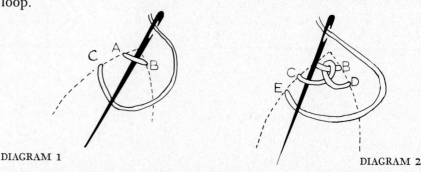

DIAGRAM 1   DIAGRAM 2

To work a large area, continue on across the row in this manner. Our diagram shows the work starting at a point which would mean you need form only one stitch here. The needle is then inserted again at the right side at D and carried to the other side, emerging at E. Repeat the procedure, going over the loops left between the edges of the work on the preceding row and the stitch that was actually made. Work over the surface thread, not through the fabric. Then insert the needle on the outside outline on the right and carry it back to the left-hand edge.

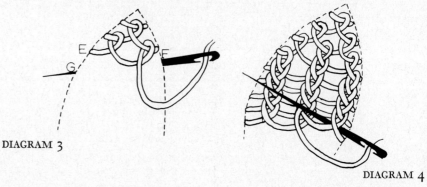

DIAGRAM 3   DIAGRAM 4

After you've established the rows as shown in DIAGRAM 3, your next row is slightly different. In the next row the needle is slipped behind the *twist* of the loop in the row above, as shown in DIAGRAM 4. Continue working the rows in this manner, going under the loops in the row above and when you reach the end of each row, put your needle in and carry it back to begin a new row.

When this stitch is worked close together, it looks almost like knitting, but when spaces are left, it gives an effect like lace. Remember, as with many of the filling stitches, this will have to be outlined in some way when the work is completed.

Left-handers will probably be more comfortable doing this in reverse—the surface work would be done from left to right instead of right to left.

46 · CHAIN STITCH

The simple Chain Stitch is one of our oldest decorative stitches and can be used with equal success for lines or fillings, including shading. Down through the ages many lovely variations have been discovered, sometimes by accident or sometimes by design. Chain Stitch is not only beautiful but also quick to work up and most economical of thread, for the larger part of the stitch is on the surface of the material. Tambour Embroidery (see Appendix A) is a form of Chain Stitch although worked with a hook instead of a needle.

In the needle-worked chain, your thumb will be used constantly. It is important to develop the ability to regulate tension and size of stitch. Opinions vary as to whether this stitch is better worked from the top down or from the right to the left. Whatever is most comfortable for you is the proper way; the more comfortable you are, the better the rhythm you can attain. Chain Stitch is used on a wide variety of embroideries, almost every type, and is effective in whatever thread you choose.

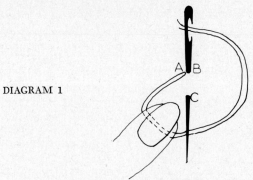

DIAGRAM 1

Work is begun by bringing the thread to the surface of the fabric at A (DIAGRAM 1). The needle is then returned to exactly the same hole, at B, and brought out at C. All the while, the working thread is being held with your thumb so that a loop will be formed as the needle is pulled on through. It is a good idea to get into the habit of placing the left thumb over the working thread, as you pull the needle through. This action will keep you from giving your thread a yank, thus causing a little pucker, or from letting your work get too loose and untidy.

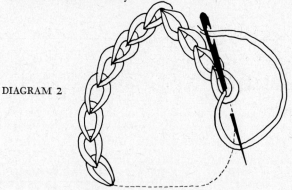

DIAGRAM 2

DIAGRAM 2 shows the stitch in progress outlining an area. As mentioned before, this stitch is equally useful for outlines or for a filling stitch. DIAGRAM 2 also shows the needle going inside a loop already worked. After the initial link in your chain, all the following links are made by the same process, but from then on you will be going back inside a loop already formed. To finish off this stitch whether you are ending a row or simply getting ready to use a new thread, take the working thread and insert it just the other side of the link, making a small tie-down stitch. If you are going to start working with another thread—and this often occurs in this stitch particularly when it is used on long outlines or solid fillings—the needle is again brought up inside the last loop, and your first Chain Stitch with the new thread is formed over the tie-down stitch.

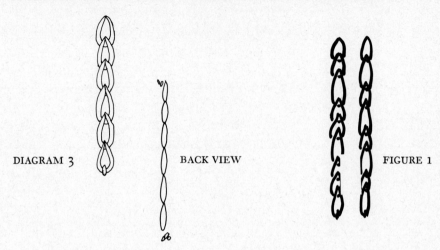

DIAGRAM 3   BACK VIEW   FIGURE 1

DIAGRAM 3 shows the tie-down loop at the bottom of the row.

The back of the work resembles a series of Back Stitches. These should be very regular in size. The size of your Chain Stitches can be varied in the same line, but make sure that it's done with a pattern in mind; if properly done, the back of your work should also reveal a regular pattern in the size of the stitches. These variations are shown in FIGURE 1.

While still playing with your basic Chain Stitch, try working one row of Chain Stitch and then a second row immediately above it in a contrasting color and perhaps a lighter-weight thread. Begin by bringing the needle out in the center of the first link. Again insert the needle in the same hole, holding the loop with the left thumb and bring it out in the middle of the second link.

Although we are not covering Canvas Embroidery in this book, this is one of the embroidery stitches that lends itself to that method of embroidery and is worked in exactly the same manner, using the threads of the canvas to regulate the size of your stitch.

For left-handers, it will probably be more comfortable if the working thread comes around to the right side, and a loop is formed from right to left.

47 · CHAIN STITCH—BACK STITCHED

This stitch, partly completed in the diagram, is a pretty addition to the ordinary Chain Stitch, easily executed. A row of ordinary Chain Stitch is worked along the outline of the design, following the method described in 46. Next, a second layer is worked over the Chain Stitch, with a change in color, and possibly weight, of thread. The second working thread emerges just outside the end of the first Chain Stitch; then the regular Back Stitch (3) is worked over the Chain Stitch, with needle emerging and returning through the material in the center of the loop of each Chain Stitch. This chain makes a decorative margin.

48 · CHAIN STITCH—BROKEN

Although there are endless varieties of the Chain Stitch, this is the first really new way of thinking about the Chain Stitch. Make an ordinary Detached Chain Stitch in the regular manner, except that, when making the tie-down loop, the needle is inserted at the end of the stitch at D and brought back in the direction you have just worked. The link is formed, and the needle emerges at E near the beginning of the stitch. This process is illustrated in DIAGRAM 1. In the next step, the thread, which emerges from inside the first link, is carried back to the end of the chain and slipped under the tie-down stitch (without going through the fabric), from the bottom up as shown in DIAGRAM 2.

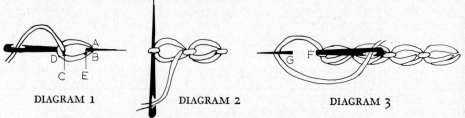

DIAGRAM 1   DIAGRAM 2   DIAGRAM 3

Work on across to the left, forming a new Chain Stitch by inserting the needle just beside or in the same hole as the little tie-down stitch. Repeat this process to the end of the row. You'll find that it makes an unusual effect and is more dramatic with a heavy twisted thread.

49 · CHAIN STITCH—BROAD

A glance at the diagram will show you that this stitch is worked in somewhat different fashion from the usual Chain Stitch. This chain is a bit firmer and has a tight, almost braided appearance, which is useful for certain purposes. However it must be worked with a strong, heavy, firm thread to get the correct effect. Smaller stitches must be taken between lengths, and I suggest that you work this with a blunt needle, for much of the action will be going under threads already worked rather than through the fabric.

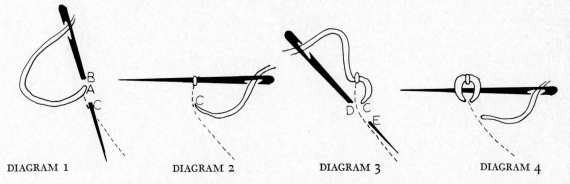

DIAGRAM 1   DIAGRAM 2   DIAGRAM 3   DIAGRAM 4

DIAGRAM 1 shows the working thread brought out at A—a very short distance from the end of the line to be worked—and carried back to the actual end and inserted at B. This forms as small a stitch as will allow the needle to slip through. The needle is then brought on back under the work to emerge at C a short distance below A. Your needle and thread are now in position to start forming the links of the chain. The needle is slipped under the small stitch you have just formed and is pulled through without entering the fabric. DIAGRAM 3 shows the thread being pulled through the loop and the needle being inserted slightly to the left of the line and brought out slightly to the right at E. Then pull it on through without tightening the loop. DIAGRAM 4 shows the second link in the process. The action of the needle is the same as in DIAGRAM 2. You now have two legs of the previous Chain Stitch to slide the needle under.

Each loop, as it is formed, is kept fairly loose, and the stitch on the back of the work is small. This keeps the stitches short and fat, which is the charm of this stitch. If your thread is sufficiently thick, you will get the proper effect. This stitch is used for lines, borders, long stems, and things of that nature.

The needle slides under as easily from one direction as the other so the left-hander should have no problems.

71

This is one of the fancy line stitches, also used for a filling, that many workers find very attractive. With a little bit of practice, it goes as quickly as the plain Chain and has great decorative possibilities. It works up well in almost any thread but a heavier twist naturally gives it a bolder effect. It is worked from top to bottom, or from right to left as is the regular Chain.

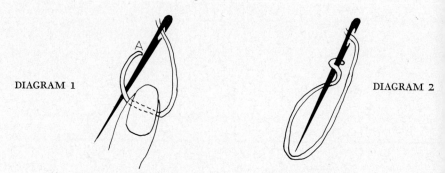

DIAGRAM 1

DIAGRAM 2

The needle is brought out at the end of the line at A. The needle is laid under the thread, which is held down just to the right of the needle with your left thumb (DIAGRAM 1). Pass the thread from right to left and under the needle, lifting it just a little, and firm up the little loop next to where the thread emerges (DIAGRAM 2). Then point the needle counterclockwise toward the right of the thread. Still holding the thread under the thumb, insert the needle just below, fairly close at B, and bring the needle out at C—the length of the next chain to be made. Next, a regular Chain loop is made from left to right under the needle, and the needle is pulled on through while the thread is being held (DIAGRAM 3).

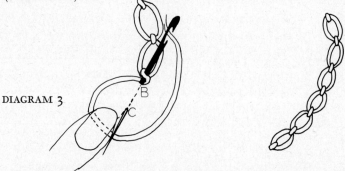

DIAGRAM 3

The first loop can also be made with the left hand holding the working thread and tightening the loop for inserting in the fabric, which method you may find more comfortable. Again go back to

Diagram 1 and repeat the twist shown in Diagrams 1 and 2, and you will be ready to start the second link in your chain.

The back of this stitch resembles the ordinary Chain Stitch except for spacing—a row of straight stitches with a space between, where the loop between the links is formed.

For left-handers, if you don't turn the illustration upside down, start at the opposite end of the line. The working thread is held with the right thumb, and the twist goes clockwise. The remainder of the process is worked the same way.

51 · CHAIN STITCH—CABLE, DOUBLE

This stitch could technically also be called a whipped stitch. Two rows of the Cable Chain are worked side by side. Make sure the stitches match each other as they go along. The loops are whipped together in contrasting color, or perhaps a metallic thread, to give a rich braid effect.

The drawing shows only the whip action, but you might try whipping in the opposite direction with a second color or using the same contrasting color again, which would give you a cross between the links to result in an even more raised effect.

Left-handers should use the directions given in stitch 50 to do the Cable Chain, and the whip stitch is worked as usual. A blunt needle would be a good idea for the whipped action. The back view would be the same as two parallel rows of Cable Chain.

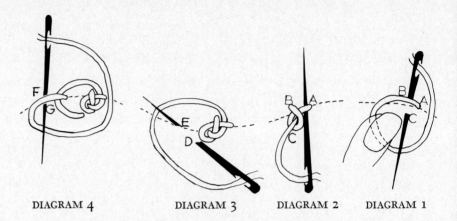

DIAGRAM 4   DIAGRAM 3   DIAGRAM 2   DIAGRAM 1

The diagrams of this stitch make it look quite complicated, but once you start, you'll be intrigued by the procedure, and it is really fun to do. Working from right to left, the thread is brought out on the right-hand end and held in position with the left thumb along the line to be worked. The needle is inserted in the fabric at B, just behind the thread, not taking up much fabric (DIAGRAM 1). It emerges at C going over the working thread which is being held in place, making a twisted chain. DIAGRAM 2 shows the needle being slipped under the thread at the beginning of the twisted chain near A. Don't pull this up too tightly, and you'll have a nice little fancy knot. For the next step, shown in DIAGRAM 3, the needle is inserted at D, just below the base of your knot, and brought out at E, allowing the space your Chain Stitch is to be. It is then pulled on through, again not too tightly. That completes the first stitch.

The thread emerging from the chain will again be held with your left thumb and the needle inserted in back of it, as shown in DIAGRAM 4. FIGURE 1 shows a completed area of this stitch.

FIGURE 1

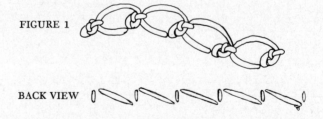

BACK VIEW

Left-handers, reverse the working of this stitch instead of using the upside-down method. The main object is to keep the tension regular, so do what is most comfortable.

This variation on the Knotted Cable Chain is seldom seen in publications but it is worth trying out.

DIAGRAM 1

DIAGRAM 2

The first two steps are worked exactly the same as your regular Cable Chain Knotted Stitch—that is, a little twisted Chain Stitch as in DIAGRAM 1. Slip the needle, without going through the fabric, back under the little beginning thread and pull on through, thus completing the knot at the start of the stitch.

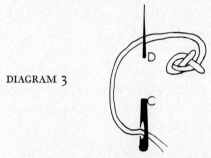

DIAGRAM 3

DIAGRAM 3 shows the departure from your original stitch. The thread is held up above the line you are working, and the needle is inserted below and brought out just above the line and a little to the left of your knot. This actually forms an upside-down Buttonhole Stitch. Pull the thread through, without stretching it in any way, and you are in the position to start your next stitch. FIGURE 1 shows several of these stitches worked.

Left-hand workers use the directions for the Knotted Cable Chain and the Buttonhole Stitch.

FIGURE 1

I found this stitch in a book published in the late 1800's, and it is one of the few really old ones I've never seen in any more recent publications. If proper attention is paid to the action and a fairly heavy thread used, this stitch really does work up into a round. Unlike other Cable Chains, this stitch is worked from the bottom up. You would do well to work this on an evenweave fabric, or mark off vertical parallel lines to guide you, for the beauty of this stitch is its regularity. You are actually working in squares.

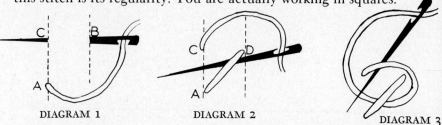

DIAGRAM 1   DIAGRAM 2   DIAGRAM 3

Bring your thread out at A on the lower end of the left-hand line, carry the needle up to the right line, and insert at B. Pass under the fabric from right to left, emerging at C, directly opposite on the left line (DIAGRAM 1). This will give you a diagonal straight stitch on the front of your work. The needle is then slipped under this stitch as shown in DIAGRAM 2 but not pulled through too tightly. DIAGRAM 3 shows the needle passing *under* the loop just made, the thread held with the left thumb, and *over* the working thread, to form another loop, again not pulled up too tightly. This completes your first round. The needle is then carried up again to the right-hand line and inserted from right to left.

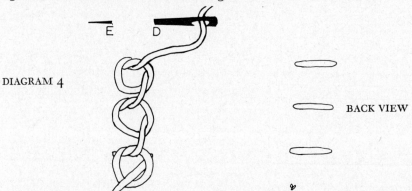

DIAGRAM 4

BACK VIEW

DIAGRAM 4 shows some stitches already worked, with the needle in position to start a new stitch. It might be advisable, if your fabric allows it, to use a blunt needle on this stitch to prevent splitting threads. The left-hander works this stitch using reverse directions.

The first slant stitch enters from right to left instead of as in the diagram, and the needle for the first insertion is carried from the left line to the right line.

55 · CHAIN STITCH—CABLE, PORTUGUESE

Unearthing old stitches no longer commonly in use is one of the things that has made compiling this book so interesting. The Portuguese Chain is a little fussy to work with but well worth the effort if you take the time to get the technique down so it is not a chore. As with most knotted stitches, a fairly stiff, heavy thread shows this stitch off to the best advantage. Perhaps use a blunt needle, because the tricky part of this stitch is where the needle goes under the thread rather than through the fabric.

Start at the position most comfortable for you when working the ordinary Cable Chain. Bring out the needle at A and form a Chain Stitch without finishing it off. DIAGRAM 1 shows the action of the needle being slipped first under the left or upper side of the loop, depending on the direction you are holding your work, and then under the working thread before being pulled through. Now the thread is twisted over the needle as for the Cable Chain, as shown in DIAGRAM 2, and inserted in the fabric. To get the full effect of this stitch, these Chain Stitches should be kept close together. Continue on in this manner.

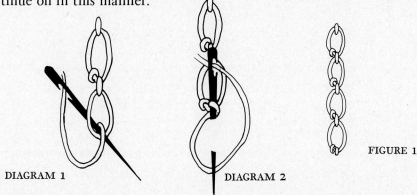

DIAGRAM 1   DIAGRAM 2   FIGURE 1

The resulting series of stitches is shown in FIGURE 1. The back of the work shows exactly what the Cable Chain shows, because the variation of this stitch appears only on the surface.

Left-handers work on the opposite side of the loop and reverse the twist over the needle for the cable part of the stitch, as in the regular Cable Chain.

77

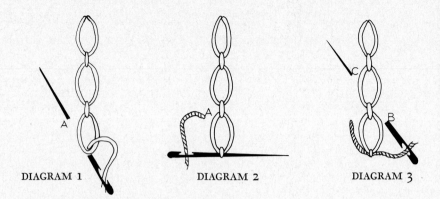

DIAGRAM 1   DIAGRAM 2   DIAGRAM 3

This variation on the Cable Chain adds extra ornamentation when you want it. As a rule, to get the proper effect, you use a different color or weight of the same color for the slipped-stitch work. As you can see by the diagram, you first work the basic Cable Chain, and then you bring out the contrasting thread to the left of the cable at A, level with the end of the actual loop at the top. Slip the needle through the stitch that lies between the cables without going through the fabric (in this case the first one, at the bottom of the row), and insert the needle on the opposite side at B level with A. The needle then emerges at C, slanting across the back of the work and up toward the top. Continue on in this manner to the top of the row of stitches. Take care not to pull the slipped-under stitches too tight, for these must lie softly on the surface of your fabric.

The back of this stitch should be a series of slanting stitches over the regular straight stitches of the Cable Chain. To make the stitch more decorative, you might try adding little Detached Chains, or French Knots in the center of your large chains.

A left-hander works the Cable Chain in the normal manner, but will probably be more comfortable slipping the thread from right to left (reverse the letters on the diagram).

57 · CHAIN STITCH—CABLE, SLIP UP

To my knowledge this is an original stitch of my own and, as has been true down through the ages, was developed by mistake. I did what many beginners do—ignored the directions and misread the diagram. The result is an interesting textured stitch, especially attractive if the basic Chain Stitch is kept rather small.

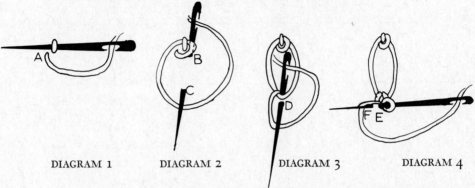

DIAGRAM 1   DIAGRAM 2   DIAGRAM 3   DIAGRAM 4

The first link of the Cable Chain is worked as described, but instead of the needle being carried down to form the Chain Stitch, it is brought around, to the left of the base, a thread or two, as shown in DIAGRAM 1. The needle is then slipped back under the stitch just formed, from right to left, on the surface without going through the fabric, and is pulled on through. Next the needle is inserted to the right of the little loop formed, so close that your needle is actually under the edge, and brought out below, the length of the basic chain that you want (DIAGRAM 2). At the base of this Chain Stitch, a small Chain Stitch is formed, the working of this shown in DIAGRAM 3. Now you are ready to start with your cable loop twist again, which is done as the tie-down stitch for your small chain and brought out to the left again as shown in DIAGRAM 4. Continue on in this manner to the end of your line.

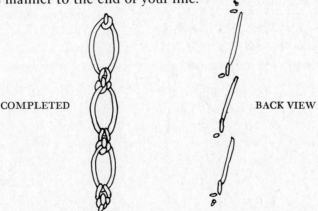

COMPLETED   BACK VIEW

This stitch has definite decorative possibilities either used in a single row or in parallel lines with angles opposing each other. As with other Chain Stitches, it can be worked either from the top down or from right to left, whichever is most comfortable for you. It is worked exactly the same as the Cable Chain Stitch, except that the stitches are at right angles to each other. The back view is a series of slanting straight lines or diagonal lines at right angles to each other. A left-hander should follow the directions for the Cable Chain, using the angle as already mentioned.

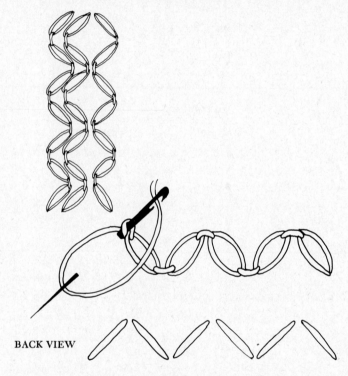

BACK VIEW

To get the full effect of this stitch you should use a fairly heavy thread with a bit of twist. The diagram shows a loop that has been pulled up tightly around the upper half of the needle and the working threads twisted around the lower end. It would be best to master the technique of the Cable Chain before attempting this variation, although once you are familiar with the basic stitch, there should be no further difficulty.

59 · CHAIN STITCH—CHECKERED
(MAGIC STITCH)

This can be a fun stitch to work, and children love it. Even before your thread is anchored and brought to the front of the fabric this stitch is different from others, because you have two threads threaded into the same needle. To get the fullest effect with this stitch, use sharply contrasting colors.

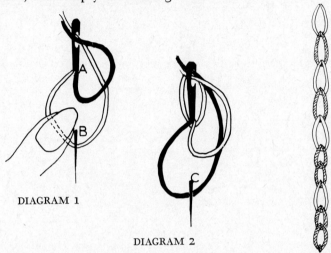

DIAGRAM 1

DIAGRAM 2

Commence working this exactly as an ordinary Chain, but hold only one of the colors under your left thumb in a loop, keeping the other thread out of the way, as shown in DIAGRAM 1. The thread is brought out at A. The needle goes into the same hole and is brought out along the working line at B, but only the white thread is held under for a loop, the black thread being kept off to the side. The needle is then pulled on through, and a second Chain Stitch is taken in the normal manner, except that this time it is the black, or alternate, thread, which is held under by the left thumb to form the loop. If, when you are making one stitch, some of the contrasting color should show on the surface, a slight pull will cause it to disappear. The thread being able to disappear is what has earned the name "Magic Stitch" for this stitch. After you have mastered the technique, try doing two or three stitches in one color before changing colors. In this manner you can get any number of variations.

Left-handers should execute the Chain Stitch in the usual manner. The back of the work appears the same as the regular Chain Stitch also, except that there is a variety of colors.

60 · CHAIN STITCH—CRESTED
(SPANISH CORAL STITCH)

This stitch is a perfect example of how fanciful variations on the Chain Stitch can get. When completed it looks almost like a Spanish Braid Stitch and is well suited for edgings. As with other Chain Stitches, this can be worked from either the top down or right to left, for right-handers. In practicing this stitch, mark out two parallel lines to work between. Heavy stiff thread gives the best results. The size of your thread will naturally determine the size of your stitches and the distance between your parallel lines, but for your first attempt work with fairly large spacing to observe the action of needle and thread.

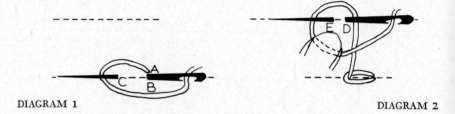

DIAGRAM 1   DIAGRAM 2

Commence work with a small regular Chain Stitch on the lower line to the right, as in DIAGRAM 1. With the thread coming out from inside the loop of the first Chain Stitch, the needle is carried up to the top line and inserted from right to left, the thread being held with the left thumb so that a loop is formed over it. Picking up a small amount of fabric as shown in DIAGRAM 2, DE, pull the needle on through. A little knot is thus formed at the top of the stitch. The next step is simply slipping the needle under the thread that lies between the two parallel lines, as shown in DIAGRAM 3, and carried on across. For the next stitch, the needle is inserted at C on the lower line, inside the original chain, and brought out along the lower line at F to form the base of this stitch. You then carry the thread on up to the top line and continue as described.

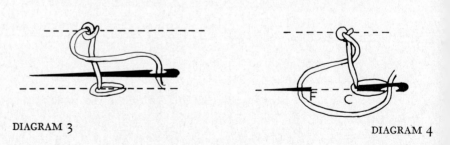

DIAGRAM 3   DIAGRAM 4

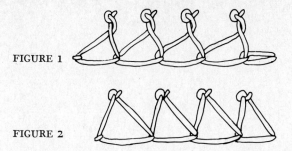

FIGURE 1

FIGURE 2

FIGURE 1 shows a series of these crested chains already worked. FIGURE 2 shows a variation that can be achieved by omitting the action in DIAGRAM 3—slipping the needle under the thread—and this can be used for a somewhat less ornate border.

61 · CHAIN STITCH—CRESTED, ZIGZAG

This stitch is a variation on the Crested Chain Stitch. Before beginning, make three parallel lines to practice on. Actually, as in most zigzag stitches, you are just making one stitch below and one above, but when you are making the small chain on the lower line, do remember to reverse the way the thread lies, as in DIAGRAM 1.

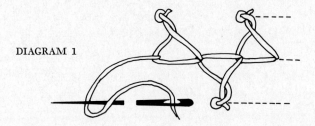

DIAGRAM 1

Although the stitches alternate, the left-hander will probably still prefer to start with the right-hand end of the work.

BACK VIEW

This little variation could, I suppose, be classified under the Cross Stitch, but since the Chain Stitch is part of the work, we will leave it as a Chain Stitch variation. This stitch produces an unusual texture which lends itself better to contemporary work than does the ordinary Cross Stitch. It is necessary to keep the squares regular, so you should have an outline to follow or should work on an evenweave fabric. This basically simple technique should be tried with several weights of thread to see what effects you get from going from the light and lacy to the heavy, almost ornate.

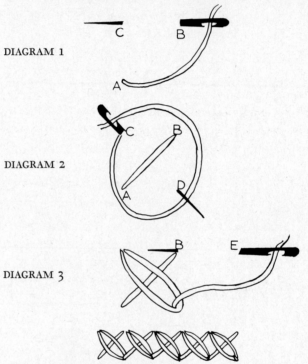

DIAGRAM 1

DIAGRAM 2

DIAGRAM 3

The needle is brought out at A on the left-hand end of the lower line and carried up to the right, inserted on the upper line at B. The thread should form a 45-degree angle with the lower line. It is brought out at C to the left, directly above A on the lower line. Now an ordinary Chain Stitch is worked in the other direction, which means that the needle is inserted again at C and a loop held with the left thumb while the needle is brought out at D on the lower line, directly under B (DIAGRAM 2). Pull the thread through, completing the Chain Stitch. You are now ready to proceed to the next stitch as shown in DIAGRAM 3. The needle is carried out again to the right, put in at E, and brought out at B.

63 · CHAIN STITCH—DETACHED
(DAISY STITCH, LAZY DAISY STITCH, KNOTTED KNOT STITCH, LOOP STITCH, PICOT STITCH, TAIL CHAIN STITCH, TIED LOOP STITCH)

Certainly one of the best known stitches in the American needle-woman's vocabulary, this simple little stitch, when combined with other stitches or with varying weights of thread, can be varied almost indefinitely. The size of this stitch is determined by the areas to be filled and the size of thread being used. The needle emerges at the required spot, and as usual the loop is held a little to the left with the left thumb. The needle is then again inserted in the same spot where it came out and emerges a little further on for the required length of the stitch. It is pulled on through over the working thread, and the loop is formed and then secured by taking the needle through to the back over the end of the loop, forming a tie-down stitch. Then the needle is brought out at whatever spot you wish to begin the next stitch.

This stitch has many decorative uses, a few of which are illustrated in FIGURE 1. When it is worked very small and tight, it takes on the appearance of a knot, but it has an advantage over a knot stitch of laundering well.

FIGURE 1

64 • CHAIN STITCH—DETACHED, FILLING

As far as the working of this stitch is concerned, the Detached Chain is not really a variation. What is different is the use and placement of the stitches. The drawings show the Detached Chain Stitch worked as a filling. As a rule, when it is used for this particular purpose, the stitches are kept fairly small and scattered over the area.

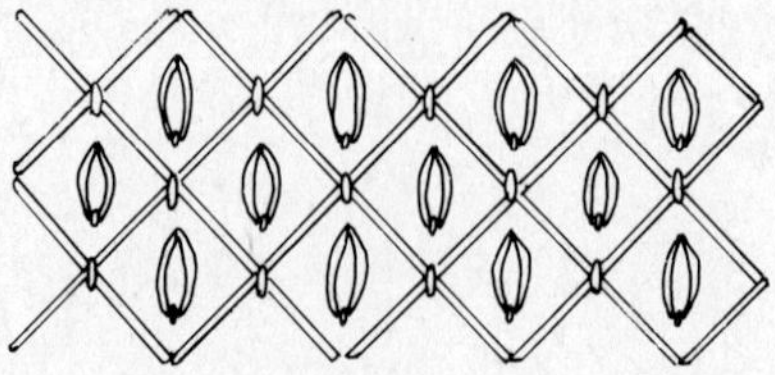

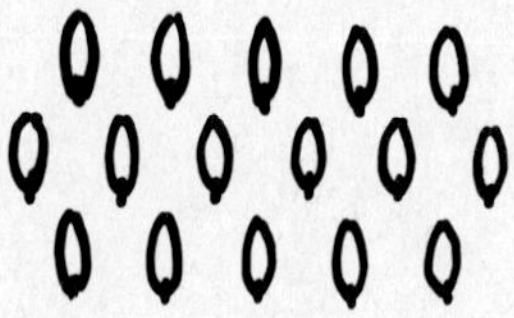

This stitch sometimes replaces the Seed Stitch or the French Knot—it is more decorative than the Seed Stitch and has less texture than the French Knot. The Detached Chain can also be useful as a filling in combination with other stitches, even the common Running Stitch, or as a small filling inside other stitches, perhaps even a larger chain.

The back of this stitch is the single stitch between the ends of the loops. If the stitch is used as an overall filling, the back runs between one Chain Stitch and another.

The left-hander simply has his loop going in the opposite direction to that of the right-hander and uses the right thumb for holding it down.

65 • CHAIN STITCH—DETACHED, LONG-ARMED
(LONG-TAILED)

The Long-Armed Stitch is a very simple variation on the Detached Chain Stitch and is accomplished simply by extending the length of the tie-down stitch. Generally, the loop of this chain remains quite small while the arm tying down the stitch is extended somewhat.

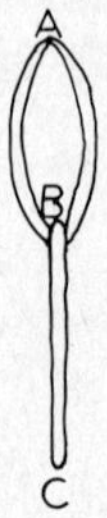

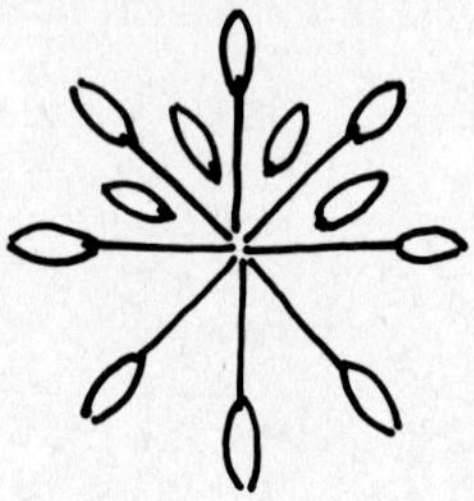

FIGURE 1

The Long-Armed Stitch can be used as a filling stitch, and it also, if all these long-arm ends are finished in the same spot and worked in a circle, makes a nice little floral effect. FIGURE 1 shows this; one half of the circle is filled with the Long-Armed Detached Chain, and the other half has small Detached Chains in each of the areas between.

66 · CHAIN STITCH—DETACHED, SLIPPED
(TULIP STITCH)

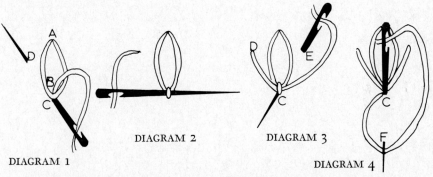

DIAGRAM 2

DIAGRAM 3

DIAGRAM 1

DIAGRAM 4

This is another of the easy variations on the Detached Chain. It has decorative possibilities, particularly when a heavy thread is used for the slipped stitches. DIAGRAM 1 shows the loop of the Detached Chain already formed and the needle going in at C to complete the stitch that ties down the loop. It emerges at D to the left of the loop and about halfway up. (Work full-sized loops with this stitch to show it off.) From D the needle is slipped, hence the name, under the little stitch that ties down the loop, pulled on through but not too tightly, and put into the fabric at E. DIAGRAM 3 shows the action of the needle if this stitch is to be worked in a continuous line. The needle comes out at C and enters the fabric again at C, and is carried along the line to emerge at F, as in DIAGRAM 4, to form a new loop.

FIGURE 1

FIGURE 1 shows various lengths and weights of threads slipped through the bottom stitch and gives you some ideas for experimenting with this stitch.

67 · CHAIN STITCH—DOUBLE

The Double Chain is very similar to the Closed Feather Stitch except that the needle is inserted inside the loop instead of outside. By altering the size of the loops, you can vary the widths of the areas to be filled with this stitch, a technique not possible with a plain line of Chain Stitches. You might need two guide lines to follow when you first practice this stitch.

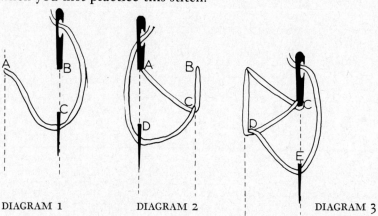

DIAGRAM 1   DIAGRAM 2   DIAGRAM 3

The work is begun coming out at the top of the left-hand line at A (DIAGRAM 1). The needle is inserted at the top of the right-hand line at B and is brought out directly below at C, the loop being held with the left thumb as always. At this point, the working of this stitch will seem a bit awkward. Throw the thread over to the left and grasp it again with the left thumb, making sure that the thread does not fall back over the left hand. You must form a loop on this side, which sometimes takes a bit of practice. If necessary, you must exaggerate the loop, as shown in the diagram, having the thread sweep clear up over the top of the line you are working, to make sure that, as your needle is inserted and comes out, it will go over the thread. The needle is inserted at A again and emerges at D which should be slightly below C on the opposite line. As you work down the lines, the stitches are staggered. The third stitch, as shown in DIAGRAM 3, is back over to the right-hand line. Go inside the loop with the needle, bringing it out farther down on the same line and over the thread at E, which will be a bit below D. Continue working on down, alternating from side to side.

FIGURE 1

88

If your stitches are large enough and you want a more textured effect, a small isolated stitch of some sort, either the Detached Chain or a French Knot, could be stuck inside each loop (FIGURE 1).

Since the work alternates from side to side, the left-hander can use the directions given for the right-hander.

68 · CHAIN STITCH–DOUBLE, ALTERNATING

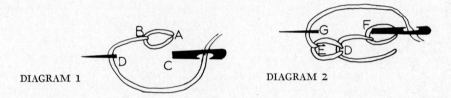

DIAGRAM 1   DIAGRAM 2

I don't suggest trying this stitch until you are comfortable with changing sides on the Double Chain Stitch. However, it is a nice variation, particularly for contemporary work. Begin by working a very small Chain Stitch and beside it another Chain Stitch about three times as long, as shown in DIAGRAM 1. With the thread coming over the loop at the end of the long stitch, now work another short Chain Stitch, and beside it, going back into the loop of the original small Chain Stitch, work another long one. Continue to repeat the combination of long and short stitches on down the row. End the work with a short straight stitch at the base of a long stitch, so you will have a smooth end.

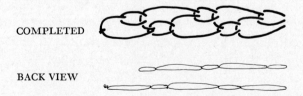

COMPLETED

BACK VIEW

The back of your work will be parallel lines of long and short stitches opposing each other. Left-handers work the same as the right-handers in this.

89

The Crested Double Chain Stitch is a Double Chain with a little extra something added, and it gives an interesting touch to an otherwise plain-looking border.

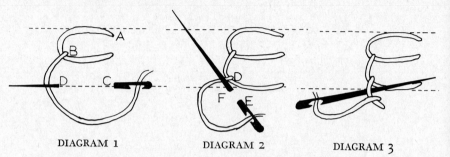

DIAGRAM 1   DIAGRAM 2   DIAGRAM 3

Begin by working two Open Chain Stitches side by side, as shown in DIAGRAM 1. In trying this stitch out for the first time, make parallel guidelines, and start work at the top of them. After the second chain has been formed, your needle is taken off to the side on which the thread is emerging and inserted perpendicular to the chain, from the outside in. Holding the thread with your left thumb, form a Buttonhole Stitch. The amount of fabric picked up, EF, will not take you clear back to D, but one third of the distance (DIAGRAM 2). The third step in this stitch is simply a whipping stitch in which the needle and thread are passed under the little loops of the Buttonhole Stitch, from the bottom up without going through the fabric. The needle is then inserted inside the loop of the left-hand Chain Stitch, and another pair of Open Chains are worked in the reverse direction, as in DIAGRAM 4.

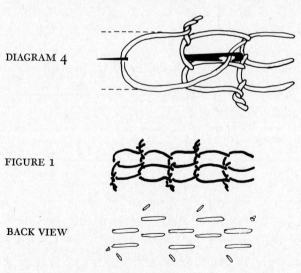

DIAGRAM 4

FIGURE 1

BACK VIEW

FIGURE 1 shows a little group of these stitches worked.

The left-hander can follow the directions as they are given, because the work is done back and forth in both directions.

70 · CHAIN STITCH—DOUBLE, LINKED

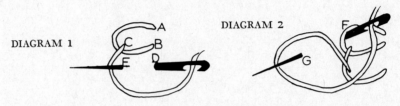

DIAGRAM 1

DIAGRAM 2

The Double Linked Chain Stitch gives a nice textured variation to a Double Chain Stitch band. It is begun like the other Double Chain Stitches by working two Open Chains side by side (DIAGRAM 1). The variation appears in the second step, where a Twisted Chain Stitch is formed, using the pair of chains as a foundation. The needle emerges from the lower chain, and it is inserted in the upper one and brought out along the line (DIAGRAM 2). This forms the Twisted Chain Stitch which links the Double Chains together. With the Twisted Chain as base, another pair of Double Chains is worked (DIAGRAM 3).

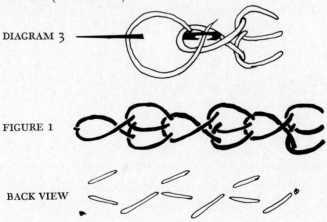

DIAGRAM 3

FIGURE 1

BACK VIEW

FIGURE 1 shows a band worked in this method.

The left-hander should start from the left-hand end of the band and reverse the working of the stitches.

91

71 · CHAIN STITCH—DOUBLE, TIED

Here is another variation achieved by working the Chain Stitch in a slightly different fashion from the usual one.

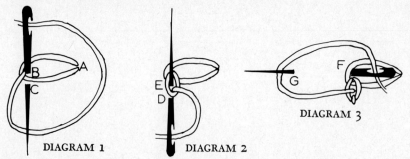

DIAGRAM 1   DIAGRAM 2   DIAGRAM 3

To start, form a regular Chain Stitch, fairly large. Now, using the thread that emerges from the chain at B, form a small chain at right angles to the first, as shown in DIAGRAM 1. This last stitch is a tie-down stitch, as in a Detached Chain, but bring the needle right on up through to the inside of the link again (DIAGRAM 2). This completes the first whole stitch. With the thread emerging from the inside of the small loop at E, the needle is then inserted inside the large link at F, beside the threads already there, and another large chain is formed (DIAGRAM 3). Repeat these two steps to the end of the line.

Do try this stitch with various weights of threads. This stitch in fine thread looks quite different from the same stitch in heavy thread. FIGURE 1 shows a series of stitches completed.

FIGURE 1   BACK VIEW

72 · CHAIN STITCH—DOUBLE, WHIPPED

This is another variation of the Double Chain. You might also try whipping the regular Double Chain, to compare results.

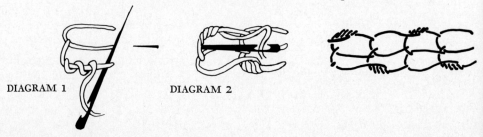

DIAGRAM 1   DIAGRAM 2

92

A pair of Chain Stitches are first worked side by side. On the side where the working thread emerges, take three or four whipped stitches around on the thread that forms the length, without going through the fabric. The needle is then brought back inside the loop nearest the working thread. Now make a Double Chain, working toward the other edge of your border, and repeat this process. Each alternate stitch will be whipped as you work along.

The left-hander works it in his normal manner for the regular Chain Stitch. The back view of this stitch would be the same as the regular Double Chain in that you simply have two rows of horizontal parallel lines, because the whipping work is done on the top surface.

73 · CHAIN STITCH—FEATHERED

When worked properly, the Feathered Chain Stitch gives you a neat border composed of a zigzag line studded with Chain Stitches. The inner zigzag is formed almost like the end of the Long-Armed Chain Stitch. To keep the work even, it is best to work on counted threads, or two parallel lines marked on the fabric.

Bring the threads through on the end of one of your traced lines and work a small Chain Stitch in a downward slanting direction toward the center of the two lines (DIAGRAM 1). Insert the needle a little lower down, slanting it in the same direction but going beyond what would be the middle point of your two lines. It then emerges on the opposite line, slanting back up toward the top (DIAGRAM 2), about level with where the previous straight stitch was brought out.

These Long-Armed Chain Stitches are worked alternately side by side in the slanting direction as shown in FIGURE 1, which gives you the view of several completed stitches.

Left-handers work as for the Long-Armed Chain Stitches.

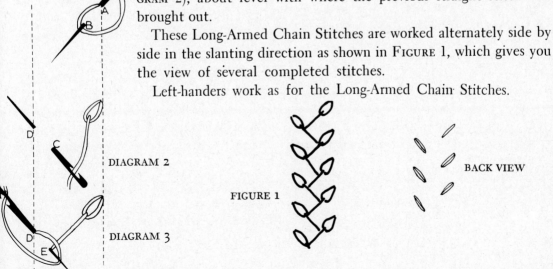

DIAGRAM 1

DIAGRAM 2

DIAGRAM 3

FIGURE 1

BACK VIEW

This stitch, which is similar to the Broad Chain, is worked in the same backward fashion but is a much heavier stitch and gives a bold decorative line suitable for thick stems.

Work is begun by forming a tiny Straight Stitch at the end of the line being worked. The needle is brought a slight way down the line, depending on the thickness of your thread, perhaps only one-sixteenth inch. (As with the Broad Chain Stitch, these stitches are kept shorter than the regular Chain Stitch, so that a heavy, braid appearance will be obtained.) The needle is then slipped under the Straight Stitch, not through the fabric, and brought down, as shown in DIAGRAM 1, and inserted in the same hole where the stitch is begun, C. It emerges again a fraction of an inch down the line at D.

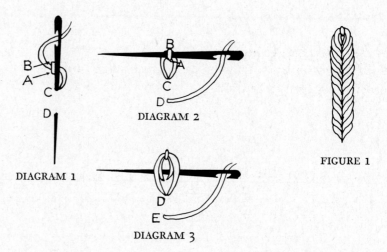

DIAGRAM 1

DIAGRAM 2

DIAGRAM 3

FIGURE 1

Now begins the part of this stitch that distinguishes it from the Broad Chain. The needle is again passed under the Straight Stitch, which makes two loops passing through the same little stitch, and brought down to be finished off in the usual manner (DIAGRAM 2). The third stitch is now ready to be formed, and in this one the needle is passed through the first Chain Stitch made and under the second Chain Stitch (DIAGRAM 3). Make each subsequent loop in that same way, always slipping the needle back under the legs of the two previous loops. Remember not to pull your thread up too tight, because part of the dramatic effect of this stitch is its heavy appearance.

The back of this stitch looks the same as the back of the Broad Chain—a series of small straight stitches.

This Braided Chain is even more effective than the Heavy Chain, although the action is very similar. Like all the Chain Stitches, it curves well and makes for a wide, thick, textured line. To show off to best advantage, work in a heavy, stiff thread and with a blunt needle.

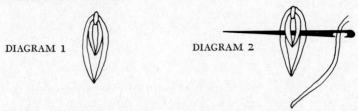

DIAGRAM 1   DIAGRAM 2

Work is begun as shown in DIAGRAM 1, and in exactly the same manner as 74, the Heavy Chain. DIAGRAM 2 shows where the difference between the two stitches lies. The needle is slipped *under* the legs of the first chain formed, but *over* the thread of the second. The working thread is pulled through and the needle inserted in the same spot where this stitch begins. Now the needle is brought out the proper distance down the line, and the above step repeated on to the end.

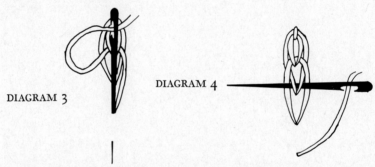

DIAGRAM 3   DIAGRAM 4

FIGURE 1 shows a series of these stitches worked. No diagram is needed for the back of the work, as it is still the same as the Broad Chain.

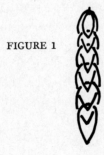

FIGURE 1

Although this stitch looks most elaborate, it is really quite easy and quick to work. It can be made very ornate-looking by the introduction of gold thread or metallic cord of some kind. One authority attributed this stitch to Mary Queen of Scots, because it was found on some of the embroideries she made during her long imprisonment. During this period, in both France and England, much elaborate work was done by royal ladies, not only for their own clothing but for church vestments.

This stitch is well worth experimenting with. To get the most dramatic effect, work the first process of the stitch with a fairly heavy thread, but not so heavy as that you intend to use for your interlacing. You can obtain a less formal but equally bold look by using raffia in the second step.

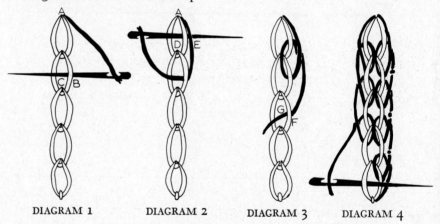

DIAGRAM 1   DIAGRAM 2   DIAGRAM 3   DIAGRAM 4

Start with a row of Chain Stitches worked somewhat loosely. When the row is completed, start again at A as in DIAGRAM 1, with a different type of thread. Pass this thread loosely from the outside in, B to C, under the right side of the second chain, without going into the fabric and with the lacing thread lying just outside the first chain. Now go back under the first chain, from the inside out, D to E (DIAGRAM 2). You will be going under both the chain and the previous lacing but not the fabric. Go behind the third chain from the outside in again, F to G, then back to the second chain from inside out and, as you did previously, going under both chain and lacing. Continue on in this manner down to the end of your row of stitches, bringing the lacing thread to the back, behind the last chain, and anchoring off.

Now with a fresh thread you begin again at A and reverse the procedure on the other side of your chain. Make sure that the two center stitches of the lacing lie side by side and are not overlapping. The interlacing thread should not be pulled tight but should lie just against the center chain. The braid is lovely just this way, but you might prefer, depending on the thread you are using and the effect you want, to anchor down the lacing thread, especially if the article being embroidered is to be laundered. Using a thread the same shade as the lacing thread, take small anchoring stitches as shown in DIAGRAM 4.

A left-hander needs no special instructions, for the chain is worked in the usual manner, and the lacing is done in both directions. The back of the work looks exactly like the regular Chain Stitch, unless you elect to do the little tie-down stitches, in which case, there will be a series of lines connecting them.

77 · CHAIN STITCH–KNOTTED
(LINK STITCH)

Like most of the fancy stitches, this decorative variation on the Chain Stitch shows off to the best advantage when worked with a stout thread.

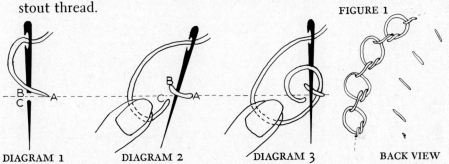

DIAGRAM 1   DIAGRAM 2   DIAGRAM 3   BACK VIEW

Start by bringing the needle out on the right-hand end of the line at A. Insert the needle a little farther to the left, just above the traced line, and bring it up just below the line, forming a little slant stitch, BC. Now throw the thread over to the left, hold it with the thumb, and pass the needle just under the slanting stitch from above downward. Draw the thread through, leaving it just a little slack. Again throw the thread around to the left and hold it under the thumb. The needle and thread are then passed under this slack loop (DIAGRAM 3). The thread is pulled carefully through, away from the worker rather than to the left. This leaves the first stitch completed. The work progresses on to the left in the same manner and will form a series of small links as shown in FIGURE 1.

The left-hander will find it easiest to work this by turning the diagram upside down. The back view is a series of little upright stitches in a line.

78 · CHAIN STITCH—OPEN
(SQUARE, LADDER)

This versatile stitch, useful for borders and fillings, is sometimes seen in the work done in India. In the diagram it is shown worked in a straight line, but the Open Chain is also very well suited to lines and shapes that are graduated. Another type of work that this stitch is often used for is Couching. This will be covered in the section on Couching, but as you can see by FIGURE 1, heavy rug yarns, bunches of thread, or even ribbons of a contrasting color lend themselves to being couched down with this stitch. Sometimes the stitches lie very close together, with no background showing through.

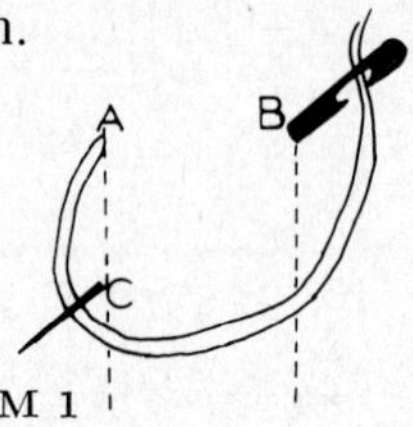

DIAGRAM 1

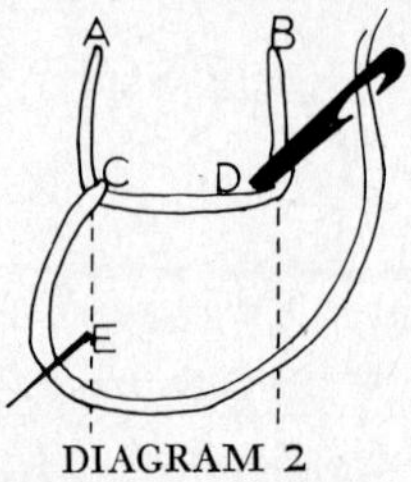

DIAGRAM 2

While learning the technique of this stitch, work between parallel guidelines. The work is done from the top down. Instead of making the Chain Stitch in the normal manner with a vertical straight stitch, the stitch is taken diagonally between the parallel lines. The basic action still resembles the regular Chain Stitch. Hold the thread with your left thumb to form a loop each time. The thread is brought out at the top of the left-hand line at A in DIAGRAM 1. The needle is then inserted opposite on the right-hand line at B, going across the back of the material, and emerges at C on the left-hand line, a short distance below A. The needle and thread are pulled through but the loop is left a little loose. Insert the needle again on the right-hand line at D just below B, *inside* the loop. Thread may now be tightened up a bit around the needle. It comes out diagonally again at E, below C, and again the needle is pulled through, leaving the thread loose as before (DIAGRAM 2).

FIGURE 1

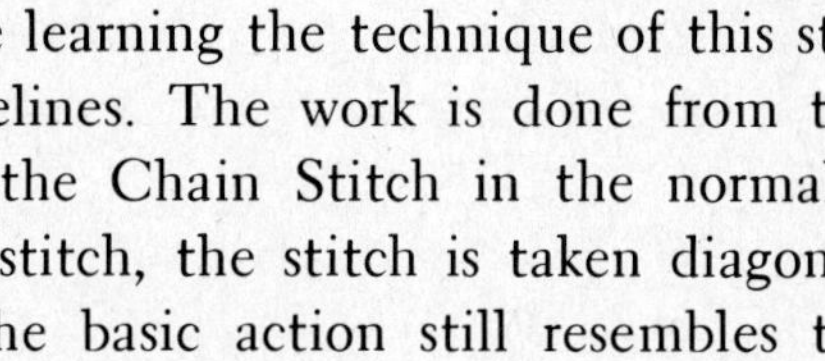

FIGURE 1 shows a combination of some of the variations that can be developed with this stitch. You will note that there are points at the ends of some of these lines. When this is done at the beginning of the line, the first chain is formed like a regular chain with the loops left loose. If it is done at the end of a series of stitches, a single little tie-down stitch is made in the center. When keeping the design parallel all the way, two anchoring stitches are necessary. Make a small tie-down stitch where the thread was on the left-hand line and carry the thread back under your work directly opposite. Bring it up on the right-hand line and insert it over the line to form the second small anchoring stitch.

The back of the work will be a series of slanting lines one under the other of equal length.

Left-handers should reverse these directions.

79 · CHAIN STITCH—ORNATE

This variation on the Chain Stitch, despite its name, is not as ornate as some of the others, but it does have a certain dramatic appearance, particularly when worked with a heavy, thick thread.

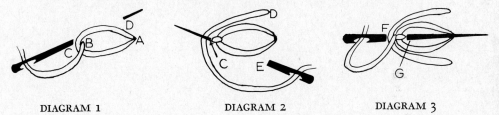

DIAGRAM 1   DIAGRAM 2   DIAGRAM 3

Work is started by making a fairly long Chain Stitch. Then bring the needle and thread out on the left-hand side of the link formed, actually almost level with the top of the chain (DIAGRAM 1). Now a Fly Stitch is made around the Chain Stitch, with the tie-down for the Fly Stitch coming out of the hole for the chain tie-down stitch at C (DIAGRAM 2). DIAGRAM 3 shows the needle being inserted to finish off the Fly Stitch and brought back inside the chain loop to begin the second Chain Stitch. These two steps are alternated on down the line to be covered.

The back of the work will be a series of straight horizontal stitches with a slanting stitch on the left side for commencing the Fly Stitch. The left-hander should reverse the procedure, forming both the Chain and the Fly Stitch in the opposite direction.

This attractive textured stitch looks quite elaborate but is really very easy to embroider and works up quickly. It's called a Band Stitch, but it can also cover complete areas, and can be varied widely, depending on the working of the stitches and the thread used. A frame of some type and a blunt needle are essential in this stitch.

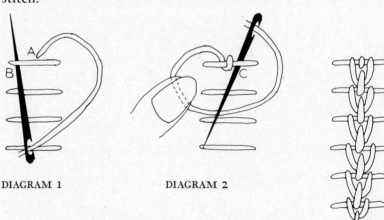

DIAGRAM 1   DIAGRAM 2

DIAGRAM 1 shows a simple band worked. This is begun by laying a series of threads fairly close together, again the distance depending on the weight of your thread. The working thread is then brought out just above the first laid thread at A, and the needle is slipped under that stitch from the bottom up. Keep your working thread out of the way, perhaps by throwing it over to the right, and slide the needle and thread through, forming a small loop (DIAGRAM 1). Now, holding your working thread with your left thumb for the loop, insert the needle to the right of the stitch just made and under the first laid stitch. Still not going through the fabric, pull the needle over the loop (DIAGRAM 2). Tighten up the stitch and continue down to the second laid thread. Again the needle is slipped under the thread on the left-hand side from the bottom up and not through the fabric. Now repeat the step done in DIAGRAM 2— sliding the needle under the laid thread from the top down, on the right-hand side of the loop formed over your laid thread. Continue in this manner until you have come down over each succeeding bar.

The back of the work shows the little stitches along the edge for your laid work and only the beginning and ending of the worked threads.

Left-handers will probably be more comfortable if they begin on the top right of the laid work and reverse the other directions.

81 • CHAIN STITCH—RAISED BAND, LINKED

This stitch is actually another variation of the Chain Band, but the diagrams are helpful in seeing the action of the needle. DIAGRAM 1 shows the evenly spaced laid stitches, fairly close together. Starting with the thread above the first bar at A, the needle is slipped under the first two bars from the bottom up and pulled firmly through. Then from the right-hand side of that stitch and downward, make the Chain Stitch over the same pair of bars, not going through the fabric (DIAGRAM 2). Proceed on down the successive bars in this manner.

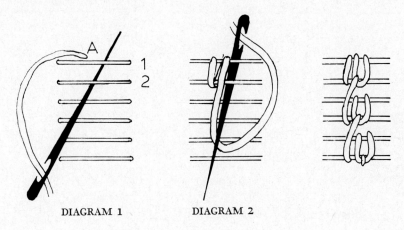

DIAGRAM 1   DIAGRAM 2

82 • CHAIN STITCH—RAISED BAND, TWISTED
(CHAINED BUTTERFLY STITCH)

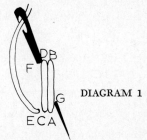

DIAGRAM 1

This is listed as a separate stitch from the Raised Band because the laid threads are done a little differently. DIAGRAM 1 shows a series of laid threads, which could even be worked as Satin Stitches, in groups of three all of equal lengths. These stitches are laid in individual groups, as the stitch is made, rather than all at once beforehand. Diagram 2 shows a group of three stitches being completed and the needle brought out at C, above the stitches. Insert the needle at D and slip it under the group of Straight Stitches, holding the thread with the left thumb, to form a Twisted Chain Stitch. Pull the thread slightly backward to tighten the knot. The needle is not inserted immediately below the loop formed, but carried a little bit farther along, where it is inserted in the fabric and brought out directly beside the parallel lines, in the same relative position as in A on the first stitch (Diagram 3). You then begin your next group of stitches. Repeat the previous step in each area until the lines to be covered are completed.

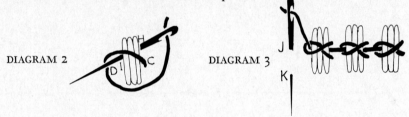

DIAGRAM 2   DIAGRAM 3

The left-hander will probably find it easier to turn the diagram upside down.

83 · CHAIN STITCH—RAISED BAND, VARIATIONS

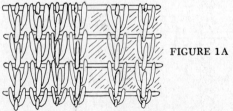 As mentioned before, there are a number of exciting variations to this stitch. The figures shown will give you a general idea of how they are worked. You can probably come up with others of your own. If the laid bars are long enough, you can work several rows of the Raised Chain Band side by side. When they are packed up close together they look quite different from the way they look spaced out between the rows so that the background fabric is part of the effect. Try it both ways. By doing exactly the same thing and changing the weight or color of thread in each row you get an unusual texture (Figure 1A).

FIGURE 1A

Another variation of this is made by alternating the direction of the chain. Instead of going back to the top each time, finish off the row of Chain Stitches, insert your needle, and bring it back up at the bottom beside the row just completed. Turn the piece around and work back in the other direction (FIGURE 1B).

FIGURE 1B

For a honeycomb appearance, try working over two bars instead of one. In this case lay the bars a little closer together when doing one stitch. Continue work over two bars for each stitch on down to the end of the row. On the second row, start by going over one bar and then proceed down, two bars at a time. Alternate the rows in this manner across the area to be covered (FIGURE 1C).

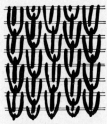

FIGURE 1C

A narrow delicate band, particularly when worked with a fine thread, is achieved by working a row of chains along each edge of the bars and leaving the center lines, which would have been laid closely together, exposed (FIGURE 1D).

FIGURE 1D

Quite an unusual appearance can be obtained by varying the length of the laid lines and working the Chain Stitches over them in a heavy thread. The length of the rows of Chain Stitches will vary according to the length of the laid thread (FIGURE 1E).

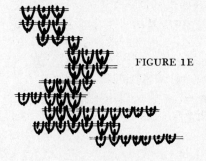

FIGURE 1E

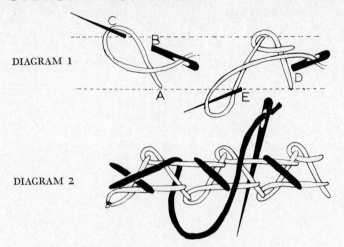

DIAGRAM 1

DIAGRAM 2

This interesting stitch looks just like narrow rick-rack braid when completed. First make a row of Spanish Knotted Feather Stitches, which in spite of the imposing name are just a variation of the Zig-zag Twisted Chain. I suggest you master that stitch before trying this variation. DIAGRAM 1 shows the variation on the Twisted Chain Zigzag. DIAGRAM 2 shows the bars that have been whipped together from right to left and the beginning of the journey back to form the last layer of this stitch. The back of the work is almost the same as the Twisted Chain, for the second step is done on the surface except where the stitches are tied down at the end. A medium-weight thread or heavier should be used for this, so that you get the textured effect we've come to expect in rick-rack.

The left-hander should work the Twisted Chain in the regular manner, and the Whipped Stitch in the most comfortable way.

85 · CHAIN STITCH—ROSETTE

The Rosette Chain Stitch is actually a twisted chain worked sideways from right to left, making a decorative line stitch. Its texture is good for edging curved geometric shapes or, when worked in a circle, for forming small flower shapes. Tension is most important in this stitch; it must not be pulled up too tight and it is not advisable to work this stitch on pieces that must be laundered frequently. A stiff thread, perhaps even waxed, gives the best results. For your first attempts at this stitch, work between horizontal parallel guidelines.

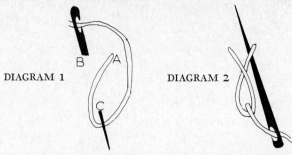

DIAGRAM 1   DIAGRAM 2

At the right-hand end of the upper line, the needle and thread are brought to the front of the fabric. Holding the thread to the left with the left thumb, insert the needle on the upper line at B, to the left of A behind the thread, and come out on the lower line at C. The needle goes over the looped thread at C when pulled through, completing a vertical Twisted Chain. Slip the needle and thread under the thread coming from A, without going through the background fabric. Then insert at D, a little farther along the upper line and, holding your thread again to the left, emerge on the lower line at E inside the loop (DIAGRAM 3).

DIAGRAM 3   DIAGRAM 4

DIAGRAM 4 shows the needle being slipped up to what is now the thread between the stitches formed. DIAGRAM 4 also shows a series of stitches that have been completed. If you wish to use this stitch to form a small flower, remember that the loops are on the rim of the circle, so that A and B, your starting points, will be at the center.

COMPLETED   BACK VIEW

The left-hander will probably find it more comfortable to work this stitch by starting at the left-hand end and reversing the lettering. The back view of this stitch is a series of slanting straight stitches, made when forming the original loop, as the rest of the work is done on the surface.

105

86 · CHAIN STITCH–RUSSIAN

In Russia the Chain Stitches are used most commonly in groups of three, both vertically and horizontally. In different books they are illustrated worked by two different methods. FIGURE 1 shows each Chain Stitch worked as a Detached Chain Stitch, but in the same grouping. FIGURE 2 shows the stitches worked by forming first a regular Chain Stitch and then working the two others from inside the loop of the original stitch. Either method makes an effective little motif.

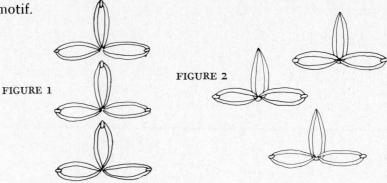

FIGURE 1

FIGURE 2

87 · CHAIN STITCH–SHELL

This is another variation of the Chain Stitch that can be changed in appearance by varying the thread. You might also want to go beyond the actual diagram, and add more loops to get a true-looking shell, as shown in FIGURE 1. As is true of all Chain Stitches, the Shell Chain follows curves nicely and adds a little extra touch to an ordinary Chain Stitch border.

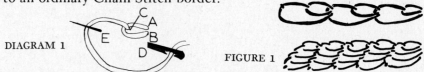

DIAGRAM 1

FIGURE 1

Beginning at the end of the line at A, make a small Chain Stitch. From B make another Chain Stitch, longer than the first one. Repeat this process, but now take the top of each stitch into the same long chain as shown in the diagram. If you are going to add extra loops to this stitch, you will have to bring your thread across the back and up inside the bottom of the second loop stitch to begin your work again.

The left-hander should work the Chain Stitches in the normal manner. The back of the work will be the straight lines with which the Chain Stitches are formed.

This stitch, a development of the Open Chain, is founded upon the traditional embroideries of Ceylon. For practice, start with a pair of straight, parallel guidelines. However, as with the Open Chain, this stitch can be varied in width and used very nicely to make a leaf shape or other lines. I wouldn't suggest trying this stitch until you have mastered the Open Chain Stitch. Before the actual stitching is begun, the extra thread, which is going to be an integral part of this stitch, is inserted into the fabric, between the two ends of your parallel lines, with the long ends left free, as shown in DIAGRAM 1. To show to the best advantage, this contrasting thread should be of heavier weight than the working thread. To keep the dangling threads from making the work difficult, either pin them down at the bottom or leave a needle threaded on the dangling end, which gives just enough added weight to keep it hanging instead of flopping.

DIAGRAM 1

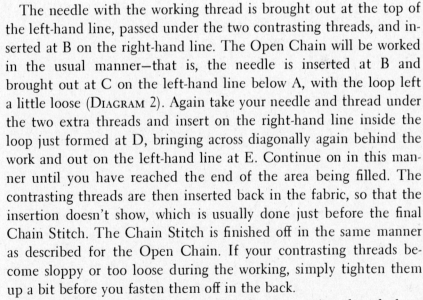

DIAGRAM 2

The needle with the working thread is brought out at the top of the left-hand line, passed under the two contrasting threads, and inserted at B on the right-hand line. The Open Chain will be worked in the usual manner—that is, the needle is inserted at B and brought out at C on the left-hand line below A, with the loop left a little loose (DIAGRAM 2). Again take your needle and thread under the two extra threads and insert on the right-hand line inside the loop just formed at D, bringing across diagonally again behind the work and out on the left-hand line at E. Continue on in this manner until you have reached the end of the area being filled. The contrasting threads are then inserted back in the fabric, so that the insertion doesn't show, which is usually done just before the final Chain Stitch. The Chain Stitch is finished off in the same manner as described for the Open Chain. If your contrasting threads become sloppy or too loose during the working, simply tighten them up a bit before you fasten them off in the back.

Left-handers slip the needle under the contrasting threads from right to left, in the direction for working the Open Chain. The back view of the work will be the same as for the Open Chain.

The Spine Chain is a useful little variation for a textured line, which lends itself to stylized stems and designs of that nature. Although it looks like a Wheat Ear Stitch with only one arm, the actual working is different.

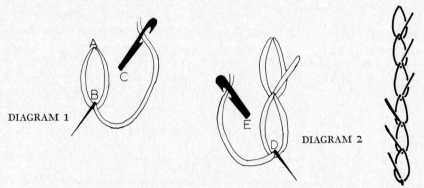

DIAGRAM 1

DIAGRAM 2

Work is begun as usual with the Chain Stitch—the needle brought to the top of the fabric and again inserted at A and brought out at B. After the thread has been pulled through at B, the needle is inserted in the fabric off to one side at C and brought out again inside the chain at B (DIAGRAM 1). Another Chain Stitch is begun at B and brought out at D. The needle is now inserted at E on the outside of the chain, this time on the left-hand side of the loop, and brought out again at D.

Continue along the line being worked in this manner, either alternating the spines or bringing them all out on one side. You can also form a pattern by having the threads in groups, some worked on one side and some on another. The effect can be varied by placing the spines at different angles to, or distances from, the Chain Stitches. Other variations used on the ordinary Chain Stitch, such as whipping, lacing, or placing a small stitch inside the loop of the chain, can be used on the Spine Chain as well.

Left-handers should work this stitch and its variations as they would the plain Chain Stitch. The back view shows the series of lines for the Chain Stitch plus the lines formed by the side stitches, in whatever direction they extend from the loop.

The title of this stitch describes it exactly—an addition to the basic Chain Stitch. There are two ways to do the actual threading: on a base of regular Chain Stitches or on a series of Detached Chain Stitches. There are diagrams for each. FIGURE 1 shows the basic Chain Stitch with one side of the thread worked and the other in the process. FIGURE 2 shows the Detached Chain Stitch. One journey of the threading has been completed and the second journey is in the process.

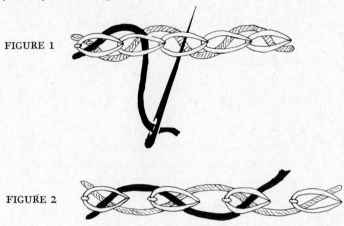

FIGURE 1

FIGURE 2

Most of the lacing or threading stitches are more easily worked on a frame of some kind, and for the second step in the process—the threading—a blunt needle is most comfortable to work with, because you don't have to worry about splitting the threads already worked. Generally the lacing thread should be heavier and darker than the chain thread for contrast, and it should be gently slipped through and not pulled tight.

The left-hander simply works in the regular manner and threads the lacing in the most comfortable way. The back of this work, except where the lacing thread is attached, is the same as the regular Chain Stitch, for all the lacing is done on the surface of the work.

91 · CHAIN STITCH—TRIPLE

The Triple Chain Stitch looks similar, in the first step (DIAGRAM 1), to the Russian Stitch but is really a combination of Detached Chain Stitches. It looks good in any kind of thread, but as you are having overstitching, it does show to best advantage in the heavier thread.

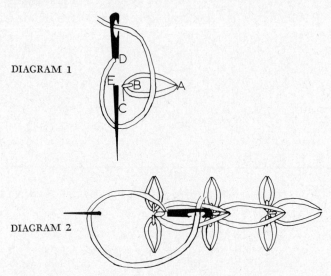

DIAGRAM 1

DIAGRAM 2

DIAGRAM 1 shows the first large chain having been worked, and one of the small Detached Chains in process of being worked from the outside toward the line. DIAGRAM 2 shows the first three complete groupings having been finished, and the thread and needle now in position to start the fourth grouping. Note that after the first large Chain Stitch, each subsequent large chain is brought up and begun inside the preceding large chain. This gives the more raised appearance to this line stitch.

Left-handers work as usual.

92 · CHAIN STITCH—TWISTED

This useful stitch looks more complicated than it is. It is most useful for lines and borders, curving nicely as do all of the Chain Stitches, and its nice textured look is simple to achieve.

The Twisted Chain is started the same as the regular Chain Stitch at the end of the line. The difference is that, instead of reinserting the needle in the same hole, you insert it to one side of the thread emerging at A, so that, when the needle is pulled through, the threads cross.

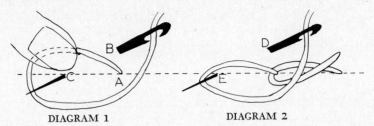

DIAGRAM 1   DIAGRAM 2

Diagram 1 shows the stitch in progress. The needle is brought out at A and put in at B, and it emerges at C with the thread being held by the left thumb. Pull the needle and thread on through, and a twisted chain has been formed. You will note that, because this stitch does not go back into the same hole, your needle will be slanting from B to C. C is back on the line and again just beyond A. Diagram 2 shows the needle having been pulled on through and inserted again at D to the side of the loop, coming out at E and on down the line.

The appearance of this stitch varies with thread and size of stitches made; parallel rows of Twisted Chain also create an interesting texture.

93 · CHAIN STITCH—TWISTED, ALTERNATING

As the name would suggest, this stitch is a variation of the regular Twisted Chain. You alternate the insertion of the needle from one side to the other, so that the twists go to the left of the loop on one stitch, and to the right of the loop on the next stitch, as illustrated in Diagram 1.

DIAGRAM 1

111

The Barred Twisted Chain is very similar to the Raised Chain. It can be worked over laid threads covering an area or with individual bars. Both types are shown in the diagram. The illustration showing the actual working of the stitch is over just one small row of bars. These bars should be laid first—fairly close together, the distance depending on the weight of the thread you are using and the effect you want. Generally this stitch, as opposed to the Raised Chain, is worked over two bars, so the laid threads should be a little closer together than for the regular Raised Chain. You might want to vary the appearance of this stitch by changing the direction of the twist if you are doing rows of Twisted Chain side by side.

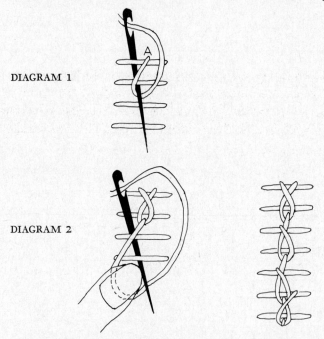

DIAGRAM 1

DIAGRAM 2

DIAGRAM 1 shows the thread being brought under the first bar in preparation for the first overstitch. DIAGRAM 2 shows the second loop formed, thread held with the left thumb in position and pulled on through to form the Twisted Chain. As in working the Twisted Chain, the insertion of the needle is different from the regular chain, the needle inserted to the left of the thread just emerging. Continue on to the end of the row of laid threads and finish off by making a little tie-down stitch.

Left-handers should do both the laid work and the Twisted

Chain in the manner already established. The back of the work, except for the beginning and ending of the threads, shows only the edging of the laid work.

95 · CHAIN STITCH—TWISTED, DETACHED

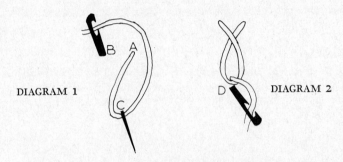

DIAGRAM 1   DIAGRAM 2

This stitch is used in the same type of work as the Detached Chain. It is not quite as well suited for flower petals as the other, however, unless you want unusual effects. It is well suited to textured powdering or filling. You anchor each stitch individually with a small stitch, and then proceed on to the next stitch.

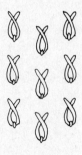

96 · CHAIN STITCH—TWISTED, LACE BORDER

This stitch is usually called the Lace Border Stitch; however I felt it should be included in this grouping as it really is a variation on the Twisted Chain Stitch. For first attempts, work between two rows of parallel guidelines if you are not using an evenweave fabric. Working from right to left, the needle is brought out on the right-hand end of the top line, and a small Twisted Chain Stitch is made. Go to the lower line directly below and make a reverse Twisted Chain (DIAGRAM 1). Now you will have a pair of Twisted Chains with the thread lying between them. The needle is carried back up again to the upper line and another small Twisted Chain made just along the line beyond the first one (DIAGRAM 2). Now the needle is passed from the right side, going up, over, and under the thread lying between the first two Twisted Chain Stitches. The needle is pulled through without entering fabric and taken down to the lower level, where you make another reverse Twisted Chain just beyond the first one on that line. Proceed down the row, alternating between the two lines, remembering that you keep the lower line with a reverse twist.

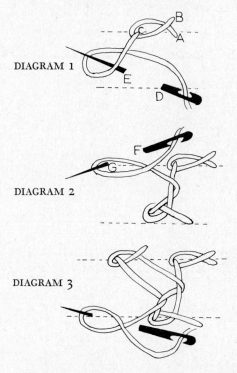

DIAGRAM 1

DIAGRAM 2

DIAGRAM 3

This is one of those twisted stitches that show up best in a lightweight thread, which gives them the full lacy effect. The back view shows simply lines slanting slightly toward the center.

Left-handers make the Twisted Stitches in the usual manner.

FIGURE 1

97 · CHAIN STITCH—TWISTED, OPEN

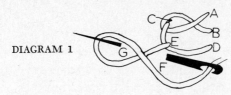

DIAGRAM 1

This stitch adds a little variety to the border stitches and is a combination of the Twisted Chain and Open Chain Stitches. Starting at your right or at the end of the line, first work a regular Twisted Chain and then an Open Chain right beside it, keeping the beginning of the stitches on the same level. DIAGRAM 1 shows the second Twisted Stitch in the process of being made, and this is on the opposite edge of the first one. Beside that, keeping the band even, you make another Open Stitch into the base of the first Twisted Chain. Repeat these alternating combinations to the end of the row.

The back of the work is formed by the two rows of Chain Stitches side by side. Left-handers work the Chain Stitches as usual.

FIGURE 1

98 · CHAIN STITCH—TIED LADDER

This is a combination of several stitches and is worked in three separate steps. It offers a good opportunity to experiment with various colors or weights of thread, or both.

The first process is the working of a Ladder or Broad Chain Stitch, which means that these are not worked in the ordinary manner. Starting at A (DIAGRAM 1), form the first two steps to start the Broad Chain line. When the first stitch is completed, the needle is carried in back of your work down to the lower line, and a second row of Broad Chain is begun. DIAGRAM 1 shows the thread being passed under the stitch just formed and then emerging on the top line, so that it will be in position to form a Broad Chain on that

DIAGRAM 1

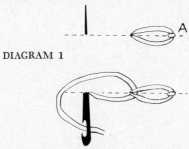

line. Work the Broad Chain alternating back and forth as diagrammed into the area to be covered. DIAGRAM 2 shows the ladder being formed, actually a type of Laid Work, by bringing the needle out in the first Chain Stitch, carrying it across the area and inserting it in the middle of the opposite Chain Stitch on the lower line and again bringing it out in the second one. DIAGRAM 2 shows the needle emerging near the center of the second chain on the lower line and getting ready to be carried up to the upper line. Repeat these steps the rest of the way down the ladder, using the centers of the Chain Stitches for the spacing. The next step is a tying and threading process, with results that look much like the Rosette Chain. The work is done over pairs of threads. DIAGRAM 3 shows a Twisted Chain being made around these without going through the fabric. DIAGRAM 4 shows several areas of the band completed and the passing of the thread. This starts at the end of the Twisted Chain, slips back under the two stitches just tied down, around over the end of that stitch and again under, coming back under the same two threads on the other side of the stitch. This is repeated on each pair of laid threads all the way down to the end of the border.

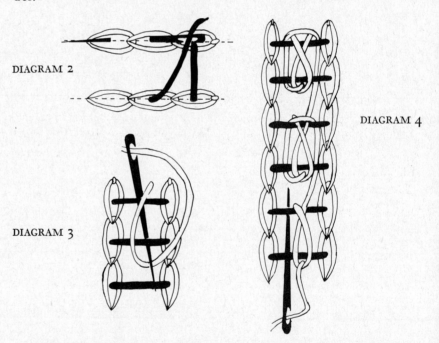

DIAGRAM 2

DIAGRAM 4

DIAGRAM 3

Left-handers should work all the stitches in the way most comfortable for them, and the threading could be reversed for ease of working. The back of the stitch is a combination of the outside edges of straight stitches used to form the chain and the Laid Work.

116

(SPANISH STITCH)

This is one of the loveliest braid-looking stitches, in appearance as close as anything to a braid that is applied separately. As do all Chain Stitches, it lends itself to curves as well as straight lines. It's not nearly as difficult to master as it looks, and really goes quite quickly once you understand the mechanics. You must remember not to pull the threads too tight, or you'll have a pucker in the fabric. A heavy twisted thread gives this its best appearance but it works up beautifully in silk or wool as well as cotton. For practicing this stitch, mark off three parallel lines, one quarter inch apart.

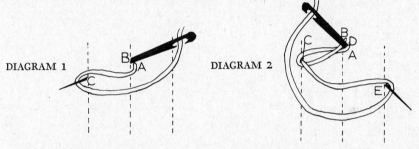

DIAGRAM 1   DIAGRAM 2

The needle is brought out at A, just to the right of the center line, is put into the fabric at B on the center line, and comes out at C on the left line, slanting downward a little, perhaps an eighth of an inch. Draw the thread through and tighten up to form a Twisted Chain. The needle is now inserted at D, which is just to the right of B, and brought out at E on the right-hand line, going down a bit below at C on the opposite line. Again tighten up and gently pull the needle and thread on through the twisted loop just formed. You may have to twist your thread over from C under the needle on these steps, for it will not fall in place as it does when worked on a straight line with the regular Twisted Chain.

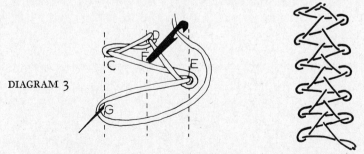

DIAGRAM 3

The needle is now inserted at F on the center line, just under the thread CE, and comes out at G, a little below C on the left line. The thread is again twisted over and the needle pulled through. Continue to work on down between the lines to the end

of the row, alternating from side to side, and not giving too hard a
tug on the needle and thread as they come through inside each
loop.

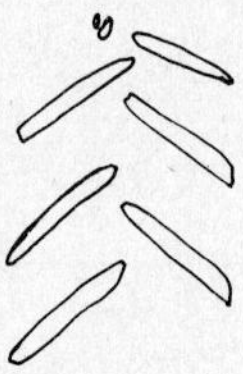

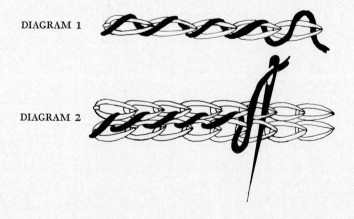

BACK VIEW

The back of the work will be stitches slanting toward the center,
alternating down the line, one beneath the other. The left-hander
can work the Twisted Chain in the reverse manner and still get
the same effect; however it may be more comfortable to work this
particular stitch with the diagram upside down.

100 · CHAIN STITCH—WHIPPED

A regular row of Chain Stitches can be whipped with a contrasting color or weight of thread. If you use the same color of
thread and pull the thread up snugly, you get a nice raised effect,
which doesn't even show it is a Chain Stitch.

The whipping thread does not go through the material except at
the beginning and the end. For this part of the stitch, use a blunt
needle. Another interesting effect, particularly if the thread used
for whipping is a heavy metallic cord, can be obtained by running
whipped thread between two rows of Chain Stitches side by side,
only going through one edge of the loop on the Chain Stitch from
each row. Naturally, the stitches of the side-by-side chains must
match each other. These methods are shown in DIAGRAMS 1 and 2.

DIAGRAM 1

DIAGRAM 2

101 · CHAIN STITCH–ZIGZAG
(VAN DYKE CHAIN STITCH)

This stitch is worked exactly like the ordinary Chain Stitch; the difference, which can be readily seen in the diagram, is simply that the chains are made at an angle to one another to give the zigzag effect. One suggestion for keeping the stitches flat and not losing the loops, is to pierce the thread at the end of the loop as you are inserting your needle to start another link in your chain. As with most Chain Stitches, the Zigzag Chain will go around curves nicely, can be worked in rows side by side and in almost any kind of thread.

The back simply shows straight stitches that form the lines going at angles to each other. The left-hander works the Chain Stitch in the regular way.

102 · CHEVRON STITCH

This stitch is used for lines, borders, and fillings, and is very similar in action to the Herringbone Stitch. It is best worked between parallel lines for practice, or on an evenweave fabric. If you want, practice with a large stitch to get the mechanics in mind, but it looks best when worked on a smaller scale.

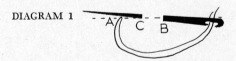

DIAGRAM 1

The needle is brought out on the lower left-hand line at A, carried to the right a bit, and inserted at B. Then the needle emerges at C, halfway between A and B. The thread is held below and out of the way while you are doing this stitch. Now, with the threads still being held down, the needle is carried up to the above line and to the right so that the next stitch will be a diagonal stitch between two parallel lines. The needle is inserted on the upper line at D, a little beyond where you think it might go and brought back out again at E, just above B on the lower line. Now throw the thread to the top of your work. While holding it up, go in at F on the same line, a little further up, along and back out at D and pull on through (DIAGRAM 3). You are now working diagonally down again so that the needle goes in at G, halfway across the stitch on the lower level, and brought out to the left at H. Again it is held down and the needle inserted at I and brought out again at G. Work on across between the two lines in this manner, alternating top and bottom for the straight stitches on the top of the work.

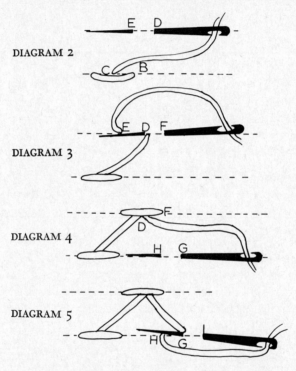

DIAGRAM 2

DIAGRAM 3

DIAGRAM 4

DIAGRAM 5

As you can see, the spacing of the stitches makes the difference in the appearance of this stitch. It does make a nice line stitch, but it doesn't do well around curves unless great care is taken as to the varying of the size of stitches.

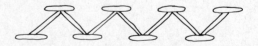

120

The back of the work is alternating pairs of little back stitches together. The left-hander will probably prefer to start this from the right-hand end and reverse the process.

103 · CHEVRON STITCH—DOUBLE

In reality the Chevron Stitch Double, which makes a very attractive filling, is just additional rows of the Chevron Stitch. As you can see by the drawing, you put the horizontal stitches together on the rows to form little squares, which make an attractive allover filling stitch. Both the back and the left-handed action would be the same as for stitch 102.

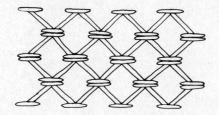

104 · CHEVRON STITCH—PAGODA

This variation on the regular Chevron Stitch is worked exactly like the simple Chevron except that the thread remains in the same position after the first horizontal stitch is made, so you have a somewhat different appearance in the texture. This can be used the same as the regular Chevron, as either a line stitch or as a filling stitch.

This stitch is not worked in the manner of the regular Chevron, but when it is completed, it looks very similar but much more impressive.

It is worked in two separate steps, the first laying a foundation of little wedges made up of straight stitches and the second step the threading. To begin the foundation layer, use three parallel guidelines, making sure they are of equal distance, for the spacing and size of the stitches in this step are most important to the overall appearance. The thread used for this should not be too fine but should be soft so that it will lie flat.

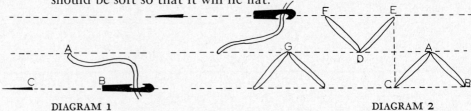

DIAGRAM 1   DIAGRAM 2

Working from right to left, bring the needle out first at A on the middle line and carry it back to the end of the bottom line diagonally to B; it emerges again at C a little further along the line. The horizontal distance CB should be twice as long as the slanting line AB (DIAGRAM 1). If you are working on a fabric without threads that you can count, mark the spots off on your upper and lower lines. The needle is taken back into the original spot where the thread emerges at A and inserted, brought out along the middle line to your left at D. (D will be the middle of the next wedge to be formed.) Again the thread is carried slantwise to the outer thread, but this time on the upper line at E, inserted and brought out along to the left at F, twice the length of the slanting line DE. Again it is inserted on the middle line at D and carried on to the left at G to start another wedge on the lower two lines. These alternating V-shapes are worked clear along the band that you intend to cover.

The next step in this stitch is almost like a lacing or threading. A blunt needle would be best for working this, and it can be done either with the same thread, a heavier or richer looking thread, or something with a tight twist. The action of the needle is the same as the regular Chevron Stitch; however it does not enter the fabric at all once it emerges at the left-hand end. It is carried up to the upper wedge and inserted under the left arm of the V from the inside out as shown in DIAGRAM 3, then carried over, holding the thread above, to the right-hand arm of that wedge and inserted from the outside in. After this has been done, drop down below and repeat the process on the lower V. Continue in this fashion until the band is completed.

DIAGRAM 3

DIAGRAM 4

The back of the work will be alternating horizontal straight stitches. Left-handers will probably find it easiest to start the foundation on the left end and the lacing on the right.

106 · CHINESE KNOT

The Chinese Knot is very much in evidence in the rich embroidery of China. At first it looks very similar to the French Knot, but a closer examination will show that it has a little stem coming out of the back of it. Many beautiful borders and solid fillings are worked with this stitch in China, and it is used in continuous flows, as our Chain and Stem Stitch are, for solid fillings. The advantage this has over the Chain and Stem Stitches is in its shading, which can vary not only from line to line but within the line. And, of course, the Chinese Knot has quite a different texture from the other two. It also has the advantage of being a little neater looking and laundering better than the regular French Knot.

The Chinese Knot is most often seen worked with silk in Chinese embroidery, but it lends itself well to contemporary work also. Practice this stitch with some of the heavier threads, and you will find that you can fill up a shape quickly. By varying the color and weight of threads, you can obtain quite unusual results with this stitch.

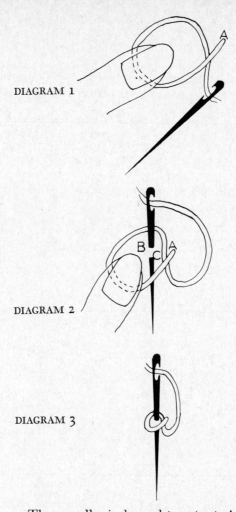

DIAGRAM 1

DIAGRAM 2

DIAGRAM 3

The needle is brought out at A and a loop formed, with the sharp end of the needle going *under* the thread, as illustrated in DIAGRAM 1. Close to A the needle is inserted inside the loop, going in at B in front of the thread, and emerging at C under the thread. The thread is tightened up at this point and pulled on through, and you are in position to start your next knot. These should be worked close together and in a line, so there is no fabric showing between. When rows are done beneath each other, the little stems don't actually show. The rows are worked from right to left, and the knots can be staggered so that they fit inside each other as each row progresses.

The left-hander works from left to right with a little more ease. The back of the work, if you are making a solid filling of it or even just a line, shows a series of tiny little stitches.

124

107 · CLOUD FILLING
(MEXICAN STITCH)

The Cloud Filling is as light or heavy as the thickness of the thread. The foundation of this pretty filling stitch consists of isolated stitches spaced at regular intervals over the surface. DIAGRAM 1 shows that these are alternately spaced in rows—that is, the little stitches in the second row are midway between the stitches of the first and third rows. When filling in a shape, you should give yourself guidelines of some sort so that this regularity can be achieved, either by running darning stitches in regular rows or marking off the design with a hard lead pencil. The little stitches are worked back and forth across the rows. To keep from puckering the surface of the work, this stitch should be worked on a frame.

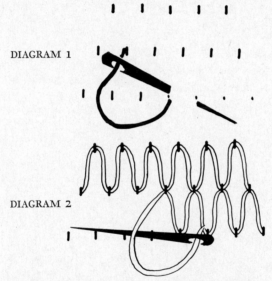

DIAGRAM 1

DIAGRAM 2

DIAGRAM 2 shows the lacing thread in progress. Working with a blunt needle and starting at the upper edge, put the needle alternately through a small stitch on the top row, then down through a small stitch on the row below and back up again to the top row, across each pair of rows. These alternate rows are laced so that the loops meet under the same stitch.

The effect may be varied considerably by the spacing of your foundation stitches as well as your choice of thread.

When this is completed all that will show on the back are the Straight Stitches and the beginning and ending of your lacing threads. As there is nothing complicated about the procedure of either of these steps, a left-hander can do them in whatever way is most comfortable.

125

108 · CORAL STITCH

(BEADED STITCH, CORAL KNOT, GERMAN KNOT STITCH, KNOTTED STITCH, SNAIL TRAIL, SCROLL STITCH)

Coral, like most of the knotted stitches, is somewhat irregular but very decorative in line, and the overall effect can be varied a great deal by the thickness of the thread and the spacing of the little knots. It is one of the many stitches used in seventeenth-century English Jacobean work, both as a little line stitch inside leaf shapes and as outlines and fillings. In some of the older books, this stitch, when its knots are worked very close together, is called the Knotted Outline Stitch.

It is an excellent stitch for use on curved lines, particularly the tight little curves, for the stitch ties itself down as it goes along. It is equally useful in solid filling. When used as a solid filling, the little knots fit inside each other as shown in FIGURE 1.

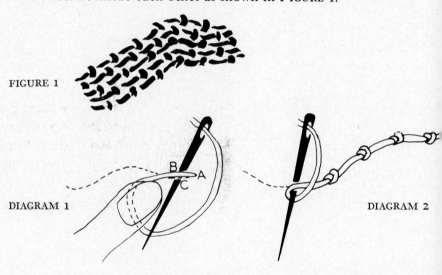

FIGURE 1

DIAGRAM 1   DIAGRAM 2

DIAGRAM 1 shows the thread emerging at the right-hand end of the line at A. It is held along the line with the left thumb, and the needle is inserted at B just above the line and brought out at C just below the line, for you are only picking up a small amount of fabric. DIAGRAM 2 shows the thread that has been pulled through the little loop formed and a row of knots already worked, with another stitch to be started.

The back view of this stitch shows a series of small stitches running in whichever direction your stitch is being worked. The diagram shows this stitch being worked from right to left; however, it is also worked easily from left to right, so there should be no problem for left-handers.

The Coral Stitch may be worked in a zigzag line to produce a pretty little border. For practicing this stitch, mark two parallel guidelines, and start at the top. You will see that the left-hand stitch is made exactly the same as an ordinary Coral Stitch. For the right-hand stitch, the thread has to be looped by carrying the thread across to the right and holding it down with the left thumb, throwing the remainder of the working thread across to the left again over the thumb, and then, after raising the thumb, inserting the needle into the loop thus formed.

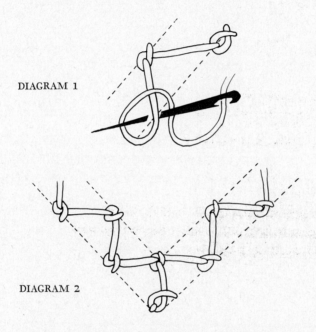

DIAGRAM 1

DIAGRAM 2

The diagram accompanying this stitch shows the left-hand knot being made and also work going around a corner. You will note that the knot in the corner has a little tie-down stitch, and the thread is brought back out to the center of the already worked knot on the inner corner, before you commence working in the other direction. As with many stitches, to achieve a sharp corner or point on your stitch, you must exaggerate or tie-down when that spot is reached. In this sort of stitch in particular, you have to finish off and begin again. By bringing it up in the middle of a stitch previously worked, you give the work a continuous appearance. Again the back shows only the small lines taken when forming your knots. This stitch is easily worked from the reverse direction for left handers.

Couching derives from the French word *coucher*, "to lay down," "to set in place." It is an easy decorative way of doing lines and filling spaces. The actual process is the tying down of one or more threads of material with another thread. This, one of the earliest forms of stitchery which dates as far back as medieval times, is closely related to Appliqué Work. The appliquéd fabric can be given a nice smooth appearance by going around the outside edge with a line of Couching. During the height of the Ecclesiastical Work in England during the eighteenth century, a particular Couching technique was used on the metallic and silk threads which was both practical and beautiful. A more detailed explanation of this almost obsolete method is given a little later. It is still used a great deal in hand-made church vestments today, but also in the more contemporary work.

Couching is the answer to those problem threads too brittle or heavy or awkward, and even sometimes too delicate, to pass back and forth through a background fabric. Couching broadens the scope of the creative embroideress, in that it gives her a number of threads and cords of various kinds that she might not otherwise be able to use. The working thread can either add to the decorative effect or be almost invisible, as when it is a much finer thread of the same shade as the laid thread, or, in the case of metallic work, by being waxed.

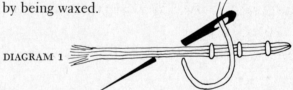

DIAGRAM 1

The simplest and most straightforward method of Couching is shown here in DIAGRAM 1. The heavy thread or threads are brought through the back of the work at the end of the line to be covered, and anchored down in some manner. They can be attached to the back of the fabric with the thread that you are going to use for the Couching under the area where the work will be done. On work that will not be having wear, such as a wall hanging—particularly in Ecclesiastical Work where metallic threads are being used—the heavy thread to be couched is sometimes anchored with masking tape or Scotch tape. Your working thread is brought through to the front of the fabric just inside the end of the laid threads, right on the line. It is carried up over the heavy thread and almost back in the same hole to form a little tie-down stitch. The needle enters the fabric and is carried on down the line a short way and brought up again.

In basic Couching Work these stitches should be spaced regularly, either in a straight line or going around curves or, for that matter, in a solid filling. The thread that is being couched down should be fairly firm, but it should not be pulled tight until the couching has been completed. I find it easiest to leave my needle on this heavy thread which gives it a little extra something for holding it in place, particularly if you are going around curves. You can hold it down with your thumb.

Before you reach the end of your Couching, the threads should again be inserted in the fabric, and when the tie-down stitches are completed, the two of them can be anchored off by whichever method you are using. FIGURE 1 shows the standard method and FIGURE 2 shows the results of varying the spacing of Couching stitches.

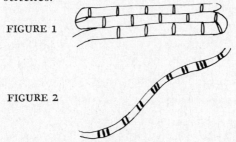

FIGURE 1

FIGURE 2

Left-handers simply work in the other direction. The back of the work looks almost like running stitches, having just a small space between the tie-downs.

111 · COUCHING—ASSORTED:

 (a) CRAZY

This is one of several Couching stitches that I will list separately, mostly because they need a detailed diagramming. If you will examine the diagram, you will see that it shows quite a wide laid thread. There are many flat or braid threads on the market which will give this effect, or perhaps a leather thong. Work the Herringbone in various widths and heights, staggered, across the line and tie it only occasionally.

(b) FRILLED (ITALIAN)

This is a modern version of an old-fashioned Couching method, which can be done with great variety. Usually used for a solid filling of some sort, as in the old medieval embroideries (Italian method), it also makes a delightful banding when done properly. It was originally used with gold thread. You can see that the laid thread is all on the top; this technique lets the light play on the gold thread. However, it has been used successfully in recent years with many types of thread, including silk.

DIAGRAM 1

DIAGRAM 1 shows strings, just pieces of heavy string or cording, being laid and couched down if necessary, depending on the size of the area; then the couching of the surface threads is done over these under threads. You will be trying to get a solid effect, so that the surface threads must be laid close together. DIAGRAM 2 shows one method of doing this, and DIAGRAM 3 shows another way.

DIAGRAM 2   DIAGRAM 3

Another method of getting a little different effect. This is done by padding certain areas. The easiest to work over are pieces of felt cut a bit smaller than the design you want. If you were doing several layers, you would cut each one progressively smaller than the one below. A variety of woven patterns or effects can be gotten by this, and many interesting shapes highlighted. If you are going to use gold thread, be sure that you get good Japanese gold, which comes in a number of weights, and the proper silk thread for couching down, or all your efforts will be wasted.

(c) LOOP

Loop Couching is a decorative stitch useful for many things. The size of your loops will depend partly on the size of the thread or the number of threads used in the laid work. This one is done a little differently as the work progresses.

130

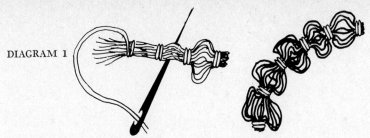

DIAGRAM 1

DIAGRAM 1 shows the Couching that has been begun. You do two Couching stitches fairly close together if your laid threads are heavy. Perhaps a pair of Couching stitches in each spot would be required. You then insert the needle under the laid thread between your two little stitches, gently lift it a bit, allowing it to puff until the required height is obtained. The thread is spread to make a loose little ball. Now take a couple of Couching stitches the same distance apart as the first ones and repeat the process to the end of the area.

This can be used as a line stitch to get a unique effect. Done in a solid fashion, it can simulate a flower with a lot of puffy petals. Heavy wool rug yarn shows a nice bold effect when used in this manner.

(d) PENDANT

The pendant effect in Couching can give a fringe appearance and can be used for either a line or a filling. When working a solid filling, it is easier to begin at the bottom of the design. We will start the diagram with the horizontal method. This is similar in some ways to doing your Rya Work, in that, if you are trying to make regular fringe, you will use either a knitting needle or a narrow straight edge of some sort to keep the loops of uniform size. Begin at the right and make sure your laid thread is firmly attached and your first tie-down stitch—or a pair of stitches if you are using heavy thread—has been made. Now loop the thread or threads around the knitting needle, or whatever you are using for a gauge, and work another Couching stitch as near to the previous loop as possible. Now move a little further along the line, and repeat the process to the end of the row. This can be worked in single rows vertically, which variation is shown in FIGURE 2.

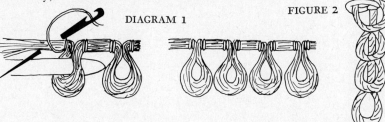

DIAGRAM 1   FIGURE 2

(e) SERPENTINE

Couching is particularly good for spontaneous and free-form design without a traced line. A good way to practice doing this and to get an idea of the possibilities is to start with a piece of string and, holding it up above a piece of fabric, let it drop in loops as it will. Pin it down at strategic spots, so that it will keep its form, and then start your Couching down. This would have to be done, as with all Couching stitches, on a tightly stretched frame. As you are working, hold the area to be couched down in place with your left hand so there will not be any slipping. Often when doing this type of work you need not necessarily insert your thread into the back of the work, if you make sure it is covered by another thread crossing over it or is tucked under. The work should be done with small stitches quite close together, so that your threads that have been dropped retain their shape. You can use various embroidery stitches for couching down in this type of work to advantage. The diagram shows one experiment in the working.

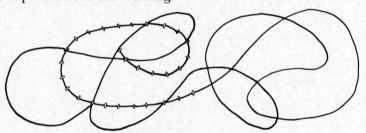

(f) STAGGERED (PARTED)

Staggered Couching is done simply by varying the lengths of the laid thread, and you can obtain some unusual results with it. This is sometimes worked in metallic thread. The diagram shows the staggering of thread with the basic tie-down stitch; however other stitches could be used to make a more dramatic effect with this method.

Parted Couching lends interest to a line that might otherwise be very dull and can also incorporate a flow into an area for a dramatic effect that might not otherwise be achieved.

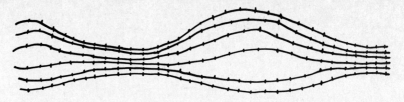

The diagram shows a group of threads done in basic Couching stitches. Start with a group of threads, side by side, couched with one or several stitches, and gradually open the group and couch down each thread separately. Then bring them together again and couch down in a group until another parting is desired.

112 · COUCHING—BOKHARA

For Bokhara Couching, as opposed to ordinary Couching, you use the same continuous thread throughout—that is, both your laid thread and the thread that makes the tie-down stitches. The diagram shows the thread being brought out on the left-hand side of the design and carried across to the right-hand side, where the needle is inserted on the outline and brought back in the direction from which the thread originally emerged. The needle comes up a short distance to the left, and the laid thread is held down below until the needle is pulled on through (DIAGRAM 1). This leaves the working thread just below a long laid thread, and you will proceed along the space from right to left making little tie-down stitches at regular intervals. These little stitches can form a pattern, or they can be put in the same spot on each row or staggered, to give you whatever effect you want. The tie-down stitches should be quite close together and pulled tight, but the thread on the back should be left just a little loose.

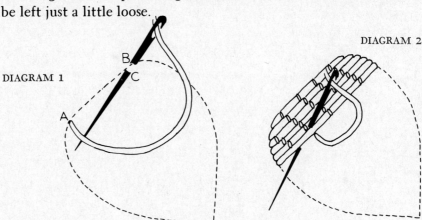

DIAGRAM 1

DIAGRAM 2

Although Bokhara Couching is very similar to Romanian Couching, the entire effect is different. In the former the tie-down stitches are short on the surface and long underneath, while for the latter it is just the reverse. This type of stitch was much used in early American needlework, because it worked up well for solid areas with very little thread on the back of the work, which was of prime importance in those days. An interesting variation with this stitch can be achieved by alternating the colors of thread (FIGURE 1).

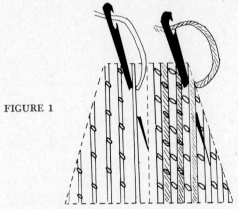

FIGURE 1

The back of the work will look almost like running stitches done in rows with tiny spaces in between. The left-hander simply reverses the procedure by placing the laid threads from right to left and bringing the needle up.

113 · COUCHING—FANCY

There are several methods of couching down, as mentioned in 110, regular Couching. This particular title covers a method of Couching which uses several specific types of stitch. You must master the technique of each stitch before attempting it on Couching. One of the fancy types is the basic Couching stitch, fancied up simply by spacing the stitches. This spacing can be done in a uniform manner—two and two or three and three—or at random, giving a variation to the appearance. The stitch can also be varied in size, which I suppose could be considered irregular Couching, but is still basically just a straight tie-down stitch over the laid thread.

Do remember the definition of Couching—superimposing something else on ground fabric with tie-down stitches. Therefore, not only thread but braid, cord, wire, leather or metal rods, twigs, even feathers can be couched. You would of course have to consider the use of the article; a metal rod wouldn't be particularly comfortable on a cushion, but would be very effective on a wall hanging or a room divider. None of these ideas is really new; they are to be found in old English, European, and Far Eastern embroideries as far back as the fourteenth century.

If you think back on the stitches you have worked with, as to which would be useful for Couching, some of them will come immediately to mind. The plain Cross Stitch, particularly with a change of thread, can give an interesting effect (FIGURE 1). FIGURE

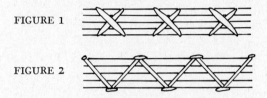

FIGURE 1

FIGURE 2

2 shows the Chevron Stitch used in Couching. The Chevron would also include plain diagonal stitches, as in the Arrowhead, which show up nicely. To get a little more complicated, the Open Chain allows the underthreads to show through to a good advantage, as in FIGURE 3. FIGURE 4 shows the plain Buttonhole or Blanket Stitch worked into the rows above as a filling stitch. You might prefer to use the Buttonhole in various combinations, in pairs or triplets.

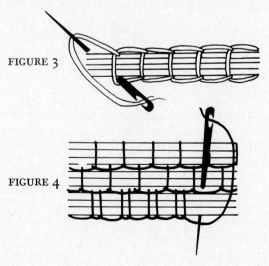

FIGURE 3

FIGURE 4

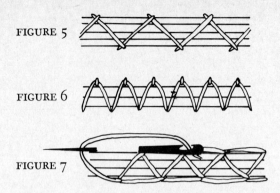

FIGURE 5

FIGURE 6

FIGURE 7

FIGURE 5 shows the Herringbone, and FIGURE 6 the Fly Stitch, which again are almost obvious types to experiment with. FIGURE 7 shows the Double Chain and the Closed Feather Stitch, both of which, having much the same appearance, will not only couch down the thread but give you a nice finished look on the edge. FIGURE 8 shows the slanting Feather Stitch worked over laid threads that have been separated, which could lead to various experiments. FIGURE 9 illustrates a couple of stitches that have been worked and then threaded, with the threading step of the stitch becoming the Couching stitch. This could lead to a variety of ideas for fancy Couching.

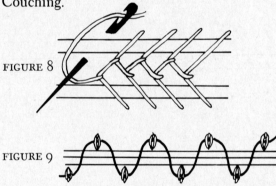

FIGURE 8

FIGURE 9

Do try these different methods of Couching, varying both the stitches and the type of thread used in your working, as well as your laid thread.

114 · COUCHING—RAISED BAND AND PLATE

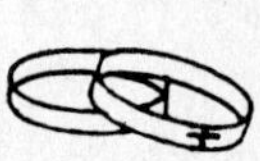

Because we are on the subject of gold thread and this method of Couching, I felt it best to include this stitch or type of work here. Originally this Raised Band work was also done with gold thread, but again it can be used with many other types of thread, including narrow ribbon. It was originally worked over laid threads but many other kinds of padding can be used, including popsicle sticks, thread, and string, and in fact anything that gives an interesting effect. It can also be worked so that the couched-down threads on the surface are solid or spaced out, but the method of doing this is worked exactly like the underside Couching.

DIAGRAM 1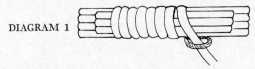

Attach to your background fabric whatever you are going to use for padding, then anchor the thread to be couched. Now, your needle is brought up to the surface at one end of the padding, passed over the laid thread, and put back in the exact same hole, and a sharp tug is given to bring the laid threads to the reverse side of the fabric (DIAGRAM 1). Now the needle is brought up on the other side of the padding, right at the end, and the laid thread is folded back in that direction and caught down in the same manner, so that it lies right beside the first stitch. This is continued on, alternating sides to the end of the band being covered.

FIGURE 1 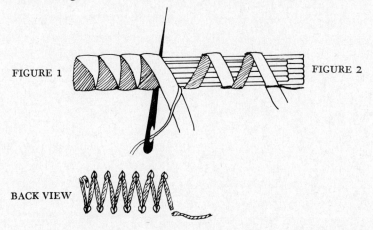 FIGURE 2

BACK VIEW

When covering a padding with plate, which is a flat piece of metallic thread or ribbon, the same action is used; however, the laid thread is not pulled to the back of the fabric. FIGURES 1 and 2 show this in process, with different spacing and the action of the needle and working thread. The term "bands" does not mean that these designs are necessarily used to outline or edge an area. There will be times when a small area of raised work, either a band or solid filling, can give much needed enrichment to the piece. Don't think of Couching as an allover thing or as an edging by itself, but do experiment with all of these methods, with both traditional and contemporary thread.

(LAID STITCH, ORIENTAL STITCH, FIGURE STITCH,
ROMAN STITCH, OVERLAID STITCH)

This form of Couching resembles your Bokhara Couching closely, but the actual working and overall effect vary considerably. It is very useful for doing wide bands or fillings and is excellent for flower and leaf shapes, particularly when flat work is needed. A slight variation on this, called the New England Laid Stitch, was used by the early American settlers, one advantage of this stitch being that most of the thread is on the surface of the piece. Work is begun on this exactly the same as the Bokhara in that your threads are brought out on the left-hand line of the area to be covered, carried across to the right-hand line, and inserted again (DIAGRAM 1). The needle is slanted slightly up in the back of the work from B, emerging at C, approximately one third of the way across the links of the line. The needle and working thread are carried on across the shape, back toward the left-hand margin and inserted above the laid thread at D, brought out on the left-hand margin at E, being right next to and under A (DIAGRAM 2). Your continuous thread is then carried across the area again and the procedure repeated on down the design being covered. FIGURE 1 demonstrates a small area of the work completed.

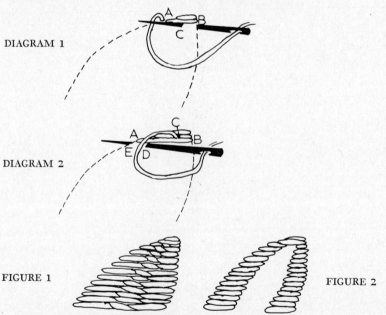

DIAGRAM 1

DIAGRAM 2

FIGURE 1

FIGURE 2

If you are using this stitch in an irregular shape, you might find that it is necessary to fill the beginning or the in-between areas with plain Satin Stitches if the space does not allow for a tie-down stitch that would be in keeping with the others.

The left-hander reverses the procedure to work this most comfortably. The back of this work shows a series of slightly slanted lines side by side along the outer edges of the shape (FIGURE 2).

116 · COUCHING–SATIN
(TRAILING STITCH)

This variation on the Couching stitch is not as versatile as some of the others but does have a definite use on occasion. It may be worked in either an upright or a slanting stitch and is very similar to the close Overcast Stitches. One of the advantages, as with all Couching stitches, is that it enables you to work a curving (trailing) line very nicely. The finished effect, particularly if properly done in a fairly tight twisted thread, whether it is lightweight or heavy, is a firm raised line almost like a series of little beads.

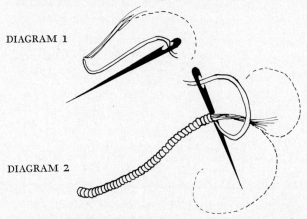

DIAGRAM 1

DIAGRAM 2

The threads for the foundation are brought up at the left-hand end of the line to be covered, and the working thread is brought out almost in the same spot, as in this case your foundation threads are going to be completely covered. A series of tiny close Satin Stitches is worked over the little bundle of thread, picking up a very slight amount of fabric as shown in DIAGRAM 2. The trailing threads should be guided by the left thumb as the work progresses.

The left-hander simply works from the opposite direction, using the same method, and the back of the work is a series of tiny little stitches side by side following the curvature of the line.

(MEDIEVAL)

This type of Couching dates from the thirteenth century, and it is with awe that we view these ancient pieces, realizing the skill it took, particularly since the steel needle was not yet in common use. The English were known throughout the civilized world for their work, called Opus Anglicanum. Most of the rich embroideries at that time were done for the church. However some was done for royalty as well. In those days Couching was worked strictly with gold thread, but until you have mastered this technique—and this will take some doing—it would be best to leave gold to the professionals and use softer thread to get your effect.

The soft threads, especially for solid fillings, should be couched with a fine but very strong thread; it should not only be worked in a frame but on a fine, closely woven linen background. Sometimes, to increase the strength, the groundwork can be done with another piece of fabric laid on the back, such as a fine, tightly woven batiste.

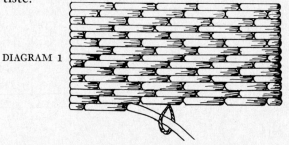

DIAGRAM 1

After the laid thread has been anchored and brought to the top, your strong working thread is brought up next to the laid threads. Regularity of stitch, whatever type of pattern you have decided to work in this method, is essential to get the full effect. The working thread is passed over the thread to be couched and inserted in the exact hole from which it emerged. It is pulled through to the back and a slight tug given, which will bring your laid thread just barely through to the back of the fabric. Continue across the line being worked at regular intervals, repeating this process.

If you turn your work over, you will see at this point that, although the surface looks as if you had a series of neat little Back Stitches, the Couching thread is continuous, almost straight, with little loops at intervals where the laid thread has been pulled through to the back. This is very similar to old-fashioned lockstitch machine sewing. In medieval times, most of this work was done in patterns such as basket weave or diamond shape, which, with the light playing on the metallic thread, gave a very rich dramatic effect. FIGURE 1 shows side view.

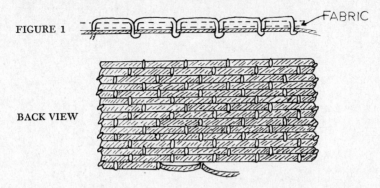

FIGURE 1

FABRIC

BACK VIEW

This method has endless pattern possibilities, and you shouldn't be intimidated by the constant mention of gold and metallic thread. Try it with string, but do try it. There are several books devoted explicitly to gold work, and some of the ecclesiastical books have detailed chapters on this type of embroidery, so I won't go into any of that, except to mention that there are many types of gold thread. Some of them have names that are unfamiliar to you, but a good needlework shop will have a supply of these and be able to explain the various methods used with the metallic threads—bullion, purl, and pearl purl.

The left-hander does this from the opposite direction, but the actual work is exactly the same.

118 · CRETAN STITCH
(LONG-ARMED FEATHER STITCH, PERSIAN STITCH)

This delightful and versatile stitch is often listed in the older books, usually as a good stitch for filling or line work, but its almost endless versatility deserves comment as an updated stitch. It is an easy, relaxing stitch once you have mastered the rhythm, with many different and elaborate variations possible, both with threads and spacing.

The basic Cretan Stitch should be tried out between parallel lines, and it might even be wise to make a series of four. On the basic action of this stitch you are picking up a small amount of fabric on the edge, and if your parallel lines are divided into fours, one fourth would be picked up on the outer edge of each side. This leaves the larger space in the center, where your threads intertwine, giving a nice lacy effect or a rich braid, depending on the slanting of your stitch.

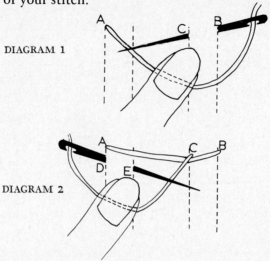

DIAGRAM 1

DIAGRAM 2

DIAGRAM 1 shows the thread being brought out at the top left-hand line. Holding the thread below with your left thumb, as you would for your other loop stitches, bring out the thread at C, slightly below B. The needle and thread are then pulled on through and carried back to the original left-hand line. In practicing this stitch and noting the diagram, you will see that the stitch between B and C is almost horizontal. Now the needle is inserted at D a short way below A and brought from the left to the right, emerging at E, with the thread held in a loop underneath the needle. The left-hand side will seem a little awkward to you until you get the rhythm of this stitch, but once this is mastered, you'll see that the action of this stitch closely resembles that of the Feather Stitch, or Double Chain, which seemed so uncomfortable when you first had to form the loop on the left-hand side of the work. Continue alternating sides as illustrated in DIAGRAM 3, on down to the end of the line, and anchor off the thread.

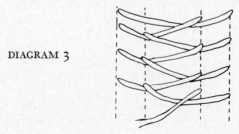

DIAGRAM 3

Before you try any of the variations, look at the figures that show a design being worked. Using the same stitch, you start this with the thread emerging at the tip of the leaf shape. It is then brought down slightly below on the right and the stitches worked down, filling the leaf shape. This illustrates the ease with which the Cretan Stitch can vary its width, whether to cover a completed shape or a border. You will also note that the inside dotted line of the design shows that the fabric picked up with the needle and thread is the same amount for each stitch. The change of size varies in the middle section, which is where your threads lace over each other, and not in the amount of fabric picked up by the needle when working.

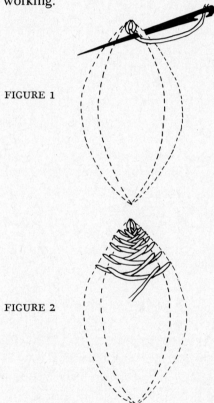

FIGURE 1

FIGURE 2

The left-hander needs no special instructions for this stitch as he is alternating sides. However just to begin with, you might feel a little more comfortable starting on the left-hand side rather than the right. The back of the work is a series of almost parallel lines evenly spaced down the outer edges of the design, whether it is a straight border line or a leaf or flower shape.

119 · CRETAN STITCH—CATCH

This is a very simple little variation on the Cretan Stitch, and the diagram illustrates it completely. In reality it's a combination of Cretan and Herringbone. Some of the old books called the Herringbone, Catch Stitch.

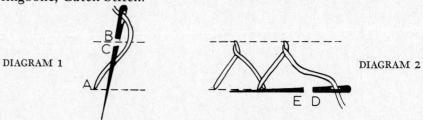

DIAGRAM 1   DIAGRAM 2

Starting from the left-hand end and working between two parallel lines, your needle is brought out on the lower line, carried up to the upper line and inserted at B. It is brought out just below B at C and carried slanting down to the lower line. A small Back Stitch is taken from right to left by inserting at D and bringing out at E. These two steps are repeated alternately on down and across your line to be filled and will carry around curves nicely.

120 · CRETAN STITCH—CHAINED
(LOOPED AND TIED)

To get the best effect with this type of Cretan Stitch, it is suggested that you use a thread with a fairly tight twist. It makes an interesting border when worked properly, and for practice in the beginning, it is probably best worked between two parallel lines. Bring your needle out on the upper left line at A, carry the needle across the space between the lines and insert at B, and bring it out at C, one third the distance between the two lines. The needle is again inserted at A and this time brought out a little below on the left-hand side at D, as in the regular Cretan Stitch. Next insert it again at B and bring it out a short way down at E. Form one more loop on each side, starting first at A, then at B, right under the loops just formed at F and G. The next stitch being formed will be an Open Chain. Your last stitch will leave the threads coming out on the right side at G, so that your Open Chain is formed by inserting your needle in the base of the last loop formed on the left-hand side at H and emerging right in the center at I. Another grouping of stitches is started now by carrying the thread over to the left line and starting the alternating stitches as shown in Diagram 2.

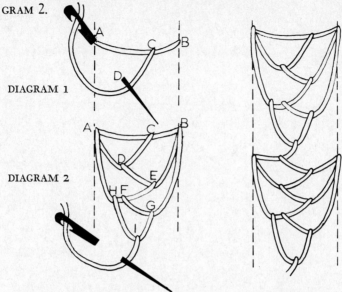

DIAGRAM 1

DIAGRAM 2

The Looped Cretan, which is a variation on this variation, is shown in the working with the letters to indicate the steps taken (Diagram 3). It is started in the same manner as the Chain Cretan, at the upper left-hand corner at A; thence follow the steps by the letters on the illustration.

The Tied Cretan again is most similar in action, but with a difference in the placing of needle and thread. The letters and action of the needle and thread in Diagram 4 will show you how this variation is carried out.

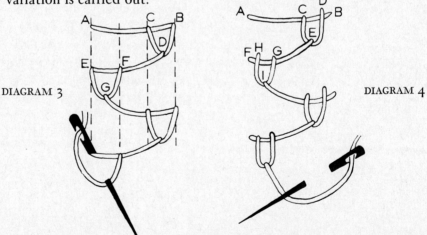

DIAGRAM 3

DIAGRAM 4

The left-hander needs no special directions for you are alternating from side to side. The back of the work varies in the different sizes of straight lines, depending on the size of fabric picked up by the stitches.

145

121 · CRETAN STITCH—CLOSED

The Closed Cretan is worked exactly the same as the regular Cretan and is generally used for filling a space where there is a border or leaf shape. The big change comes in the amount of fabric picked up and the angle of the needle between inserting and emerging. As the name "Closed" indicates, stitches are worked as close together as possible without overlapping. To give a completely closed effect when filling a leaf shape, start this at the tip with a Chain Stitch, as shown in DIAGRAM 1. DIAGRAM 1 also shows the first stitch being taken on the right-hand side and, as in all the loop stitches, with the left thumb holding the thread below, the needle will be sure of passing over the thread to form the loop. DIAGRAM 2 shows a series of these stitches having been worked and the action of needle and thread when coming in on the left side. You will see that, in working this stitch closely, the center, instead of being the open lacy effect of the regular Cretan, has really a braidlike appearance. This is enhanced when a heavier thread is used.

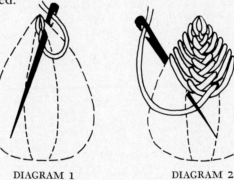 

DIAGRAM 1   DIAGRAM 2   BACK VIEW

The alternating action of the needle indicates that the left-hander can follow the directions as given. The back of the work is a series of slanting straight lines close together.

122 · CRETAN STITCH—CROSSED

In working the Crossed Cretan, you will discover after the first few steps that it is actually the combination of the Cretan and a Cross Stitch, so that a loop is not being formed with every insertion of the needle. This can fill areas of varying widths and should be practiced, to start with, between parallel guidelines.

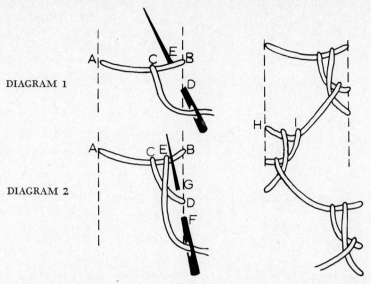

DIAGRAM 1

DIAGRAM 2

The needle is brought up on the upper left-hand line at A. A loose Cretan Stitch is formed by carrying the needle across, inserting it at B, and bringing it out at C, which is to the right of the center of the space. The needle is next inserted at D and brought out at E, as shown in DIAGRAM 1, but not looped under the needle. Now the needle is inserted at F and brought out at G, again without using the left thumb to form a loop (DIAGRAM 2). Take the needle to the opposite side of the band being formed and make one Cretan Stitch comparable in size to the original one, and repeat the other steps of the movement before crossing back to the right side again.

The left-hander follows the steps mentioned with no changes except that to get the feel you might want to start first on the left.

123 · CRETAN STITCH—FRENCH

Several of these Cretan Stitches have names of countries attached. Whether they actually originated there or not doesn't matter. They do give us some more interesting variations to this versatile stitch. Start between parallel guidelines, as is usually suggested in trying the Cretan Stitch. The needle is brought out on the left-hand line at A and carried across the area, inserted at B and brought back out at C, the distance between being about one third the width of the entire stitch. A Cretan Stitch is worked by carrying the needle back over from C to D, emerging at E (DIAGRAM 1). With the thread at E, the needle is taken over a short slanting stitch taken from B to F, with the thread being held below to form a loop so that you are actually doing a Cretan Stitch. The next looped stitch, again using B as the beginning, is really a Buttonhole Stitch so that the needle being inserted at B comes directly below, this time emerging at G, on the right-hand side. The needle and thread are carried back over to the left-hand end to begin this series of stitches again, and a small space is left between the groups.

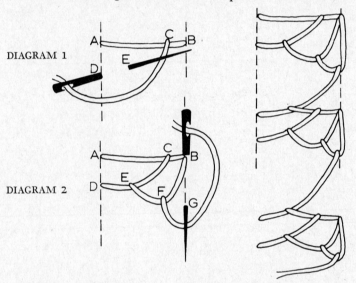

DIAGRAM 1

DIAGRAM 2

This is one case where you are not alternating back and forth constantly, so perhaps the left-hander would prefer to reverse the process in this particular method. Or perhaps it would be best to turn the diagram upside down.

124 · CRETAN STITCH–IRISH

The Irish Cretan looks best with a tightly twisted or round thread. The manner of working this stitch is completely different from the other Cretan, and it would be essential to have mastered the basic stitch before starting.

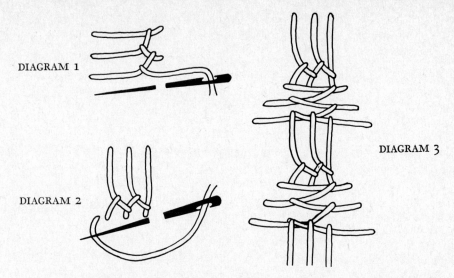

DIAGRAM 1

DIAGRAM 2

DIAGRAM 3

Starting on the left, the thread emerges. A Cretan Stitch is made with a long arm on the left and a short one on the right (DIAGRAM 1). Repeat twice more, directly under each other (DIAGRAM 1). Turn the work completely around at a right angle, and the next series will be in the same direction. DIAGRAM 2 shows the first stitch being made and covering the short ends at the base of the stitches that form the plait of the first series. These three stitches are balanced, each a bit larger than the previous one. The work is now turned to the original position, and three long-armed Cretans made again. This time insert the needle on the left so that it goes over the lower stitch in the previous series to link them together as shown in DIAGRAM 3.

The left-hander works best in the reverse with the aid of a mirror. The back is straight stitches, the size and direction of the Cretan Stitches taken.

125 · CRETAN STITCH—LACED
(DOUBLE PEKINESE STITCH, INTERLACED BAND STITCH, LOOPED AND TIED STITCH)

The Lace Cretan Stitch is actually a Laced Stitch worked between bases of another type of stitch, which can be your Back Chain or even a Running Stitch. The stitches of the two rows you are lacing must be equal in length and must be placed so that the midpoint of one row of stitches is directly below the end of the stitch on the opposite row. As indicated, you would form two parallel lines and make your base stitches of whatever type you desire, being careful to keep the size regular. The diagram shows the Back Stitch.

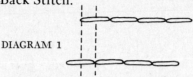

DIAGRAM 1

Once your lacing thread has emerged, no fabric is picked up. The tension should not be too tight. The needle, as shown in DIAGRAM 2, picks up the Back Stitch from the outside in, and is pulled over the working thread. If your line stitches are very small, the overall effect is almost like a solid braid. When larger spacing is used, a little more open effect is obtained.

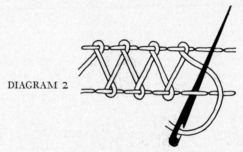

DIAGRAM 2

The interlacing is usually worked from left to right; however it can be done from the other direction with ease, so that the left-hander could simply start that way.

126 · CRETAN STITCH—LONG-ARMED
(SPINE STITCH)

The diagram shows quite clearly the working of this stitch, which could also be classed as a type of Feather Stitch. The action is the same as the regular Cretan Stitch. However your fabric is picked up right down to the center of the openings between the two parallel lines, and if you want to keep a good straight line down the center, you must make a series of three parallel lines, as shown in the dia-

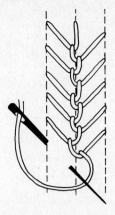

gram, before starting to work. The size of these stitches can be varied, for both borders and to fill shapes like leaves.

Because of the alternating action, the left-hander follows the diagram as illustrated.

127 · CRETAN STITCH—OPEN

DIAGRAM 1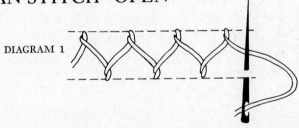

Yet another variation forming a simple Border Stitch is the Open Cretan. The working of this is similar to the ordinary Cretan Stitch except that the needle is inserted quite straight into the fabric, instead of at a slant, and a space is left between each as shown in the diagram. This form of Cretan Stitch can be used to build up interesting border patterns by inserting other stitches in the spaces left. Whichever side you are working from, the needle always comes from the outside in and passes over your thread to form the loop. Loops can be worked in rows side by side or so that they cross each other as in FIGURE 1.

FIGURE 1

One of the most attractive of the open filling stitches is the Cretan Stitch. It must be worked upon a foundation of vertical stitches formed by a very stout thread. These are laid across the area to be worked. The area can be any shape, but the foundation threads must be laid at regular intervals and not too far apart. DIAGRAM 1 shows the thread emerging on the upper right hand corner and the beginning of the Cretan Stitch being worked over the threads and not going through the fabric. As the second step of this stitch is done only over threads, you will probably find it easier to use a blunt needle and, because the foundation threads must be kept taut, a frame is absolutely necessary.

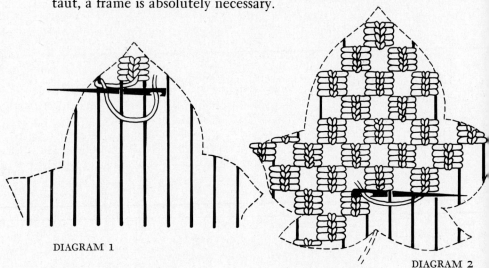

DIAGRAM 1

DIAGRAM 2

This bold and effective filling is shown in DIAGRAM 2, with the needle passing from one group of stitches, which have just been worked in the beginning of the second row, to another. As you complete a group of stitches, the needle is passed under the thread on the left and carried completely over to the next thread. Then pass it from the outside in as in your Cretan Stitch, using threads 3 and 2 as your base threads.

When one series of diagonal clusters is completed, go back up to the upper right-hand edge and begin the process again so that you have spaces between your groups from the outside in as in your Cretan Stitch, using threads 3 and 2 as your base threads. The overall appearance will have a checkered effect.

The left-hander starts in the upper left-hand corner, but as with the right-hander, the regular Cretan Stitch is worked between a pair of the foundation threads doing four stitches, one directly below the next and edging them up close together with your needle. The back of this work would only show the laying of your foundation threads and the beginning and ending of your thread for your surface work.

129 · CRETAN STITCH–REVERSED

This stitch could be practiced between parallel guidelines, as with most Cretan Stitches. However it lends itself to distorted work in the varying of the sizes once you have the technique mastered. The diagrams will show the work being done between parallel lines. It is begun on the upper left line coming out at A. A regular Cretan Stitch is formed, with the thread emerging at C. Next a Straight Stitch is taken, CD, the needle emerging at E. But no actual loop is formed, and E is about the center of the distance between the ends of the stitch (DIAGRAM 1). Now another straight line between E and F, and the thread comes out at G without a loop actually being formed; however, the needle is to the top of the stitch at G (DIAGRAM 2). The needle and thread are carried over the left line and inserted at H, which is the beginning of the repetition of these steps, so that H would take the place of A in DIAGRAM 1.

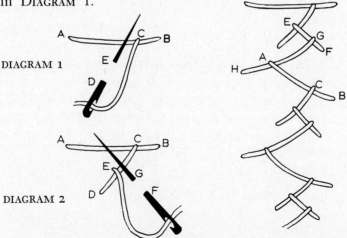

DIAGRAM 1

DIAGRAM 2

The left-hander might be more comfortable working in reverse; however no loops are being formed, so it might not be too awkward to follow the directions given for the right-hander.

130 · CRETAN STITCH–SCOTCH

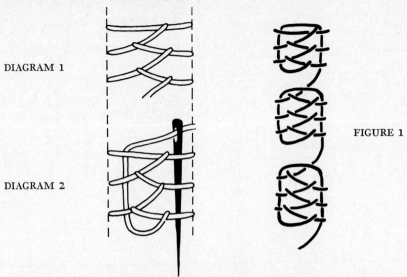

DIAGRAM 1

DIAGRAM 2

FIGURE 1

The Scotch Cretan resembles little thistle heads, which is perhaps how the name came to be used. Working between your lines, three pairs of complete Cretan Stitches are worked fairly close together as shown in DIAGRAM 1. The needle is passed up under the arms on the outer edges on the left-hand side and down under the arms on the right side. Pull the thread firmly but not tight (DIAGRAM 2). Leave just a little space and repeat the process. This forms an interesting grouping as shown in FIGURE 1.

131 · CRETAN STITCH–SPLAYED

The Splayed Cretan is one variation that can be very useful for certain effects. It shows up best when worked with fairly firm thread. Because of the variations in sizes, it doesn't work up well between lines.

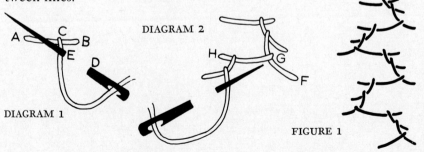

DIAGRAM 2

DIAGRAM 1

FIGURE 1

A regular Cretan Stitch is made, as shown in DIAGRAM 1, which also shows the second step of this stitch in process. After your needle has emerged at C, it is carried on down to D on the right-hand side and inserted a little farther out at D and brought out at E, to form a small Cretan Stitch on the right-hand side. Directly below this another small Cretan Stitch is formed but with the arm a little bit farther out an the right than at DE. The thread then emerges at G, is carried over to the left-hand side, and a series of three Cretan Stitches of various sizes are formed on that side (DIAGRAM 2). The pattern is repeated, alternating sides, and gives a rather casual appearance (FIGURE 1).

132 · CRETAN STITCH—TRIPLE

The Triple Cretan is worked by doing one row of widely spaced Cretan Stitches to start the work. DIAGRAM 1 shows the second row being worked directly over the first row and a little bit to the right. DIAGRAM 2 shows the third one again over the rows previously worked and a little more to the right, with different shadings of color or weights of thread giving interesting variations. This stitch is particularly effective when started in a heavy thread and worked up in a lighter weight.

No special directions are needed for the left-hander; as with basic Cretan Stitches, you alternate the sides.

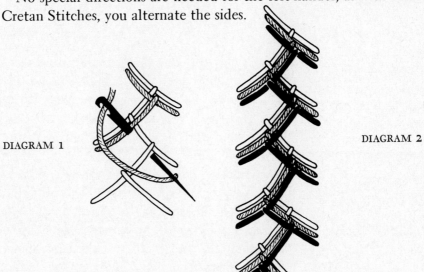

DIAGRAM 1   DIAGRAM 2

(FILLING STITCH, SAMPLER STITCH)

The Cross Stitch is certainly one of the best known and most widely used stitches in the world. This type of embroidery has been used as a basic stitch and a variation for centuries by the rural people of many European countries, for enrichment of all types of embroidery, and was very much in prominence in the United States during the nineteenth century, in the American version of the sampler. This type of sampler, it might be added, was really not a needlework sampler as much as it was an aid in teaching neatness or learning the alphabet and numbers. The neatness of plain straight stitches was of great importance during this period, for nearly all garments were made by hand, at home. Likewise hand stitchery was needed for enrichment.

The idea, unfortunately in widespread use at the present time, of the prestamped cross-stitch pattern has done much to put the Cross Stitch, which can be such a decorative thing, in disfavor. When properly done, whether a basic Cross Stitch or some of the variations, it can be made a most interesting and even exciting stitch by varying the placement of stitches and threads. This stitch was originally worked on evenweave fabric by counting the threads for regularity of stitch and is equally adaptable to Canvas Embroidery.

Another method, still in common use in Europe on a fine or delicate fabric, is to baste a certain kind of canvas onto the fabric, and to work the Cross Stitch through both, without piercing the threads of the canvas. When the work is completed, the canvas can be gently pulled out or if the fabric to be used can be laundered, launder carefully and the canvas almost disintegrates. This special canvas, which contains a good deal of sizing, comes in various sizes and can be obtained in fine needlework shops. It is called Penelope Canvas for Cross Stitch.

Many beautiful pieces can be done with a remarkable amount of shading using the plain Cross Stitch. There are numerous charts and books that give patterns to follow, either for a motif or actual objects done in the Cross Stitch. The important thing to remember in Cross Stitch is that the top layer of the stitches must all cross in the same direction. The Cross Stitch can be worked as an individual stitch, with each cross completed before you go on to the next, or, when filling large areas, can be worked in a series of slanting lines in one direction and then in the other.

DIAGRAM 1 shows the cross being completed in itself. DIAGRAM 2 shows the two steps in working a complete row of half Cross Stitches, before coming back and completing the entire row. This second method is the obvious one to use in Assisi Embroidery. This interesting type of embroidery is done in squares as is all Cross Stitch embroidery, but what makes it unique is that the shapes are left blank on the fabric, and the background is filled with Cross Stitches, as shown in FIGURE 1.

To work a complete Cross Stitch the needle is brought out at A on the lower left-hand edge and carried up diagonally to B. When working on evenweave threads, it would be the same number of threads up as to the right. The needle is inserted at B and emerges directly below at C on the same level as A. Then the needle is carried diagonally in the other direction to D and brought out again at C. This completes the cross, and you are in position to start your next one in the line (DIAGRAM 1).

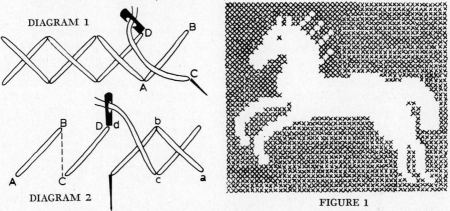

DIAGRAM 1

DIAGRAM 2

FIGURE 1

If you are doing large areas of Cross Stitch in the same color, the work goes faster, and you are likely to have a smoother tension, if you work in the second method (DIAGRAM 2). The thread is brought out and carried across diagonally the same as the first step in method 1, and brought directly below the half stitches as shown in DIAGRAM 2, continuing across the whole line to be covered in the Cross Stitch. When that end is reached, the work is simply reversed, and a straight diagonal row of stitches, which completes the crosses, is worked back in the opposite direction. However, your needle should enter and emerge from exactly the same holes that it did on the original journey. Whether done in small tight little stitches or with large bold stitches and heavy thread, the action on this work is exactly the same.

Because this is worked in the reverse, the left-hander uses the same directions. The back of your work is just a series of vertical double lines.

134 · CROSS STITCH—DOUBLE
(LEVIATHAN STITCH, SMYRNA STITCH)

This makes a nice change from the regular Cross Stitch, and is again used equally well in Canvas Embroidery and Surface Embroidery. Because of the nature of this stitch, each stitch as a rule is completed before going on to the next one. However an interesting result and texture can be gotten by doing half in one color of thread and half in another.

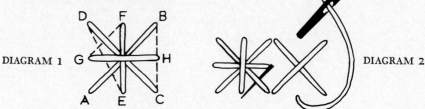

DIAGRAM 1

DIAGRAM 2

The working order of the stitches is shown in DIAGRAM 2 with the completion of the second cross in the works. On inspection you will see that this is actually the regular diagonal cross with an upright cross on top. This creates a charming little pattern, and when a solid area is worked using two colors, an interesting effect is obtained.

A variation on this is called a Star Stitch, in which a third small cross is worked over the upright cross, giving a heavier, fuller stitch (FIGURE 2).

FIGURE 1

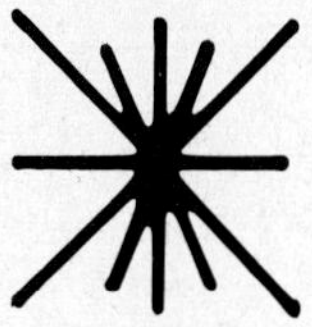

FIGURE 2

135 · CROSS STITCH—ENRICHED

This stitch, the Enriched Cross Stitch, is actually a combination of two stitches, the foundation being an oblong Cross Stitch. These have to be fairly large size and with fairly heavy thread to show to the best advantage. They work out nicely as either a border or filling for an area.

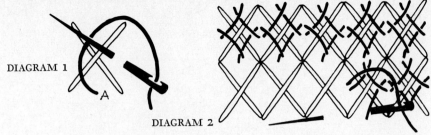

DIAGRAM 1

DIAGRAM 2

Diagram 1 shows the foundation laid with Cross Stitches and the beginning enrichment step of this stitch, which in reality is a series of Buttonhole Stitches worked into the four corners of the Chain Stitch. The needle is brought out at A in the middle of the right-hand end of the Cross Stitch, and, moving counterclockwise, the Buttonhole Stitches are worked over each arm of the Cross Stitch. Then the threads are carried across the back to the next one for the following series of stitches.

Diagram 2 shows the needle being inserted over the first straight thread to complete the appearance and carried on to the next square in the working of this stitch.

136 · CROSS STITCH—ITALIAN
(ARROWHEAD CROSS STITCH, TWO-SIDED ITALIAN STITCH)

This stitch, which is alike on both sides, can be worked either on loosely woven linen or upon canvas. The Italian embroiderers of the sixteenth century used this stitch a great deal and worked it on the evenweave linen. The completed stitch consists of a cross with straight stitches surrounding it on all four sides.

A characteristic of the older work, which you don't notice until you actually try working it, is the tiny perforation between the stitches, caused by making a slight pull on the thread as each stitch is taken. To show this work to best advantage, there should be a certain proportion between the working thread and the ground fabric, which can only be discovered by trial. If the thread is too coarse for the background material, the perforation will be filled up and the effect lost, while if it is too fine, the threads will not completely cover the ground, and again the effect will be lost.

I suggest you work this stitch with a fine blunt-point needle. There are two methods of working it. One entire stitch can be completed before going on to the next, or the completion can be carried out in the return journey. I'll show diagrams of both methods, but I find the second one a little faster to do, and as a rule am able to keep the tension a little smoother, using it.

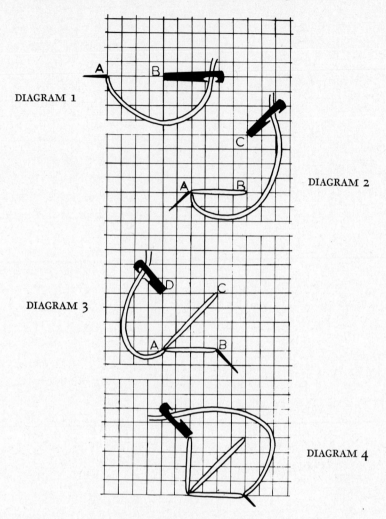

DIAGRAM 1

DIAGRAM 2

DIAGRAM 3

DIAGRAM 4

DIAGRAM 1 shows the beginning of the stitch in which you are actually doing a horizontal Back Stitch, so that your needle comes out at A and goes over the number of threads desired, and is inserted at B and emerges at A. DIAGRAM 2 shows the next step in which the slanting stitches are taken up and away from the starting point to C. Again the needle emerges at A on the completion of the stitch. DIAGRAM 3 shows the third stitch being taken, which is an upright stitch with the needle slanting in back of the work and emerging this time at B. The fourth step in this stitch is shown as the stitch slants back to the left to form the cross, the needle again emerging at B. The needle and thread are now in position to begin the series of steps over again.

The second method of working this stitch means leaving out the fourth step, the final cross, and completing all three steps of each stitch completely across your row. Then do a return journey, making only the top cross stitches, and when the needle is brought down the desired length, you are in position to start another row across. FIGURE 1 shows both how the work looks on completion and the second method in the final step.

Left-handers would probably find it easier to reverse the directions of these stitches than to turn the diagrams.

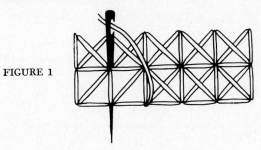

FIGURE 1

137 · CROSS STITCH–KNOTTED

The Knotted Cross Stitch is another stitch that can be worked in two journeys. However like the basic Cross Stitch, each complete stitch can also be worked on its own. The main advantage of doing it in two journeys occurs when you use contrasting threads for the knotted part. Use a fairly heavy thread, and bear in mind that, when you start distorting your Cross Stitches, they don't always have to be worked on evenweave fabric. This stitch can go around curves and lends itself to various shapes.

Begin by forming the Cross Stitch as shown in DIAGRAM 1, from A to B and C to D. As the Cross Stitches are completed, the needle emerges at E. Now your Cross Stitch is complete, and you are ready to start forming a Twisted Chain Stitch which is worked over the cross just completed, not going through the fabric, as shown in DIAGRAM 2. When this is completed, tie down the Twisted Chain by inserting the needle at F and carrying the thread to the top of the line, to start knotting your next Chain Stitch.

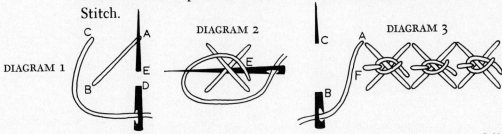

DIAGRAM 1   DIAGRAM 2   DIAGRAM 3

The left-hander works the Cross Stitch in the most comfortable manner and probably will find it easier to work the Detached Twisted Chain from the left to the right, so that the overall work goes from left to right.

138 · CROSS STITCH–LONG ARMED
(PLAITED SLAV STITCH)

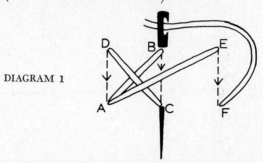

DIAGRAM 1

This is an interesting Cross Stitch variation, which shows how a stitch can be enriched merely by changing the length and placement of the stitches. It is a popular Canvas stitch and is particularly useful for rugs, for it gives a padded textured effect. This stitch needs to be worked with evenly spaced stitches to get the best effect. The first two movements of the needle and thread are the same as for the regular Cross Stitch. However the Cross Stitch is completed by bringing the needle up directly below at A as shown in DIAGRAM 1, and carrying it across twice the length of the original diagonal stitch to E on the upper line, straight down to F on the lower line and then back to B on the upper line and in the same hole. The needle goes from B straight down to and out the same hole at C and clear over to G on the upper line and down directly below to H, as shown in DIAGRAM 2.

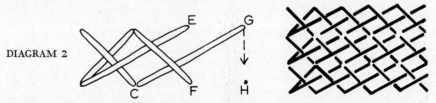

DIAGRAM 2

The reverse side shows upright stitches at regular intervals. The left-hander will find it easier to work this by either turning the directions upside down or reversing them.

This is another of the stitches most commonly used on canvas, but it works up well as a border on fabrics and is particularly good for rugs, because of the heavy backing.

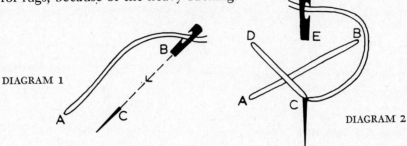

This stitch is worked from left to right, but the original Cross Stitch is started with the Long Armed. DIAGRAM 1 shows the thread emerging on the lower left line at A and carried twice the distance of the squares to the right and up to the upper line. The needle, instead of going down as in most Cross Stitches, slants back half the distance of the original stitch and is brought out on the lower line as shown in DIAGRAM 1. The second action of this stitch is the needle being carried up to the left directly above A and slanting backward to where the thread has just emerged at C and brought out the same hole. Next an upright stitch is taken, inserting the needle directly above C, where the thread is inserted at E, and bringing it down again in preparation to start the next stitch (DIAGRAM 2). Now this process is repeated.

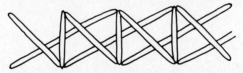

The reverse side of this stitch also makes a pleasing pattern.

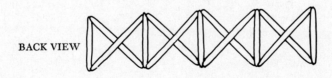

140 · CROSS STITCH—MOORISH DIAGONAL

I found this stitch in an old Victorian English pamphlet. It is not worked strictly in the Cross Stitch manner, more of a Cretanlike Stitch, but it isn't that exactly either. I will leave it labeled as a Cross Stitch.

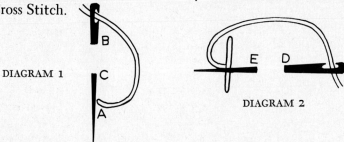

DIAGRAM 1

DIAGRAM 2

DIAGRAM 1 shows the thread emerging at A and the needle being inserted directly above at B and coming out directly below at C, C being about halfway between A and B. DIAGRAM 2 shows the next step, the thread held above the working area and the needle inserted to the right at D and brought back, taking a horizontal stitch. The needle is brought back toward the vertical stitch just made, emerging at E, about half of the distance of the entire stitch and pulled on through. FIGURE 1 shows a series of these stitches worked.

Left-handers, to work at the same angle, turn the diagram upside down. The back of the work is a series of little horizontal and diagonal stitches.

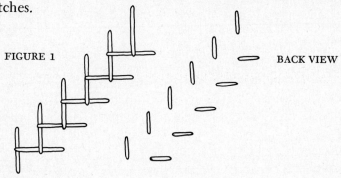

FIGURE 1

BACK VIEW

141 · CROSS STITCH—ORIENTAL
(CHINESE)

Although this isn't a regular Cross Stitch in the accepted sense, the end result is an upright Cross Stitch. There is a definite pattern to the steps of each pair of upright Cross Stitches, and for practicing this particular stitch is probably best worked on evenweave fabric. The diagrams and the initial directions will be given for the evenweave.

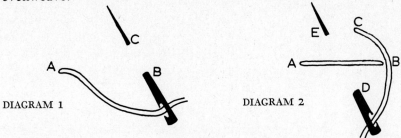

DIAGRAM 1   DIAGRAM 2

Note DIAGRAM 1; the working thread has emerged at A, and the needle and thread are carried over six threads to B; the needle is coming out at C, which would be *up* two threads and *to the left* two threads. Now make a single straight stitch directly down, with the thread leaving the fabric at C and the needle entering the fabric at D, four background threads below. The needle from this point emerges two threads *to the left* and four threads *up* at E. Another straight stitch is made equal to CD, with the needle going in at F and emerging at D (DIAGRAM 3). The next set of stitches is shown in DIAGRAM 4, two threads below the original set, so that, as the needle is carried across the six threads to G and brought out at H up above, it will be level with the straight line of the original group of stitches.

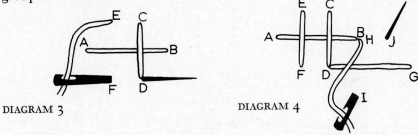

DIAGRAM 3   DIAGRAM 4

Repeat the process through from A to F to complete this stitch. When the second upright stitch is completed, the needle is brought out up above in the same hole as H, in preparation for starting another group of stitches on the upper level. FIGURE 1 shows these stitches grouped in various ways with a definite Oriental flavor.

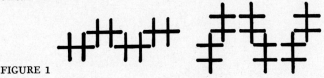

FIGURE 1

165

This is a very descriptive title. The stitch is a Cross Stitch, but it is worked so that both sides of the work look exactly alike. This method is not used as often as it once was, but is still a good stitch to be able to refer to if the occasion should arise for enriching a garment or curtain which must be seen back and front. This stitch has to be worked in four journeys to complete a whole row and to get the proper effect. The secret of getting the exact appearance on this stitch is taking a couple of little half stitches when the work is being reversed as will be noted when we arrive at that point in the journey.

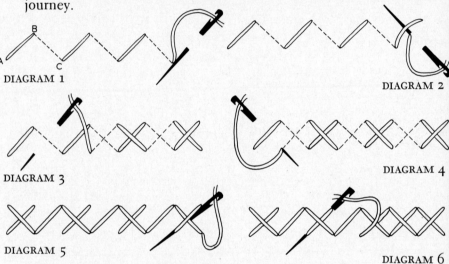

DIAGRAM 1

DIAGRAM 2

DIAGRAM 3

DIAGRAM 4

DIAGRAM 5

DIAGRAM 6

The beginning work is shown in row 1. The needle and thread are brought out at A on the lower line, and a slanting half Cross Stitch is taken and the needle inserted at B. It emerges at C an equal distance away, on across on the lower line, so you have slanting stitches of equal size, one on the front and one on the back of the work at this point (DIAGRAM 1—the stitches on the under side are indicated with dotted lines). A series of these stitches is continued on across the row. DIAGRAM 2 shows the procedure to the end of your first journey.

As you reach the end of your first row of stitches, the needle is only brought halfway down, directly back in the direction from which it came, and emerges. Now the needle is put in on the lower line directly below the long slanting stitch just completed and brought out again in the same hole from which the thread has just emerged (DIAGRAM 2). DIAGRAM 3 shows the second return journey in progress so that you are completing the process started on your first journey. DIAGRAM 4 shows the beginning of the next journey from left to right with the stitches slanting. You will be constantly using the same hole formed on the first journey. The work is carried completely across the row, and DIAGRAM 5 shows the finishing up of that journey and the beginning of the next return journey, in which another little half or auxiliary stitch is taken to complete the appearance on the back of the work the same as on the front. DIAGRAM 6 shows the final journey being completed across.

The left-hander simply reverses all the directions, starting at the right side rather than the left.

143 · CROSS STITCH—TWO-TRIP

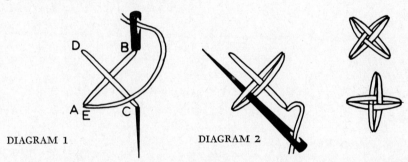

DIAGRAM 1   DIAGRAM 2

This stitch is called the Double Cross Stitch in French books. However, since we have a different meaning for the Double Cross Stitch in English books, I have named it thus. There are two trips in each direction of this stitch so that it is really as good a name as any. It is a lovely individual stitch when made with heavy thread, but works well as a solid filling or in groups and even with extra stitches added to it. DIAGRAM 1 shows a regular Cross Stitch made, ABCD, and the thread emerging again at A. The original stitch is under the thread CD. Now on this stitch you will take another stitch exactly like the first one from A in the same hole at B and out again at C as on your first journey. Going back to cover the second stitch, your thread has been brought out at C, and your needle is placed under your first stitch, AB, which will put the needle going over this stitch just made, under AB. Now pull on through and insert again at B. Should you be turning your work around to work at different angles, do remember that on the very last stitch in this series, the needle will always go *over* the last stitch made on the second trip and *under* the first thread.

If the left-hander reverses the directions in making the stitches, he will find it a little easier going over and under in the second trip.

144 · CROWN STITCH

There are two methods of working this little stitch, which is definitely a separate stitch, but works well when used in groupings. One is German and one is Swedish. Although they are worked quite differently—and I will give you both methods—the end appearance is exactly the same.

The German method (DIAGRAM 1), starts with the thread being brought out at A and a Fly Stitch made with a long tail, as shown in DIAGRAM 1. The other two straight stitches are taken over the original legs of the Fly Stitch, one on each side of the tie-down stitch.

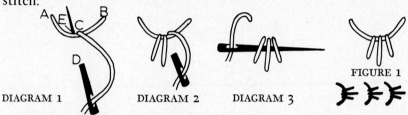

DIAGRAM 1   DIAGRAM 2   DIAGRAM 3   FIGURE 1

In working the Swedish method, three straight stitches are worked, as in DIAGRAM 2, with the bases close together and the outer edges spaced a little apart. DIAGRAM 3 shows the needle passing under these stitches to form the base of the crown. FIGURE 1 shows the end results of these stitches, which as I mentioned before are exactly the same.

145 · CROW'S FOOT STITCH

Although I suppose technically this would be considered a dressmaker's stitch, it can be very useful at times in your surface stitchery, and of course you might one day embroider a garment where this would come in handy. This stitch almost needs no text to go with it, for by following the diagrams, you can see what needs to be done. If you want to be sure to keep a definite triangular shape, it would be well to mark it; however, once the actual work has been started, you will follow the pattern established on the first layer.

The needle and thread are brought out at A, the lower left-hand point, carried up to the peak of the shape and inserted, picking up a tiny bit of fabric from right to left at B. (I will be using arrows with these diagrams to help you keep the direction, because you will need to continue repeating this process in the various steps.) The needle is carried down to the lower right-hand point and a tiny bit of fabric picked up in the direction of the arrow shown at C. Now the needle and thread are carried across the bottom of the shape and the same stitch taken in the direction of the arrow again at A. You repeat these three stitches around the edge of the shape, making a stitch at each corner within the last one made and always *in the direction of the arrow*. As the work progresses, each stitch will approach nearer and nearer the middle until the whole triangle is filled.

The left-hander reverses the directions.

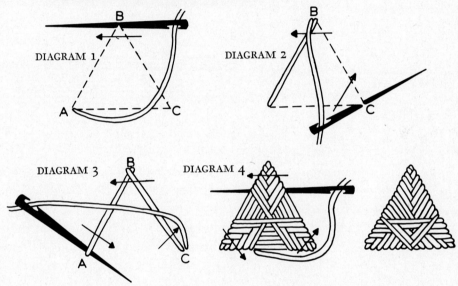

146 · DARNING STITCH

In reality the Darning Stitch is just an old-fashioned sort of a basting stitch except when used for surface embroidery. Of course there is a certain regularity and sort of a pattern, so it does have a decorative touch. This is sometimes used interchangeably with the term Running Stitch; however, although the action is the same, there is a difference in the two stitches, and they are used for different things.

Darning embroidery can be done with various weights of thread for different effects. A bold type, suitable for work carried out on a large scale, would be of coarse thread, either the pattern or background being solidly filled in by this means. Another is finer work with fine threads. Although the work is done the same, the overall effect is quite different.

The direction of your stitches is very important in this work, and many sophisticated pieces of embroidery have been done almost entirely with this very simple stitch. As a general rule, this should be worked on fabric with the weave loose enough so that the stitch can be picked up easily, and you can judge the size of your stitches by the number of threads.

DIAGRAM 1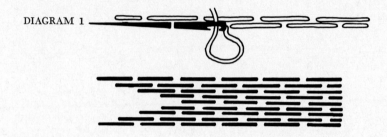

Darning Stitch as a rule is done over three or four threads, up to six, only one or two threads picked up in between the long stitches. The rows are worked very closely together, as shown in DIAGRAM 1. Although the stitches are of the same size, you alternate the spacing, brick-fashion, so that you are picking up your thread or two in the middle of a long stitch of the row previously worked. For practice on your sampler, it might be preferable to do a few rows of staggered lengths until you get used to the idea of how this could be used both as a filling or a background effect on your creative embroidery. This will probably show you that you can't pick up more than two little threads between stitches and keep the size and tension even on this stitch. (It is really best to pick up only *one* thread between two stitches.)

A little playing with this stitch will show you that it has almost no end of possibilities in design, and you will probably become aware that you have seen a lot of this used in patterns. One of the most common uses, and one of the best known in the United States a few years ago, was a type of darning called huck weaving in which the actual weave of the fabric was incorporated into the pattern.

The left-hander works the Darning from the left-hand direction for more comfort, but the picking up stitches would be exactly the same. The back of the work shows only the tiny little stitches where a thread or two has gone under.

Damask Darning is a development of Pattern Darning. However there are some old samplers that have areas simply covered with Pattern Darning. The name would lead us to think that this technique was originally developed to mend damask table linen. The figure will show it is a simple Darning Stitch taken in both perpendicular and horizontal directions, and if two suitable colors are used, it gives a charming effect of shot damask silk. There is no diagram on this because you know what the darning action is, and the figure illustrates the end result of the thread. It is obvious that this particular type of work should be done with great care and regularity.

148 · DARNING–DOUBLE
(PESSANTE)

The special characteristic of Double Darning is that it is exactly the same on both sides of the fabric, and in some cases this is very useful and thrifty. It is often found on work in the Near East—Turkey, Persia, and the Greek Islands. The stitch itself consists of the basic row stitches—more Running Stitch than Darning, for you pick up exactly as much fabric as you need between the stitches. When you reach the end of the space being covered and start the return journey, you reverse your procedure, so that the needle at this time picks up the fabric covered by the stitch on the previous row and covers the gaps left on the first journey (DIAGRAM 1).

DIAGRAM 1

A somewhat different stitch can be obtained, exactly like the stitch in FIGURE 1, by moving the stitches over half the length with each succeeding row. This way you get a diagonal effect instead of ribbed rows.

FIGURE 1

149 · DARNING—JAPANESE

The Japanese Darning is actually a type of Pattern Darning. Rows of darning with the alternate spacing are done—with, however, a little more fabric left between the rows than those you worked for a solid darning filling. DIAGRAM 1 shows these rows having been worked and the start of the second process in this stitch. It emerges at the beginning of the first stitch on the second row at A and is inserted at the end of the first stitch on the top row at B. It emerges at C, the beginning of the second stitch on the top row, alternating the stitches between the two rows. DIAGRAM 2 shows the pattern being formed, and the action of the needle and thread making the next row of Pattern Darning. This stitch is very useful for a light filling for any shape.

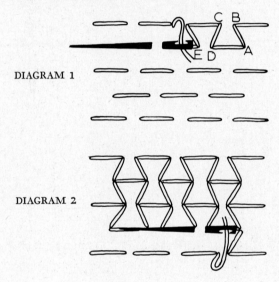

DIAGRAM 1

DIAGRAM 2

150 · DARNING—PATTERN

Pattern Darning is exactly that. It is a simple form of enrichment of fabric that has been used in all countries for centuries as a filling or background. The size of the stitches varies, but accuracy is most important. An evenweave material is essential unless you work on the same spaced canvas as was suggested in your Cross Stitch work, which can be easily removed when the design is finished. In that case the stitches are worked carefully into the rows without piercing the threads of the canvas. I will not do any more diagramming but will just give you the figures and some of the darning patterns and variations that can be used for ideas.

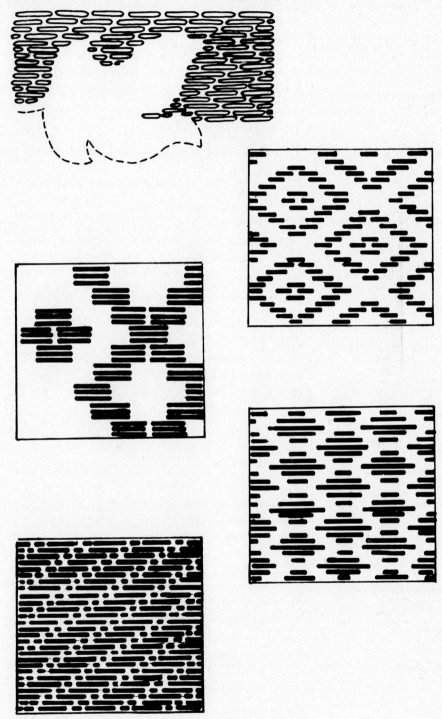

This band really has to be worked to see the proper effect. It is listed in all the old embroidery books as a band; however, an area can be worked in the same method for an interesting effect. The work is begun with a base layer of stitches, which, unless you are using very heavy thread, should be fairly close together, about one-sixteenth inch. These can be seen underneath the beginning of the work in DIAGRAM 1, and they are done like all Laid Work by carrying a thread across and inserting and bringing it out on the same side and then bringing back in the other direction.

This is one of the stitches for which a frame must be used. For the surface layer it would probably be best to work with two needles and two different threads of sharply contrasting color to work up the best effect. Both colors will be threaded, and you will work with two needles all the time, and as you are working only on the surface, going under the threads, it would be best if both of these needles were blunt or tapestry needles.

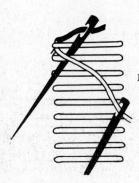

DIAGRAM 1

The needle with the lighter thread is slipped under the first cross bar and left lying. The needle with the dark thread is carried *over* the first cross bar, so that it actually hides the light thread, then *under* the second cross bar, and down on through. Now the dark thread is left lying to one side while the light thread is passed *over* the second cross bar, *under* the third, and then *under* the dark thread. The weaving movements are continued in this manner, alternately picking up dark and light threads, until the bottom of the area is reached. The same process is begun again at the top; however, this time the order of the colors is reversed. The needle with the dark thread is slipped under the first cross bar, the light thread going over it, and on down to the end again. The third row is the same as the first, beginning with the light thread, and the fourth is the same as the second.

DIAGRAM 2

In this way the two colors will come alternately across the bar and in diagonal lines down the length of it. Sufficient lines of weaving should be worked to cover the cross bars completely, and it is probably a good idea to use your needle or fingernail to pack them over tightly together, so there is absolutely no background showing. If a raised effect is wanted, a preliminary padding of long straight stitches could be put down on the work before the cross bars are laid. If you are making a long band, it is best to be sure that your threads are long enough to complete the whole weaving band each time a new line of work is started.

Left-handers work the same but will probably be more comfortable starting on the right-hand side of the area. The back of the work merely shows the beginning of the threads at each end of the band, and the stitches on the edges made by the Laid Work.

152 · DIAMOND STITCH

This is an attractive border stitch, which you would probably do well to practice first between a pair of parallel guidelines. The needle is brought out at the top of the left-hand line and carried directly across and inserted at the top of the right-hand line. The needle comes out just below, a thread or two, on the same line at C, and is then in position for the first knot. Holding the working thread down on the fabric toward the left with the thumb, pass the needle under the two threads as shown in DIAGRAM 1. When the thread is pulled through, a knot will appear on the right-hand side of the first stitch. You will then be in position to start your second knot. (These knots do not have to go through the ground fabric but it is a good idea, on the first two, to pick up a bit of the background material at the same time.)

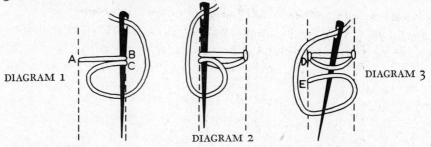

DIAGRAM 1   DIAGRAM 3

DIAGRAM 2

The second knot is formed on the left-hand parallel line as shown in DIAGRAM 2. The knot is formed in the same manner as your original one with the direction reversed. Now the needle is stuck back immediately under the second knot at D and brought to the surface a slight way down on the left-hand line. DIAGRAM 3 shows the third knot being made, and this definitely doesn't go into the background fabric. The needle will pass under the threads left slack above and under the working thread that you are holding with your thumb, to form a knot in the center of your two parallel lines. Your needle then goes back to the right-hand line and starts the process over again. FIGURE 1 shows a series of stitches that have been worked.

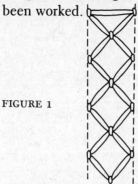

FIGURE 1

Left-handers start on the right-hand parallel line, making the right-hand knot in reverse order. The back of this work shows only the tiny stitches along the edge of your parallel lines.

153 · DIAMOND STITCH—FILLING

DIAGRAM 1

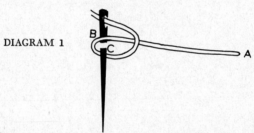

This stitch is used in needlepoint lace, but is equally pretty for embroidery work. To commence the work, the needle is brought out at the top right-hand side of the area to be filled. The thread is carried across the entire area and inserted on the left-hand outline at B and brought out directly below, no more than one-sixteenth inch. Form a little Coral Knot right there, using your left thumb, with the working thread and needle going over the thread that has just been laid (DIAGRAM 1). Continue across, making Coral Knots at regular intervals, not going into the fabric and leaving loops between each two knots as shown in DIAGRAM 2. When the upper right-hand corner has been reached, a final knot is made in the corner. The needle passes to the back of the work and is brought up (depending on the weight of the thread) generally about one-eighth inch below and in position for casting the second line of thread from side to side.

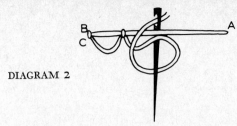

DIAGRAM 2

After this is done, the needle is brought up to the front again, on the left-hand side immediately below where it has just passed through. A second line of knots and loops is now formed and the upper row of loops is stitched down at the same time (DIAGRAM 3). Technically the needle doesn't pass through the fabric while you are doing this, but it can be done, and sometimes the filling is a little more regular, particularly if you are doing it on a large scale, if the needle does stitch the thread to the fabric at the knots.

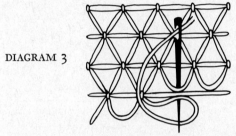

DIAGRAM 3

Because of the basic action in this stitch, the left-hander will be more comfortable doing the actual working from right to left, meaning that the original thread is brought out on the left-hand side of the area. The back of this work, unless the knots are anchored down, shows only stitches along the outline where the rows are finished and begun again.

154 · DIAMOND STITCH–KNOTTED

This is a handsome stitch when worked with a heavy, coarse thread, and the diagrams pretty much show the working of it. Start at the left-hand end of the line. If you want to be certain to keep your stitches regular, draw a pair of horizontal parallel guidelines to work between.

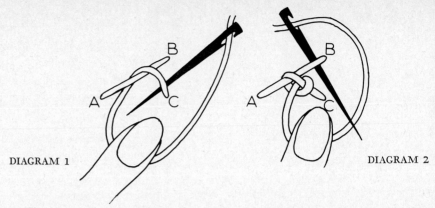

DIAGRAM 1   DIAGRAM 2

The thread is brought out of the lower line on the left-hand end and carried slantwise up to the upper line AB (DIAGRAM 1). After the needle has been inserted at B, it emerges directly below on the lower line at C. The rest of this stitch is worked on the surface over the threads, and it's a good idea to use a blunt needle. The working thread is passed from the top down over line AB and pulled on through. It is then held down below with the left thumb and inserted from right to left under the loop just formed, as in DIAGRAM 1. Next the needle is passed under the thread AB, to the right of the knot already worked, and the thread again is held below as in a Buttonhole Stitch. The needle passes under the stitch and over the working thread (DIAGRAM 2). Do not pull the thread too tightly when forming these knots. In the last stage, the needle again passes under the thread that emerges at C, and a loop is again held as for a Buttonhole Stitch—this time in the same direction as in step 1, from the top down, under the stitch and over the working thread.

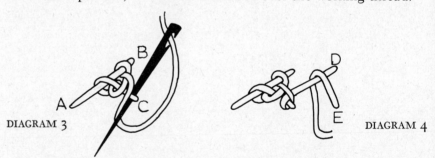

DIAGRAM 3   DIAGRAM 4

DIAGRAM 4 shows another base stitch made, with the needle carried over to the right, slanting upward, inserted on the top line and brought out on the end of the line. It is really difficult to picture what an interesting effect this stitch has until it's been tried.

The left-hander will probably find this stitch easier to work by turning the diagram upside down; start at the right-hand end of the upper line to work this stitch. The back of the work shows only vertical straight lines.

178

155 · DOUBLE KNOT STITCH
(TIED CORAL STITCH, OLD ENGLISH KNOT STITCH, PALESTRINA STITCH, SMYRNA STITCH)

This lovely stitch is known throughout Europe as the Palestrina Knot, after the town in central Italy. It is an attractive and easy way of getting knotted lines with a textured, beaded effect. Besides being decorative, it is a practical stitch, for it stays in place and launders well. Besides giving a rather unique line stitch, it lends itself to solid fillings very nicely, as used by the women in Palestrina. They also like to form rows of the Palestrina Knot separated by a line of Bokhara Couching.

As a rule these designs would be outlined with a stem stitch, and the work is generally done with a heavy white thread on a colored linen. Try practicing with a pearl cotton, which has a nice tight twist, to bring out the beauty of this knotted stitch. Start your work from the left.

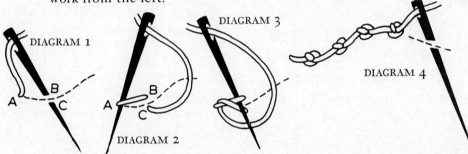

DIAGRAM 1 shows the working thread brought out at the end of the line at A and inserted just above the line at B and coming out just below the line at C. After the thread has been pulled through, the needle is inserted from the top down in the diagonal line formed at AB, without picking up any fabric (DIAGRAM 2). DIAGRAM 3 shows the needle again being inserted in the same manner, but this time the working thread is held with the left thumb so that the needle passes over the working thread after going under the stitch. Once this has been pulled on through—and not too tight—you are then ready to start your next stitch as shown in DIAGRAM 4, with the needle being inserted again to the right of the stitch just worked, above and coming out below the line. The left-hander will find this stitch easier to work if he turns the entire diagram upside down and starts on the right-hand end of the line.

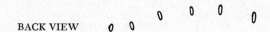

BACK VIEW

179

156 · EDGING STITCHES

I did not draw any diagrams of stitches for this first section, but I do want to reiterate that, of all the Edging Stitches, the Buttonhole Stitch is the best known. This includes all variations on the basic Buttonhole Stitch, but not the distorted ones.

Remember, when using the Buttonhole Stitch as an edging, it must actually provide for the hem as well. Care must be taken, when the needle is inserted and brought back to the lower edge of the fabric, that the thread goes completely over the folded-back fabric to insure that the hem is caught down properly all the way around the edge.

All of these edging stitches, whether incorporating hemming or just for a decorative edging, can be used either for finishing a needlework project or on a garment to add an extra touch. Although most of these are quite old in terms of use, it might surprise you how well they work, particularly with the heavier threads, for edging embroidery projects.

157 · EDGING STITCH—ANTWERP
(KNOT STITCH, KNOTTED BLANKET STITCH)

This little stitch is worked from left to right. The thread is anchored securely beneath the material and brought downward through the edge of your fabric. This is a better decorative stitch than a hemming stitch, for there are spaces and loops between the stitches. However, it is a wonderful base for a fringed edging. You will also see this same stitch described in the Insertion section, for it is useful for joining two pieces of fabric.

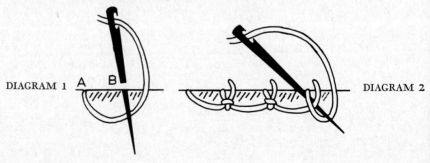

DIAGRAM 1 A B   DIAGRAM 2

Starting from the left, the thread is at the lower edge of the fabric. The needle is inserted off to the right a bit (DIAGRAM 1), and a Buttonhole Stitch is made. You don't actually hold the thread down with your left thumb, but it will be needed in there to help you keep the thread below, so the needle can be passed under, from left to right. DIAGRAM 2 shows a series of these stitches worked on the edge, the needle taking the second step of this stitch—sliding under both threads of the cross made by the previous stitch and over the working thread. These two steps are continued on across the edge, the spacing depending somewhat on the size of thread being used.

The left-hander will find this more comfortable to work starting from the right hand and working the Buttonhole Stitch by sliding the needle from right to left.

158 · EDGING STITCH—ARMENIAN

This decorative edging shows up to best advantage when worked with a really heavy thread, and is another pretty edging. Working from left to right, the thread is anchored at the edge of the material. The needle is inserted a little farther along the edge, from the back to the front of the fabric (DIAGRAM.1). The thread is not pulled completely through; a loop is formed by twisting the thread to the right. Holding the loop in the left hand, insert the needle from the top down, *over, under,* and *over* the working thread (DIAGRAM 2). Now the thread is pulled up tight before the next stitch is begun.

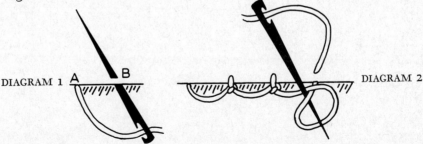

DIAGRAM 1   A   B   DIAGRAM 2

Left-handers will find it easier to execute this stitch by starting on the right-hand edge and reversing the direction of the needle.

(a) PICOT BULLION

There are several Picot Edgings, all of which add really decorative effects to your embroidery work. Most of them were originally used in Richelieu and Italian cutwork; however, with the proper weight of thread—that is, usually heavy—they can add a delightful finishing touch to a piece of today's embroidery. This edging is worked from left to right and along the edge of the material. It can be used—as can all Buttonhole edgings, which most of your Picot Stitches are—to incorporate the hem also.

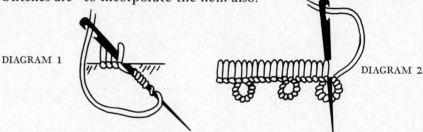

DIAGRAM 1

DIAGRAM 2

Start by working a few Buttonhole Stitches very close together until you reach the spot where you want to make your first Picot. The needle is then inserted back into the upright part of the last Buttonhole Stitch formed (DIAGRAM 1). Now hold the head of the needle down without pulling through. Twist the working thread around it five or six times, as shown in DIAGRAM 1. The twist is held with the left thumb and forefinger as the needle is pulled through. Tighten up the Bullion, and secure it in place with the next Buttonhole Stitch, which must be worked very close to the last one. These stitches must be worked with a tightly twisted thread to look good when finished.

The left-hander works from the opposite direction and does the Buttonhole Stitch and twists in reverse.

(b) BUTTONHOLE PICOT

In the Buttonhole Picot, it is more comfortable to work from right to left. It may seem a bit awkward for the Buttonholes but you will find it is much easier for executing the Picots themselves. Having reached the point on your edge where a Picot is required, place a pin in the edge of the material very close to the last Buttonhole Stitch, as shown in DIAGRAM 1. The needle is then inserted into the material at A and emerges below the edge. The working

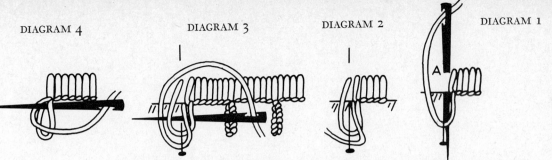

DIAGRAM 4   DIAGRAM 3   DIAGRAM 2   DIAGRAM 1

thread is then pulled through until the desired length of Picot is left in the shape of a loop under the pin (DIAGRAM 2). The thread is then taken under the pin again, from the right to the left, and the needle slipped on to the right side of the loop, *over* the pin but *under* the left side of the loop and *over* the working thread. It is then pulled on through, up taut and firm, to form the end of the Picot (DIAGRAM 3). DIAGRAM 4 shows the Buttonhole Stitch being worked over the thread of this loop, which is continued until the edge of the fabric is reached. Now start working the Buttonhole into the edge of the fabric, and continue again until the spot where the next Picot is to be done.

The left-hander simply reverses this procedure.

(c) LOOP PICOT (PINNED PICOT)

As with the Buttonhole Picot, this variation is best worked from the right to the left because the working of the Picot is easier from this direction. The Buttonhole Stitch is used for the edge of the fabric between the Picots, and when the spot for a picot is reached, the needle is inserted into the material, as shown in DIAGRAM 1. The thread is then passed under it from right to left, and a stitch is taken into the material at A. The needle is brought below the edge of the material and slipped under the loop, *over* the pin and *under* the first part of the working thread, but *over* the second part as in DIAGRAM 2. This forms a Buttonhole Stitch. When pulled on through tightly, it secures the loop against the edge of the fabric. The Buttonhole Stitch is then continued to the next spot where a Picot is wanted.

The left-hander reverses this procedure.

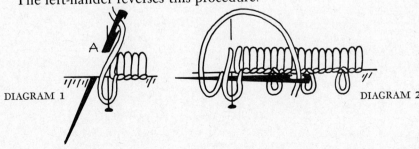

DIAGRAM 1   DIAGRAM 2

183

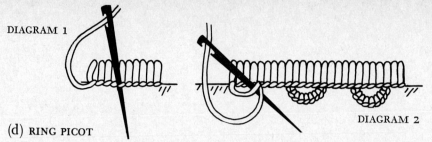

DIAGRAM 1

DIAGRAM 2

(d) RING PICOT

This is the easiest of the Picots to work, but it does have a heavi-er result than the others. The Buttonhole Stitch is started at the right-hand end of the edge and worked until the spot where a Picot is required. Remember, when doing this one, you will be using sev-eral Buttonhole Stitches to form the Picot, so work a few Button-hole Stitches beyond the exact spot where you want the rings formed before starting the ring. The needle is inserted three or four stitches back to the right and into the looped edge of a Buttonhole Stitch. The working thread is pulled on through but a small loop is left. Unless an exceptionally large ring is required, the loop really should be drawn almost as tight as the distance along the edge, for the subsequent buttonholing enlarges the space surprisingly. The needle now will work Closed Buttonhole Stitches onto this loop, back from right to left, until the edge of the fabric is reached again. The ring is secured by the Buttonhole Stitch and taken back into the fabric. Proceed on across the edge in this manner.

Left-handers will probably prefer to work this from the opposite direction.

(e) WOVEN PICOT

This variation produces a larger Picot than the others and definitely needs to be worked with stiff thread. The diagrams show an individual Picot being worked; however, it is very effective when worked in combination with the Buttonhole edge also.

The thread is anchored under the fabric, and you will find it eas-ier to execute this if the edge is held away from you. After the thread has been brought through the edge, the needle is inserted from the edge out but not pulled up tight, as shown in DIAGRAM 1. Next a pin is slipped over the loop and into the fabric, with the working thread passing behind the top of the pin from left to right and pulled on through to firm up the loop. The needle is passed through the loop, as shown in DIAGRAM 2, and pulled on through. The diagram shows it left rather loose, but it should be pulled up tight, using either your needle, which should be blunt, or a thumb-nail to keep these stitches up close to each other.

Next a weaving movement from left to right is performed, the

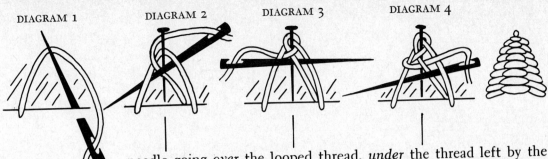

needle going *over* the looped thread, *under* the thread left by the last stitch formed, and *over* the looped thread on the outside again (DIAGRAM 3). DIAGRAM 4 shows the weaving movement from right to left. These alternate weaving movements are continued until you have a tightly woven Picot and have reached the edge of the fabric. Each stitch should be pulled up snug, and the result is the finished Picot.

The left-hander follows the same directions except perhaps that the original anchoring might be reversed. The weaving stitches are worked alternately, so there should be no problems with them.

160 · EDGING STITCH—BRAID

This Edging Stitch takes a little practice to do well and uniformly. It is most effective when done with a tightly twisted thread and is also a bit easier to work if the edge is held away from you.

The thread is anchored on the right-hand edge and brought on toward the left in preparation for the beginning of the stitch. A loop is formed with the left hand and will have to be held in place while the needle is working. The needle is then put through this loop and inserted on the back of the fabric and brought out again a short distance below, on the edge and over the working thread (DIAGRAM 1). The needle is then pulled through, but not quite tight. At this point, if the loops left between the knots are at all irregular, they should be adjusted with the needle, for regularity of size is part of the beauty of this stitch. After the loop is adjusted, the thread is pulled away from the work and a firm knot is formed against the edge. Practice is required to master the technique, but it is well worth the effort.

The left-hander will find this stitch easier to do by turning the diagram upside down and starting from the right-hand edge. However, the edge of the work will be facing you.

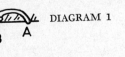

B A   DIAGRAM 1

161 · EDGING STITCH—LOOPED

This is one Edging Stitch that incorporates the hem and is most commonly used for various types of cutwork. It makes a nice firm Buttonhole edging, but is stronger than the ordinary Buttonhole Stitch. The reason for using this with cutwork is that it gives a strong edge, so that when a section of fabric is cut out, you still have a firm line to work into. Looped Edging Stitch is generally worked over a tiny turned-back edge, which is shown by the dotted lines in the diagram.

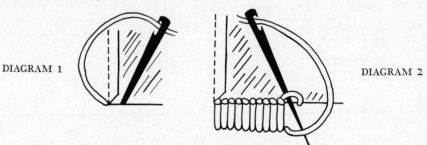

DIAGRAM 1   DIAGRAM 2

The work is begun on the left-hand end of the line, and the threads are anchored as near to the edge as possible. The needle is then inserted from behind upward, the length of this stitch being worked (DIAGRAM 1). Before this thread is pulled completely through, the needle is slipped under the loop on the edge as shown in DIAGRAM 2, and pulled sharply away from the edge. This forms a tight edge. You are then in position to start the next stitch, which should be as close to the previous stitch as possible.

The left-hander works this from the opposite direction, but slides the needle under the loop in the same manner.

162 · EDGING STITCH—PLAITED

This decorative edging is generally worked over a raw edge. It makes a neat, firm finish and prevents fraying.

DIAGRAM 1   DIAGRAM 2

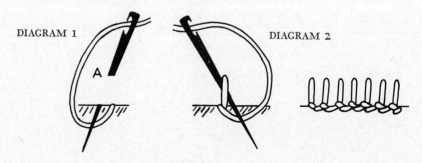

Working from left to right, the thread is fixed at the back of the material, in from the edge of the fabric. Take a few running stitches along the edge to be covered, and finish with a Split Stitch, the thread emerging in the proper position. The needle is then inserted at the right side and pulled through from underneath, leaving a Straight Stitch on both sides of the fabric. Next the needle is slipped under the Straight Stitch and pulled over the working thread, but does not enter the material (DIAGRAM 2).

The stitches can be left with a little space in between, as shown in the diagram, or, to get a heavier close effect, they can be worked so that none of the background fabric shows.

The left-hander will be most comfortable starting this on the right hand and working the needle from right to left through the Straight Stitch. The back of the work shows the same Straight Stitches that you have on the front.

163 · ERMINE FILLING STITCH

This stitch, when used all over, makes a delightful filling, and when worked in black on a white ground, it gives very much the effect of ermine tails, hence the name. The diagram shows that it is a series of straight stitches crossing each other, so it could be considered a kind of Cross Stitch.

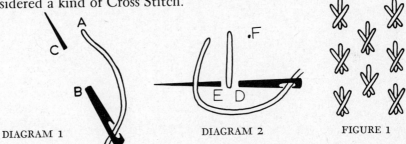

DIAGRAM 1   DIAGRAM 2   FIGURE 1

The work is begun with an upright Straight Stitch. The needle emerges up on the left about two thirds the length of the original Straight Stitch (DIAGRAM 1). FIGURE 1 shows some of these stitches having been worked as a filling. DIAGRAM 2 shows the needle being inserted at D and emerging at E to form the first little Cross Stitch. The dot at F is where the needle is inserted to complete the entire stitch. The thread from there is carried on to the spot where the next stitch is to be worked.

The only change the left-hander need make will be in bringing the needle out on the right of the upright stitch, to commence the second stitch, instead of to the left.

(SINGLE CORAL STITCH, SLANTED FEATHER STITCH)

This stitch has been in common use down through the years, particularly in the United States. A few generations ago it was used exclusively in infants' clothing. It is used a great deal with the addition of French Knots and a Chain Stitch in the spaces left between the Feather Stitch. The name "Feather Stitch" is sometimes found in the very old embroidery books for the Long and Short Stitch. The stitch is also known as the Plumage Stitch, owing to its frequent use for working up feathers. In some provinces of Hungary an interesting variation of this stitch is called the Rosemary Stitch, in which it is worked between parallel lines of Chain Stitch, with each Feather Stitch running through the center of each chain, resulting in a beautiful border.

There really is no limit on the uses of this stitch as interesting borders and straight lines. When the technique has been mastered, you can comfortably try some distortions of your own, filling in shapes such as leaves. In learning the technique of this stitch, put in four parallel guidelines to follow, as shown in DIAGRAM 1. Once you have mastered this stitch, you would, as a rule, have only a line to follow to give you the direction or curve.

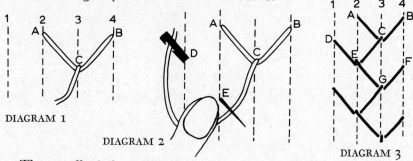

DIAGRAM 1

DIAGRAM 2

DIAGRAM 3

The needle is brought out at A, which is the top of line 2, and inserted on line 4, right opposite, with the needle slanting downward, emerging on line 3 below A and B, and pulled on through as in DIAGRAM 1. The awkward part comes on the second step of this stitch. The thread is now carried over to the other side and the loop held below with the left thumb. You must remember, when you are going to the awkward side, that the working thread must be carried completely around so that a loop will be formed when the needle is inserted and brought out over it. Don't let the working thread flop back over the hand holding the loop or you will lose your loop. This step is illustrated in DIAGRAM 2. The action of the working thread should be exaggerated until this becomes a natural action.

Next the needle is inserted at D which is exactly opposite C, on line 1, and emerges down below, slanting at about a 45-degree angle, line 2 at E, forming a loop on the left (DIAGRAM 2). From E the needle is carried over to line 4 again, and the stitch is repeated on the right-hand side. These two steps are worked down to the end of the row.

The left-hander will probably want to start working between 1 and 3 with the needle emerging on 3 and inserted on 1.

165 · FEATHER STITCH—CLOSED

The Closed Feather Stitch resembles the Double Chain Stitch, and the action of your needle is exactly the same, the difference lying in the insertion of the needle. The loops must be held with the left thumb as in both the Feather and Chain Stitch. In practicing this stitch, draw two parallel guidelines for working.

The needle is brought out at A on the left-hand line and inserted at B on the right-hand line, which is slightly above A as shown in DIAGRAM 1. The needle emerges at C on the same line and is ready to be carried over to the left-hand line. DIAGRAM 2 shows the needle being inserted at D, brought out at E on the left-hand line, D being directly under A, as close as you can get it, and pulled on through to form a left-hand loop. The needle is again inserted and emerges on the same line with F, as close to C as possible. These two steps are alternated to the end of the area to be covered.

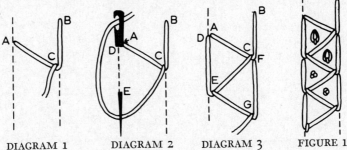

DIAGRAM 1   DIAGRAM 2   DIAGRAM 3   FIGURE 1

If the stitches are made large enough, an interesting variation can be made by inserting little French Knots or Detached Chain Stitches in the spaces left. This works nicely around curves, for forming borders or monograms. On curves you would have to remember that the inside stitches will be shorter than the outside stitches; however, keep the point of the loop staggered.

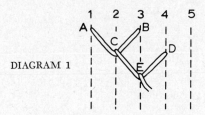

DIAGRAM 1

The Double Feather Stitch is simply a variation on the basic one, and to practice the working, make five parallel lines fairly close together, as shown in the diagram. The work is begun on the first line. The needle is brought out at A and inserted at B and emerges at C. For the second stitch, begin to form between lines 2, 3, and 4, so that the needle is inserted at D on line 4 exactly opposite C and emerges at E, on line 3, slanting at a 45-degree angle (DIAGRAM 1). At this point you have formed two stitches in the same direction, using only the four lines. Now the fifth line should be used to form another Feather Stitch in exactly the same direction as the previous two, with F being on the same level as E, and the needle emerging at G as shown on the diagram. With the thread at G, you are now ready to start back in the other direction, to swing the loop completely around, inserting your needle at H on line 2 and emerging below at I on line 3, to form the first stitch in the other direction. DIAGRAM 2 shows the needle being inserted at J and emerging at K on line 2 below. Continue alternating in this manner to form a regular border. Variation of threads and size of stitches can result in some interesting effects, when doing three and four stitches in one direction before starting back in the other direction.

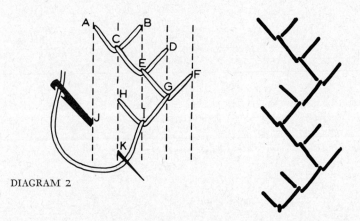

DIAGRAM 2

on down the length of the area to be covered (FIGURE 1). This makes a rich-looking braid effect, particularly when worked with a heavy thread.

Left-handers reverse the directions, starting on the left side rather than the right.

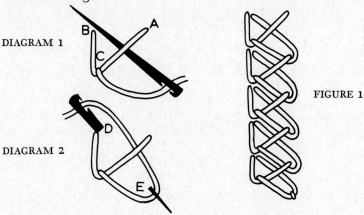

DIAGRAM 1

DIAGRAM 2

FIGURE 1

170 · FEATHER STITCH–KNOTTED
(CHAINED)

The work is begun on this as for a regular Feather Stitch, and can be done either slanting or straight. However, the straight seems to come off with the best effect. At the base of the Feather Stitch, as shown in DIAGRAM 1, a small Chain Stitch is formed over the thread, and the needle is carried over to the left to begin the next Feather Stitch. These two stitches are worked on down the line, and FIGURE 1 shows a group of these having been worked.

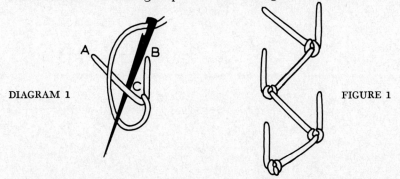

DIAGRAM 1

FIGURE 1

The left-hander will follow the same directions, for the stitches are worked alternately.

171 · FEATHER STITCH—PLAITED

This particular variation of the Feather Stitch gives you a really handsome raised effect. It can be made very delicate by the use of fine thread or look quite heavy and rich with heavier thread. An interesting texture can be achieved by a combination of the two.

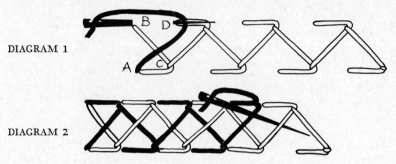

DIAGRAM 1

DIAGRAM 2

First work a row of straight Feather Stitches, leaving a distance between each stitch of at least half an inch, so there is a working space for the second layer. Now another row of Feather Stitches is begun, as shown in DIAGRAM 1, over the base stitch, using the same hole. The direction is exactly the opposite so that, instead of the thread emerging as originally at A, it emerges on the right-hand side at D, and a straight Feather Stitch is worked over the original one, as in DIAGRAM 1. DIAGRAM 2 shows that the thread has been passed under the slanting thread of the second Feather Stitch on the original layer, and an upright straight Feather Stitch has been worked to the right, in the space left between the first two stitches on the original. Continue working down in this manner with the second color, remembering to slide the working thread under the slanting bar when carrying the needle over to begin the work of the Feather Stitch on the right-hand side.

The left-hander does exactly the same.

172 · FEATHER STITCH—RAISED BAND

The Raised Feather Band is worked over a layer of laid threads done in two directions, and is really a band or an area covering. Thread is first laid lengthwise on the bar to be filled—a tight, round variety is best—then with the same thread, a ladder of evenly spaced laid stitches is worked over the under layer, as shown in DIA-GRAM 1. Now, with a tauter and fairly thick thread, the Feather Stitch is begun over the bars, as shown in DIAGRAM 2. Alternating from side to side, remember to hold the thread with the left thumb so that the loop will be formed as the work progresses down the ladder. The entire top layer is worked over the horizontal bars laid.

Left-handers work this exactly the same.

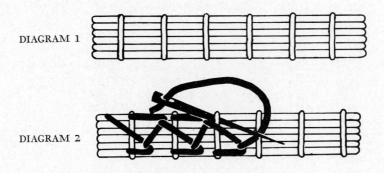

DIAGRAM 1

DIAGRAM 2

173 · FEATHER STITCH—SINGLE

The Single Feather Stitch is just the Feather Stitch worked without carrying the thread over to the other side, and could easily be called a slanting Blanket Stitch. As the diagram shows, the arms are at an angle, but the spacing and the manner in which the loop is formed is very similar to the Blanket Stitch.

This is a nice little border stitch. A pair of them could be used sloping in toward each other, with the second row of stitches entering the spaces left in the first row. This is often used singly in smocking.

Left-handers work in the other direction.

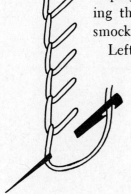

195

The Spanish Knotted Feather Stitch does seem at first a little difficult to keep even. The secret in this lies in the diagonal angle of the needle. Once you have mastered this, the result is a slightly raised decorative line. In reality the working is more of a twisted chain, but because it alternates from side to side, the name "Feather Stitch" was given to it.

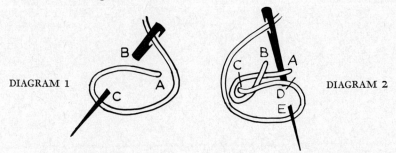

DIAGRAM 1   DIAGRAM 2

DIAGRAM 1 shows the work being started for the first knot, the thread emerging at A and the needle inserted at B, up above A and slanted slightly to the left of C under the first stitch, and being carried over the working thread. The working thread is held with the left thumb while the needle is drawn on through. The working thread is then laid over to the right, forming a large loop, again held with your left thumb, while the needle is inserted at D above and over the threads coming out at A. It emerges in the loop made by the working thread and is drawn on through and over the loop, as shown in DIAGRAM 2. This process is repeated from side to side, the needle always inserted into the fabric just above the last stitch. FIGURE 1 shows several completed stitches.

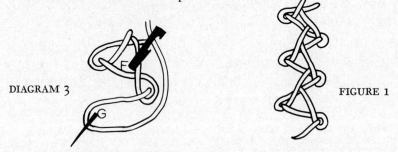

DIAGRAM 3   FIGURE 1

The left-hander needs no special instructions, for the work is done from side to side.

175 · FEATHER STITCH—SPINE
(LONG ARMED)

This stitch is really just a slanted Feather Stitch worked on three lines instead of four, and as can be seen in the diagram, the needle always comes out on the center line to form a spine. It is a quick and easy way to fill a leaf shape, with the spine part of the stitch becoming the center line in the leaf. Make sure that D is opposite B and F is opposite C, right on down your lines.

The left-hander works this in exactly the same way because of the alternating action of the needle and thread.

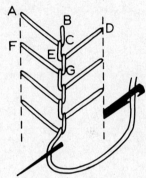

176 · FEATHER STITCH—STRAIGHT

The Straight Feather Stitch is worked exactly like the regular Feather Stitch, the only difference being the angle of the needle. When working on two lines to form this stitch, the needle is inserted in and out on the same perpendicular line, as the diagram shows. DIAGRAM 1 indicates the working of the stitch on the left-hand line after a few other stitches have been worked. The needle is always inserted on the same level as the thread emerging from the previous stitch.

Left-handers work in the same manner.

DIAGRAM 1

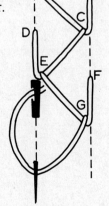

177 · FEATHER STITCH—SWINGING

This is a simple Feather Stitch variation that can be worked in a single line or in a border composed of two lines of stitches worked side by side. There is nothing unusual in the action of the needle and thread, it is simply the spacing. FIGURE 1 shows the double row worked.

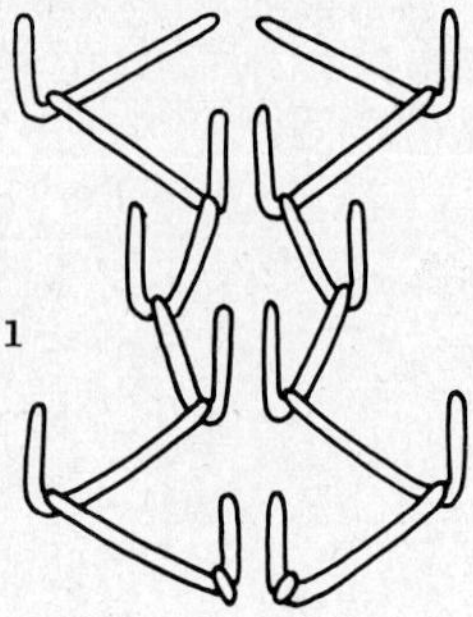

FIGURE 1

178 · FEATHER STITCH—TRIPLE

This little variation on the Feather Stitch can give you ideas for developing other variations. The work is begun by doing an upright Feather Stitch as in A, B, and C of DIAGRAM 1. Right beside this, and a bit longer, another stitch is taken. This time it will be worked as a Buttonhole Stitch, right beside the upright section of the stitch just worked, with the needle going in at D and coming out at E. Now another Buttonhole Stitch is formed to the left of the one just worked. This stitch is not anchored down. The thread is carried on down to the level below and off to the right, so that the original Feather Stitch will be going in directly underneath A. A series of Buttonhole Stitches of varying heights is worked side by side.

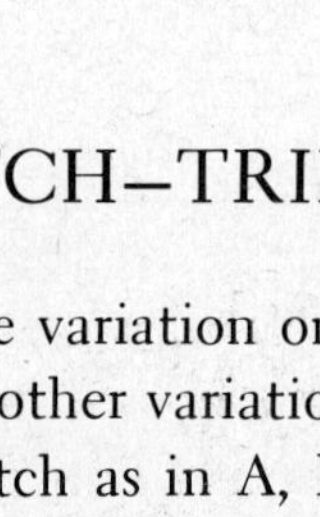

DIAGRAM 1 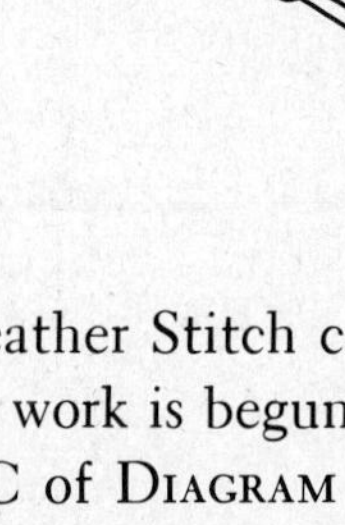   DIAGRAM 2 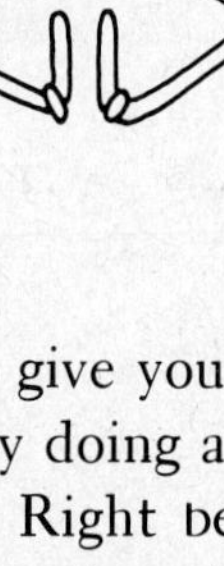   FIGURE 1

You will note that the top of the tallest stitch in the second grouping is begun on the same level as the base of the previous stitches. FIGURE 1 shows a series of these stitches worked to form a little border.

The direction in which the Buttonhole Stitches are worked changes with each group of stitches, so that the left-hander needs no special directions.

179 · FEATHER STITCH—ZIGZAG

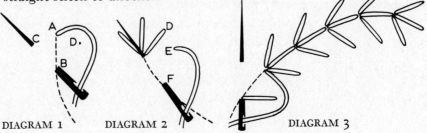

The Zigzag Feather Stitch is a combination of the Single Feather Stitch and the Spine Feather Stitch. If you take a look at the diagram, you will see that you have three Single Feather Stitches worked in one direction, A through G. The needle and thread are now carried over to the other direction, and three Single Feather Stitches worked from the left-hand side. The alternating of these groups of Single Feather Stitches gives you one more variation of the Feather Stitch to add to your vocabulary.

The left-hander uses the same directions for this particular stitch.

180 · FERN STITCH

This is a simple stitch that is useful for working fernlike sprays or leaf veining. The working is simply a combination of straight stitches. These straight stitches are used in groups of three all exactly the same size, entering the same hole at the base with each action. DIAGRAM 1 shows the beginning at A, the original stitch on your outline being formed. The needle is emerging at C where it will be in position for working the second straight stitch. The dot at D shows where the third stitch will be worked. All of these come back into the hole at B on the line.

DIAGRAM 2 shows the procedure for working the second group of stitches. The needle is brought out from D to E and inserted on the line at F up in the hole at the base of the previous group of stitches. DIAGRAM 3 shows a series of these stitches worked, the needle in the process of working the second stitch in the grouping and getting in position to do the third one.

There are no special instructions for the left-hander except that you might want to vary the order of doing the straight stitches. The back of the work will just be straight lines leading from one straight stitch to another.

DIAGRAM 1   DIAGRAM 2   DIAGRAM 3

Fishbone Stitches are generally used for filling a small area such as a leaf, but are also effective as a border if the stitches are kept an equal length. In working the Fishbone Stitch, if you find you are losing the angle of your slant as you work downward, try leaving a little more space between the stitches in the middle of the work. In the case of the Raised Fishbone, spaces are left between the lower insertions, which will be covered in any case. This will help to keep the thread slanting sharply downward, which is a large part of the effect of this stitch.

The first three diagrams show the work as it would be for a border between parallel lines, with spacing left between the stitches. This is a good method for practicing, but in actually working this stitch, there is no background showing through.

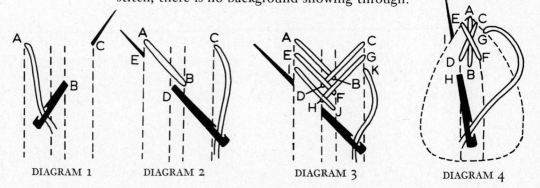

DIAGRAM 1   DIAGRAM 2   DIAGRAM 3   DIAGRAM 4

FIGURE 1

BACK VIEW

DIAGRAM 1 shows the thread being brought out on the top of the left-hand line at A, so the first stitch lies diagonally down at B and emerges at C on the top of the right-hand line. The second stitch is formed by inserting the needle, after bringing it across from the right hand toward the left, at D to the left of the center and bringing it out at E on the left-hand outline. The stitches are worked alternately in this manner, as shown in DIAGRAM 3, always crossing over just a bit off the center.

DIAGRAM 4 again has the stitches spaced so you can see the actual working of the needle and thread, as if you were making a leaf-shaped stitch. It can be seen that, in forming a leaf design and having the entire area closed with point included, your first stitch will be an upright stitch from A to B. Then the alternating Cross Stitch starts. Again these are worked with C and E close to A, without actually overlapping. FIGURE 1 shows some completed leaf shapes filled with the Fishbone as it would appear if you put your stitches as close together as they should be.

The left-hander needs no special directions, for the stitches alternate from side to side.

182 · FISHBONE STITCH—OPEN

This is one of the few stitches where the open version, usually just a matter of spacing, is worked in a completely different method from that of the closed stitch. Look over the diagrams carefully before starting work. You might want to try this stitch in the border form before starting to work the leaf shape, as it is generally used.

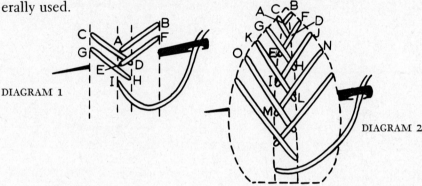

DIAGRAM 1

DIAGRAM 2

The needle is originally brought out in the middle of the shape or border as in A (DIAGRAM 1) and carried slanting up to the right and inserted at B. The needle and thread then go across the back of the entire design. The thread slants slightly downward as can be seen clearly in the illustration which shows the appearance of the work on the back. This is to stagger the stitches so that you can get the proper spacing. The needle emerges on the left-hand side, on a level with the base of the stitch on the right-hand side before the one just worked. DIAGRAM 2 shows the working of a leaf shape. You can follow the action of the needle by following the letters. If you want a closed peak on the design, you would have an extra stitch, illustrated in FIGURE 1, which shows the complete stitch having been worked.

FIGURE 1

BACK VIEW

183 · FISHBONE STITCH—RAISED
(OVERLAPPING HERRINGBONE STITCH)

The Raised Fishbone Stitch is done with another change in the action of the needle and thread from the two previous stitches. This stitch is commonly used in small leaf-shaped areas and in petals, but can also be used for a heavy border. You will do well to practice this as a border before you attempt to fill in a curved shape. DIAGRAM 1 shows the needle emerging at A and carried over diagonally to B, then brought directly across the back of the work, emerging back on the left-hand line at C. It is carried down so that it will be inserted opposite A at D, and emerges again in the same hole as A. The next diagonal stitch is inserted just below and very close to B at F, and carried back across the area, emerging at G just under C.

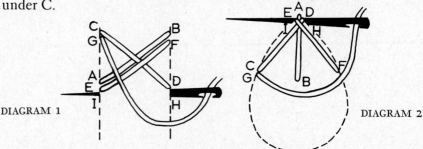

DIAGRAM 1   DIAGRAM 2

DIAGRAM 1 shows the needle being inserted at H which is just under D and brought out on the opposite line at I just under A. The two actions, first up and then down, are the motions used in the stitch and are worked so closely together that none of the background shows. DIAGRAM 2 shows a leaf shape having been started. You will note that, to get the closed effect, a straight stitch is taken first before the alternate crossing motions are started on the work.

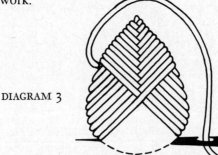

DIAGRAM 3

The back of this work is a series of straight stitches.

The left-hander might want to start with the needle coming out on the right-hand side of the design and insert it from left to right, so that it won't be quite so awkward in the working.

The working of this stitch is very similar to that of the ordinary Fishbone Stitch. There is merely a change in the direction of the needle when inserting and bringing it out. DIAGRAM 1 shows the needle being inserted just to one side of the center of the shape and emerging on the outline, with the stitches alternating from side to side. You will have the same center crossing as in the Fishbone Stitch.

This is a nice filling for small shapes or borders, and can have quite a heavy appearance when worked with heavy thread. An interesting variation on this stitch can be worked, sometimes called the Double Flat Stitch, for covering wider border areas. The surface stitches are absolutely flat. DIAGRAM 2 shows some of these stitches worked and what the action of the needle is from side to side.

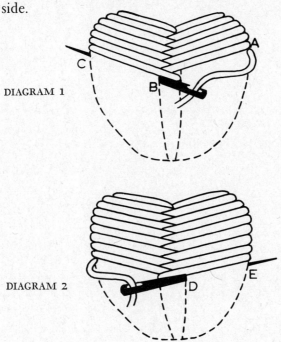

DIAGRAM 1

DIAGRAM 2

Directions for the left-hander are exactly the same, as they are for all alternating stitches. The back of the work appears the same as the regular Fishbone, except that the direction of the stitches corresponds to those at the top of the work.

185 · FLY STITCH
(OPEN LOOP STITCH, TIED STITCH, Y STITCH)

The Fly Stitch is really an Open Detached Chain. You can imagine that you are just making a V shape that is going to be tied down at the point of the V. The needle is brought out to the front of the fabric at A, and inserted over to the right on exactly the same level at B, and slanted down at a 45-degree angle, so that your working thread forms a V, and is brought on out at C. You can see that the V has already been formed, and in most cases a very tiny little tie-down stitch is made by inserting the needle at D just next to the loop that has been formed.

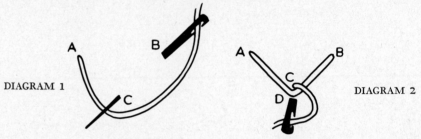

DIAGRAM 1   DIAGRAM 2

Any number of variations and effects can be produced by varying the length of the tie-down stitch to give a definite Y to this stitch. The placement on the background material also varies the appearance, as does changing the size of the stitch.

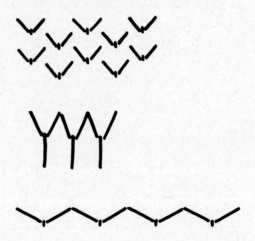

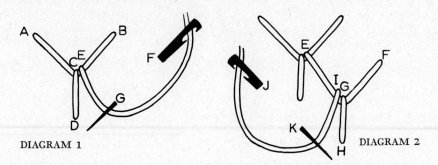

DIAGRAM 1   DIAGRAM 2

The Broad Double Fly is exactly that. It consists of a double row of Fly Stitches. Each one is linked into the last stitch made. In some respects the working of this stitch resembles that of the Feather Stitch, in that you are alternating directions, and the thread emerges from the preceding stitch. DIAGRAM 1 shows the Fly Stitch with a long tail completed and the thread again brought up inside the loop at E. The needle is then carried to the right again and inserted in the fabric on a level with E, at F, slanting down toward the center and emerging at G. When this stitch has been completed, the needle is again brought out inside the loop just formed, which is at I. Now the work is carried to the left and the loop formed. The loop must be held so that the needle goes over it, as shown in DIAGRAM 2, with the needle entering the fabric at J and emerging at K. These two steps are alternated, first on the left and then on the right, on down to complete the row.

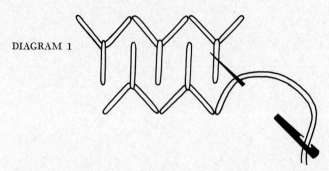

DIAGRAM 1

This interesting variation makes a rich-looking border, particularly when it is done with heavy thread. The first step is taken by working rows of joining Fly Stitches in both directions, as illustrated in DIAGRAM 1, so that the long tails head in toward each other and form a row of bars for the second step to be worked over. DIAGRAM 2 shows the process for working the second step. The thread is brought out above the top bar. You slide the needle under the bar from the bottom up, as shown in the diagram, and you will have a loop over that bar. Now the needle is inserted from the top down, with the thread held by the left thumb forming a loop underneath, so that a Chain Stitch can be worked by pulling the needle on through over the working thread. None of this step goes through the fabric except where the thread originally comes out and where the final tie-down stitch is taken to anchor the Chain Stitches. Do try this with various weights of thread and spacing.

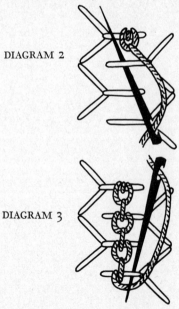

DIAGRAM 2

DIAGRAM 3

This method of working the Fly Stitch is interchangeable with other solid fillings on leaf shapes and is also useful as a border. It would be easier to work the shape of the leaf if a line were drawn down the center so that you would have something to follow for the tie-down stitches, illustrated in DIAGRAM 1. The work is begun, for completely solid filling, by taking a straight stitch as shown in DIAGRAM 1. The thread emerges at the tip of the leaf shape and is carried straight down and inserted at B. The needle emerges at C just to the left of A, as close as possible without overlapping on the left-hand side of the leaf shape. The needle is then carried over to the other side by a straight stitch, inserted at D and brought out at B in exactly the same hole, with the thread being held by the left thumb to form a loop over which the needle passes. The stitches are tied down in the usual manner with the Fly Stitch, and as the needle goes in at E, it slants down and emerges on the left-hand side again, as close to the previous stitch as possible—in this case F (DIAGRAM 3).

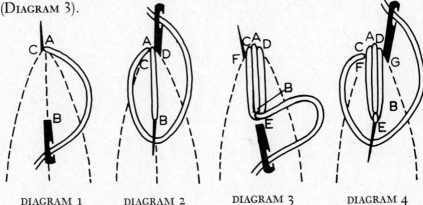

DIAGRAM 1   DIAGRAM 2   DIAGRAM 3   DIAGRAM 4

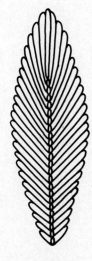

Another Fly Stitch is formed directly under the one just worked, the needle going in on the right-hand side at G and emerging in the hole at E—the end of the previous tie-down stitch just worked. Continue down the entire shape of the leaf, forming Fly Stitches just underneath each other, as closely as possible so that no background fabric shows, keeping your slant at a sharp angle all the way down.

The left-hander will be more comfortable working the loop by bringing the thread out on the right-hand side and inserting the needle on the left to form the loop for the Fly Stitch.

189 · FLY STITCH—DOUBLE

As with many stitches, the name is very descriptive. The Double Fly Stitch is a series of Fly Stitches with the second row worked right on top of the first row. To have the stitch show up to best advantage, your first row of Fly Stitches should be fairly wide. These rows are spaced equal distances apart, with a long tie-down stitch. However, in this case the legs on the loop are longer than the tie-down stitch. A space is left between these wide Fly Stitches, equal to the tie stitch just made, as shown in DIAGRAM 1. In the next row of narrower Fly Stitches, the thread is brought up inside the loop, about halfway up the length, and inserted in the same spot on the right-hand side with the tie-down stitch coming out of the hole formed by the tie-down stitch on the first layer. DIAGRAM 1 shows this step in the working and also shows it done with a contrasting thread—contrasting either in color or in weight. FIGURE 1 shows a series of these stitches completed.

The left-hander works from right to left.

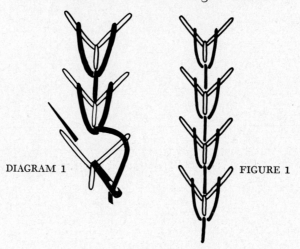

DIAGRAM 1   FIGURE 1

190 · FLY STITCH—FILLING
(CROSSED)

This Fly Stitch makes an attractive filling for a trellised effect and is very simple to work. A row of Fly Stitches is made in the ordinary way across the area to be filled. In the second row the Fly Stitches are inverted, as shown in DIAGRAM 1. However, I find it easier just to turn the fabric upside down and work in the normal manner.

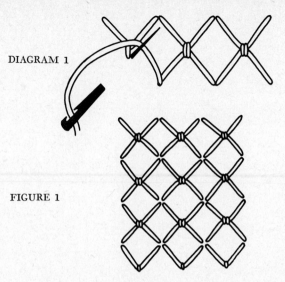

DIAGRAM 1

FIGURE 1

Note that the tie-down stitches are done exactly alongside the tie-down stitches in the previous row, so that you have a series of little double stitches linking the rows together. Rows are repeated in this order alternately, until your design is filled. FIGURE 1 shows a group of these worked.

The left-hander simply reverses the directions.

191 · FLY STITCH–INTERLACED

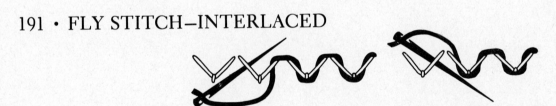

This embellishment is another of the variations on the Fly Stitch which add dimension. A row of Detached Fly Stitches is worked horizontally, almost touching, as shown in the diagram. Then with contrasting thread, either in color or weight, the work is begun from the right-hand end, and once the thread has emerged, it doesn't go through the fabric again until the end of the row. The needle shows the action, merely slipping the thread from the top down under the stitch and slanting up to the right, carrying it on over, not pulling too tightly, and then slipping it from the bottom up over the stitch. Continue down the row until you reach the end. The Interlaced Fly can be combined with other stitches, such as an outside row of Chain or hemstitch, to form an interesting border.

Although you don't change your thread, the overlap of this stitch gives a heavy effect. It can be used either for a line stitch or a solid filling. It is also one of the stitches that makes a good strong fabric filling. To have the work show up to the best advantage, it is best to take all the stitches fairly large.

A Fly Stitch is worked and the needle emerge at the completion of the tie stitch directly above, which would be halfway across the loop. As the next stitch is being worked, the needle is inserted directly below the end of the first stitch, on a level with the beginning of the tie-down stitches at C. If you follow the letters on the diagram, you can see the progression of this stitch. The second row is worked directly underneath. The second stitch on the second row starts at D, at the bottom of the tie-down stitch on the first stitch formed. The diagram shows the action of the needle in forming the stitch on the second row.

The left-hander reverses the procedures and works from right to left.

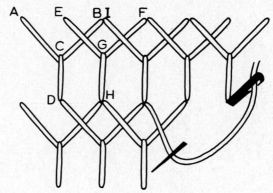

193 · FLY STITCH—REVERSED

This stitch is worked all in one color, although on completion it gives the appearance of having been done in two different sections. The action is to form a regular Fly Stitch and then a Reverse Fly Stitch right beneath it. The main thing to remember about this stitch is to make sure that all of the tie-down stitches meet to form the center line, to give the best effect. DIAGRAM 1 shows a Fly

Stitch completed and the tie-down stitch formed. The thread is brought out at E on the left, the needle carried over to the right and inserted at F, and brought out at G which would be the same as C, the beginning of the first tie-down stitch. You must hold your working thread up above to form the loop for the Reverse Fly Stitch. After the tie-down stitch has been made, the needle is carried down and to the left to begin another Fly Stitch in the regular manner. FIGURE 1 shows a series of these stitches worked in a line.

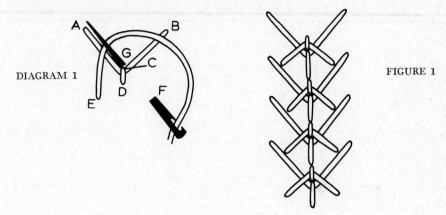

DIAGRAM 1

FIGURE 1

194 · FLY STITCH—WHIPPED

To form a foundation for the Whipped Fly Stitch, a series of Fly Stitches is worked in a line, as shown in the diagram, with the tie-down stitches touching and directly under each other. Then another thread is brought out at the end of the line, and the needle is slipped under the tie-down stitch of each successive Fly Stitch, without going through the fabric.

The left-hander works in the same manner.

195 · FOUR LEGGED KNOT

The Four Legged Knot is a small stitch most effective when worked with a tightly twisted thread so that the knot shows up well. The work is begun with a upright stitch. After the needle is inserted at B, as in DIAGRAM 1, it emerges at C, halfway between A and B, and to the right. In reality, to have an upright Cross Stitch, both lines are the same size; however before you complete the second half of the Cross Stitch, a little knot is formed in the center. This is illustrated in DIAGRAM 2. The needle is slipped under the upright stitch, but over the loop of the working thread held by the left thumb. After this is pulled on through, a little knot is formed in the center, and the needle is inserted at the other end to form the stitch shown in FIGURE 1. These stitches should be kept fairly small, and if you are working a complete area with them as a powdering, the needle, after being inserted at D, goes on to the next spot where a stitch is to be worked.

The left-hander simply reverses the procedure, bringing the needle out on the left first, instead of the right.

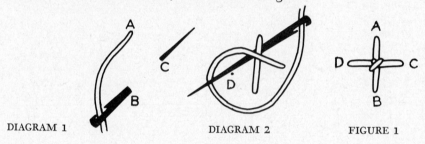

DIAGRAM 1   DIAGRAM 2   FIGURE 1

196 · FOUR SIDED STITCH

This stitch consists of a series of straight stitches forming a box. It is best worked over an evenweave fabric and is often used for Drawn Fabric Work. It makes a nice allover filling or a border stitch. Spaces can be left to give a geometric effect when used to fill solid areas or even to form a design.

There are two methods of working this stitch. The first is to make a horizontal line, starting at the right-hand end. DIAGRAM 1

212

shows the first stitch being formed and the needle emerging at C to be in position to form the next stitch. DIAGRAMS 2 and 3 show the action of the needle and thread in forming the first three sides of this square stitch. DIAGRAM 4 shows the needle and thread completing the square. When the thread is brought out at E, it will be in position to start forming the second square in the row.

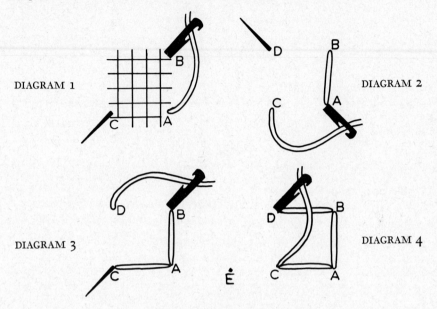

DIAGRAM 1

DIAGRAM 2

DIAGRAM 3

DIAGRAM 4

FIGURE 1 shows a group of stitches worked together.

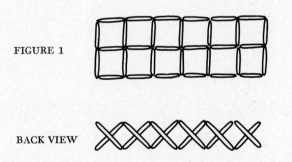

FIGURE 1

BACK VIEW

The left-hander follows the same directions by reversing the procedure and starting on the left-hand end.

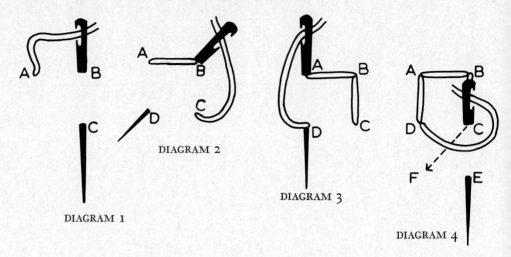

DIAGRAM 2

DIAGRAM 3

DIAGRAM 1

DIAGRAM 4

The diagrams show quite clearly the working of this stitch, which is very similar to the regular Four Sided Stitch. However, this one is worked vertically rather than horizontally. The work is begun by bringing the thread out at A. The needle is inserted at B and emerges directly below at C, as shown in DIAGRAM 1. DIAGRAM 2 shows the needle being carried back up to the hole and inserted at B, then emerging at D on the opposite side of the square. DIAGRAM 3 shows the needle and thread going back up to the top again at A and brought out at D. DIAGRAM 4 shows the action of the needle completing the square, with the stitch from D to C, and being brought out below in position to start the next square. FIGURE 1 shows a completed row of these squares.

Left-handers simply reverse the procedure, with A at the top on the right rather than on the left.

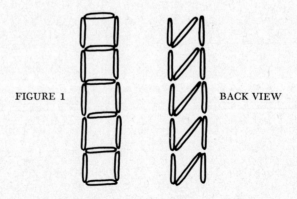

FIGURE 1   BACK VIEW

(FRENCH DOT, KNOTTED STITCH, TWISTED KNOT STITCH)

The knotted stitches form a distinct group of great interest, both historically and technically. The irregular texture that they give to the surface is often useful in making a contrast to smoother flat stitches. The French Knot should be done either in a hoop or a frame, as the material needs to be kept taut once you begin working with the thread. It is often used for an accent as a single stitch in combination with other stitches, sometimes as a scattered, powdered filling or for filling in solid areas.

It is a more versatile stitch than most people suspect. Think of a sheep with an entire coat made with French Knots. This stitch is surprisingly useful for shading also.

Keep in mind, while working this stitch, that your thread must be held taut throughout. After the thread has emerged from the fabric, it is pulled to the left and held between the left thumb and forefinger, with the needle slipped under it. The thread can be given a twist with the left hand or the needle can be revolved in a circular motion to the right so that you will end with one twist of thread on your needle (DIAGRAM 1). No more than one twist should ever be used, so as to keep the knot neat and firm. If a heavier knot is required, either use a heavier thread or add threads to the one already in use. Your knot will become loose and irregular when extra twists are used.

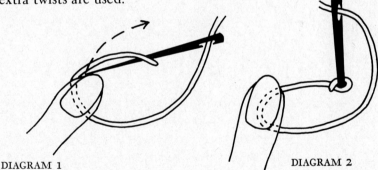

DIAGRAM 1   DIAGRAM 2

The needle is inserted next to the spot where the thread has emerged, and the working thread is still held with the left hand. The needle is eased on through to the back of the fabric, and the working thread is not released by the left hand until the thread is almost completely through. The needle is then brought to the surface in the next spot where a knot is required.

Left-hander would hold thread in right hand and needle in the left.

199 · FRENCH KNOT—BORDER STITCH

This stitch makes an unusual border and is useful both in straight lines and around curves. It can be used for floral designs to good advantage. A frame is needed to work it properly. For practicing this stitch, make a pair of horizontal, parallel guidelines.

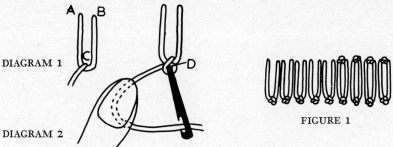

DIAGRAM 1

DIAGRAM 2

FIGURE 1

Start on the left-hand end by bringing the thread out on the top line at A. Holding the working thread with the left thumb, insert the needle at B, very close to A, and bring it out at C on the lower line, with the working thread under the needle. Pull the thread on through and make a French Knot as shown in DIAGRAM 2, inserting the needle at D just outside the loop formed. FIGURE 1 shows a series of these stitches worked. If you will look at the right-hand end, you will see that some French Knots have been added to the top of the border as well, which gives a nice finished filling. However this stitch can also be used without this added touch.

200 · FRENCH KNOT—BUTTONHOLE

This is a Buttonhole Stitch with a knot at the tip. Its obvious use is for an edging, but it can also be used for flowers or other growing things, particularly if a delicate effect is wanted. Because the Buttonhole Stitch goes in and out in the same action, a hoop cannot be used, so a little extra care will be needed in executing this stitch, to keep the knot firm. Work from left to right. DIAGRAM 1 shows the thread, having emerged at A, being wrapped around the left thumb, with the needle inserted from the bottom upward. The loop is slipped off the thumb, and the working thread still held with the left thumb while the needle is inserted at B above, and brought out at C below, without losing the loop. The thread is tightened up next to the needle insertion, and the needle is pulled on through. The process is begun again on along the line.

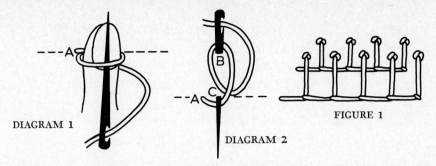

DIAGRAM 1

DIAGRAM 2

FIGURE 1

FIGURE 1 shows a row of these stitches worked over another row in the background, to suggest how this stitch might be used either in a border or for a floral effect. You might try working it with two different weights of thread also.

The left-hander reverses the directions.

201 · GUILLOCHE STITCH

Several stitches go into the making up of the border known by this name. The Guilloche Stitch was inspired by an architectural ornament consisting of waved, interlaced bands. The stitch is usually worked in two colors. The various steps are indicated on the diagrams by the letters. First a pair of Stem or Chain Stitch lines is worked on the outside borders, as shown at A. Next, groups of Satin Stitches in threes are worked at intervals as indicated at B. These can also be worked as Running Stitches in three separate rows if desired. Next comes the threading, which should be done with a blunt needle, as indicated at C and D. The needle is slipped under the Satin Stitches already worked, without going through the fabric, and worked alternately up and down. At the end of the area, turn around and fill the spaces left on the return journey. A French or Bullion Knot is often placed in the center of these circles to complete the band.

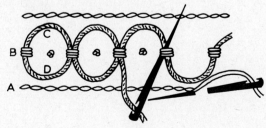

(CATCH STITCH, MUSSUL STITCH, RUSSIAN STITCH,
RUSSIAN CROSS STITCH)

This simple stitch has been used down through the ages, and appears in the fourteenth-century paintings of the Last Supper by Giotto at the Arena Chapel in Padua. Both the regular and Double Herringbone Stitch are represented in this fresco in great detail, illustrating the most effective manner in which this stitch can be worked.

The Herringbone is a most versatile stitch, both for decorative work and tailoring. Sometimes known by the name "Catch Stitch," it is useful for hemming clothing or attaching an interlining to a garment. It works particularly well on bias hems for easing in the fabric. An entire sampler could be worked up in variations on this stitch; its appearance changes greatly from thread to thread and with different spacings. Try varying the amount of fabric picked up by your needle on the back of the stitch, and see how the appearance changes.

To get the rhythm of this stitch, work between parallel guidelines, perhaps even squares between these lines for your first practice. Once the stitch is mastered, you can work irregular lines and many varied designs.

DIAGRAM 1

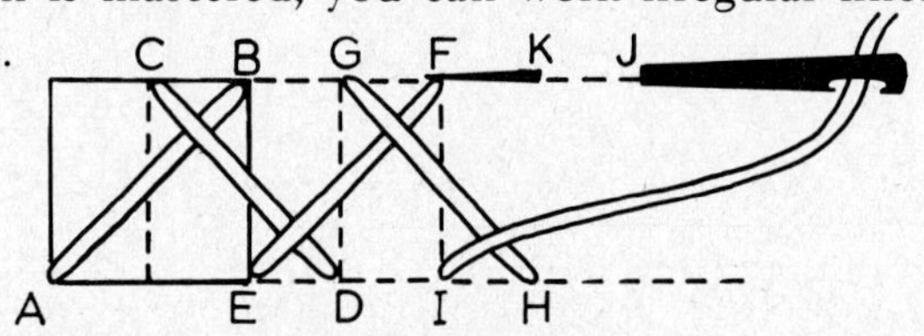

The needle is brought out on the left-hand end of the line. In the diagram it is shown on the lower line; however, it can be begun either top or bottom, for the action alternates. From A your needle is carried upward to the right at B, diagonally crossing a square so that it will be up as far as over. The needle is inserted at B and emerges back to the left at C, half the distance between A and B. Next the thread is carried down, the same length as the stitch just formed, and the needle inserted at D. It emerges again back to the left at E directly under B. These two alternate movements are continued on across the line and end with the effect given in FIGURE 1.

FIGURE 1

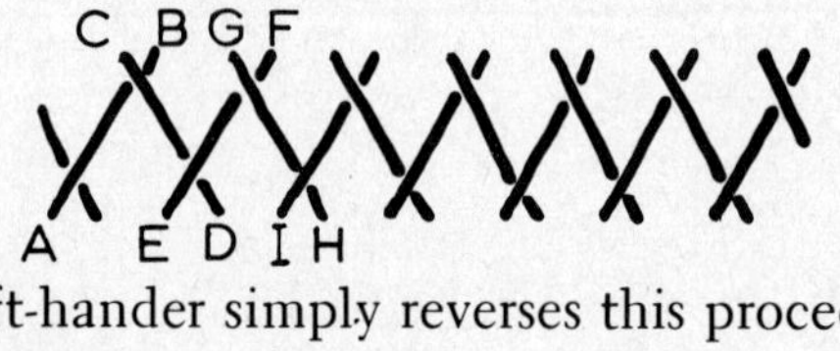

The left-hander simply reverses this procedure and starts at the right-hand end, with the needle working from left to right.

203 · HERRINGBONE STITCH—CLOSED
(DOUBLE BACK STITCH)

This is another stitch recorded for us in art, in this case by Fra Angelico, whose paintings illustrate this stitch beautifully. It is worked much the same as the regular Herringbone, the difference being that the needle comes out the same hole as that of the previous stitch of the same level. This makes a beautiful filling for a border, and the character of the stitch will vary with the angle that you cross your stitches.

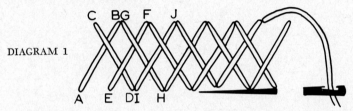

DIAGRAM 1

For practice again start between parallel lines as shown in DIAGRAM 1. As can be seen, the action is exactly the same as for the regular Herringbone, except for the needle coming back out the same hole at the end of the previous stitch. Once you have mastered this rhythm, the stitch will go very quickly, and you might want to attempt something with a design, as illustrated in FIGURE 1.

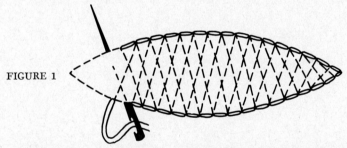

FIGURE 1

FIGURE 1 also shows, as indicated by the dotted line, what this stitch looks like on the reverse side. When used in this manner on fine transparent fabric such as organdy or lawn, the work is done so that the threads show through from the back of the work. It is called Shadow Work, and gives a lovely, delicate effect, excellent with curtains, sheer blouses, and children's party dresses. In the days of handmade lingerie, this stitch was very popular.

This is a very useful stitch for covering large areas quickly, once the action has become comfortable. As with the other Herringbone Stitches, it would be advisable to practice between parallel guidelines at first, and again to think in terms of squares—this time perhaps a square divided into three sections by the stitches, to get the interlacing effect of the Crisscross.

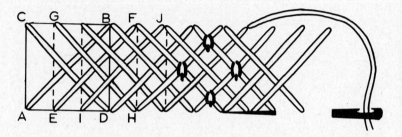

The diagram shows the needle having been brought out at A and carried up to the top line at B, emerging at C, and back down to D, which forms the basic square. From D it is brought back two thirds of the distance between D and A to E, and carried up to the right beyond B to what would be one third of the distance between the squares. The dotted lines on the diagram indicate the division of the squares that outline A, B, C, and D.

When done on a frame, this stitch can cover large areas. You can divide your squares into fourths if you choose. You may also want, when covering large areas, to tie down the threads with a Chain Stitch or French Knot, as is illustrated toward the right-hand end of the diagram.

205 · HERRINGBONE STITCH—DOUBLE

For this stitch, two rows of Herringbone are worked separately in contrasting shades, to show it up to the best effect. There are two methods of working the stitch, and both are illustrated. DIAGRAM 1 is a little more elaborate, and is the foundation used for the Interlacing Stitch and Twisted Lattice Band. The second is really quite simple and is merely used as a decorative border. In the first method, it is most important to get the interlacing correct with the sequence of under-and-over in the proper effect.

First study the diagram, which will reveal that the light-colored thread is on the basic row. After each stitch is taken on the *top* line, the needle is slipped *under* the last stitch, instead of taken over in the usual manner. The bottom action on this row of stitches is done as usual. This row is worked with fairly wide spacing so that you will be leaving room in between your stitches for the color that follows.

DIAGRAM 1

On the second step of this stitch, the needle, after having completed the stitch on the bottom, is slipped underneath the light stitch on its way to the top to make the next stitch. This is shown by the stitch lying loose at the end of the diagram with the dark thread. Continue, when making the top stitch, to slip the needle under the stitch just made, illustrated in the same area of diagram.

DIAGRAM 2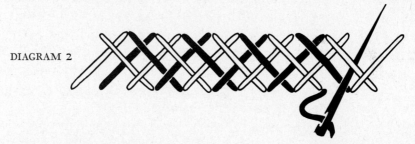

For the second method, notice that there will be two rows worked exactly as for the regular Herringbone Stitch, but they interlace where they cross each other. This is shown by the action of the needle at the end of DIAGRAM 2. The first layer in the light color is worked in the regular manner, leaving the space between the stitches for the working of the second color. When the second color is worked, the needle is slipped under the stitches on the first layer, after the stitch on the lower level has been worked as shown at the end of the diagram.

The left-hander reverses these directions.

206 · HERRINGBONE STITCH—LACED
(GERMAN INTERLACING STITCH)

This is a lovely decorative stitch, and can be quite important looking if the interlacing is done with metallic thread, which is perfectly feasible, because once the work is begun on the second step, the thread does not enter the fabric again. The foundation for this stitch should be checked in DIAGRAM 1, for it is worked somewhat differently from the regular Herringbone in order that the interlacing will work out properly. Note the arrows in DIAGRAM 1. They show that, instead of laying the thread over the stitches worked, your needle is slipped under to form the proper interlacing.

DIAGRAM 1

This stitch should be kept quite regular and really is only effective as a border stitch. The working of this stitch is the result of turning the Herringbone Stitch upside down, and it could be done that way if you prefer, which means starting from the right-hand end.

Now the second step in this stitch is begun, and because you are going under the stitch and not through the fabric, a blunt needle is recommended. The thread is anchored at the left-hand end and carried up to the first crossover, and the needle is slipped *under, over, under,* and *over* the stitches laid in the first layer; then it goes *under* the thread just brought up from the lower level and *over* the threads which were previously passed under.

DIAGRAM 2

Continue around the intersection until your working thread is ready to pass over itself. Now the working thread is carried down to the next intersection, which would be on the lower level, and slipped *under* the first thread, *over, under,* and *over* the threads on the first layer. Now go *under* the working thread just brought down, *over* and *under* the thread of the first layer, and pass up to the top again to start your next weaving action. The working thread makes two complete circles around each upper cross, and one and a half around each lower cross, always interlacing *under* and *over* the foundation stitches and *under* and *over* itself. To obtain the best effect, the foundation stitches should be kept not less than three-quarters inch long.

The left-hander reverses this procedure. The back of the work looks the same as the regular Herringbone, except for the beginning and ending of the weaving threads.

207 · HERRINGBONE STITCH—LADDER FILLING
(INTERLACED BAND STITCH)

The foundation for this stitch consists of two rows of Back or Double Running Stitches. However, they must be placed so that the center of the stitch in one row is above the end of the stitch in the other row—that is, they are placed alternately, brick fashion. The needle that interlaces the thread should be a blunt one, for once the foundation is laid, you are not going through the fabric. A good heavy thread works best in this, and the density will depend on the size of the foundation stitches.

The needle emerges on the left-hand end, inside the bottom line. The thread is carried over the foundation stitch and slipped under. Now, carry it up to the top layer and slip the needle under the foundation stitch from the top down, but hold the threads to the right, so that your working thread will pass over itself and be in position to go down to the lower level again, as illustrated at the end of the diagram.

This can be worked up to an interesting effect if you are making something like a scarf, where you want to have the same effect on both sides. For, if the foundation is laid in a Double Running Stitch, this interlacing effect can be done on both sides.

The left-hander reverses the procedure.

208 · HERRINGBONE STITCH—PLAITED
(RAISED)

In this stitch, the action of the needle and thread will be the same as in the basic Herringbone Stitches, and again you must think in terms of squares between parallel guidelines to practice the work. When working this stitch on a leaf shape, you will note that the ends are automatically filled in, so that no special care needs to be taken with this.

This stitch shows off to best advantage if kept sharply slanting, so it might be well to remember, when the needle goes into the fabric, that the stitches should be kept slightly apart and almost touching up tight, as the needle comes back up on the edge. Practice working this between straight parallels, but remember that it makes an attractive raised filling for small leaves.

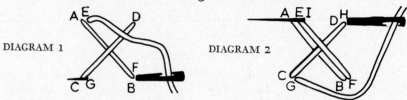

DIAGRAM 1   DIAGRAM 2

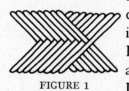

FIGURE 1

DIAGRAM 1 shows the action of the needle. Having come out at A, it is carried diagonally across and inserted at B, emerging again at C. The second part of the cross is formed by the thread being carried across from C and inserted at D. When it emerges at E, it is as close as possible to A without actually going in the same hole. It is carried down and inserted behind and to the right of B at F, and brought out behind C, as close as possible, at G, as shown in DIAGRAM 1. DIAGRAM 2 shows the second half of this step being taken, with the needle inserted on the upper line at H, and brought out again at I. Continue alternating these top and bottom actions on down your row, and after a short period of time you will see that you are covering the back half of your original stitches. This helps to give a padded effect. Your needle goes just outside your under layer of stitches. An area of this work is shown in FIGURE 1.

FIGURE 2

FIGURE 2 shows a leaf shape worked, and the stitch at the top of the motif is a straight stitch. Note the stitch pointing out at the tip of FIGURE 2; that will be your first stitch. Your lines will be slanting, so that you alternate from side to side, and the back of your work is a series of overlapping stitches on the outline of the shape.

The left-hander works this stitch exactly the same as the regular Herringbone, starting from the right-hand end but alternating the stitches in the same manner.

This little area filling I found in an old Victorian publication and have not seen it elsewhere. This makes an interesting squared-off filling to be used in isolated spots. It works up best with a fairly heavy thread. The diagrams show the action of the needle and thread at each corner as the work progresses.

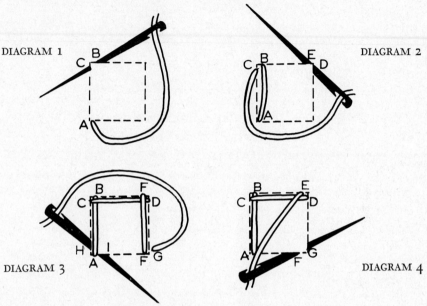

DIAGRAM 1

DIAGRAM 2

DIAGRAM 3

DIAGRAM 4

The thread is brought out on the lower left-hand edge at A and inserted, picking up a bit of fabric at the corner above, from B to C as in DIAGRAM 1. DIAGRAM 2 shows the needle being carried over to the next corner on the right and the needle inserted upward from D to E, again just picking up a small bit of fabric. On the two lower corners the needle goes first from F to G on the right hand as in DIAGRAM 3, then is carried over to the left-hand corner again, stuck in at H, and brought out at I. These four steps are repeated around the outline of the square, placing each succeeding layer just inside the previous one. This is continued on around until the entire square is filled, with the final appearance shown in FIGURE 1.

The left-hander reverses the directions.

FIGURE 1

This is an effective stitch worked over a base of ordinary Herring-bone Stitches. The threading can be done comfortably from either direction, as shown in the diagrams.

DIAGRAM 1

After the foundation of regular Herringbone has been worked, a contrasting thread is started at one end and a blunt needle used, for once the thread emerges, the needle does not go back through the fabric. The threading process is shown in DIAGRAM 1, with the needle simply slipping up and down under the slanting threads made in the Herringbone Stitch. To give the best results these should not be pulled up too tight.

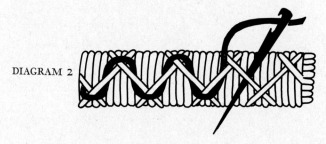

DIAGRAM 2

DIAGRAM 2 shows the stitch when a raised effect is desired. First lay the padding threads, long stitches worked horizontally, and then another layer of Satin Stitches is worked vertically over this. On top of all this, a line of Herringbone Stitching is placed, worked back and forth over the padding stitches. The final layer is done in the same manner as the Threaded Herringbone, simply lacing the contrasting threads in and out under the slanting threads of the Herringbone as illustrated in DIAGRAM 2.

The left-hander needs no special directions.

This embellishment of the Herringbone Stitch can be done in two different ways giving two quite different effects. The method shown in DIAGRAM 1 gives almost a smocking effect. You have a simple little tie-down stitch at each intersection of the threads crossing in the basic Herringbone. These can be straight vertical stitches or Chain Stitches or even French Knots if you want something more ornate. The needle and thread simply go from one intersection to the next, as illustrated in the right-hand end of the diagram.

DIAGRAM 1

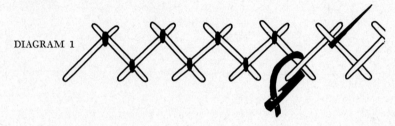

You might want to try this with the Closed or Crossed Herringbone foundation also for a richer effect. For those who are familiar with the plain Herringbone and Coral Stitch, this variety needs little explanation. The work consists of a Zigzag Coral Knot, worked upon a Herringbone line. The foundation of the Herringbone Stitch must first be worked. Next with a contrasting thread, begin the work at the right-hand end of the line, and do a Zigzag Coral Stitch directly on top of the Herringbone Crosses, as shown in DIAGRAM 2.

The left-hander works these by reversing directions for each step.

DIAGRAM 2

212 · HERRINGBONE STITCH—TRIPLE

The name of this stitch indicates exactly what it is. However, as opposed to the Double Herringbone, these layers are worked directly over each other, rather than side by side. The diagram shows one layer of regular Herringbone Stitches worked, and at the end of the diagram you will see exposed the second layer in the dark thread worked directly over the first layer, but just a trifle smaller, and the stitches inside those on the original layer. The third layer is shown in the working. At the left-hand end you can see the total effect of this stitch.

It is very interesting when done with different weights of thread as well as different colors, and you might try having your last layer come out not directly under the previous ones but spread out a little to give a somewhat more decorative effect.

Left-handers work the Herringbone in the usual manner.

213 · HIGH PYRAMID CHAIN

Several rows of Chain Stitch of a good size are worked to lay the foundation of this stitch. Succeeding layers are worked in the spaces left between the rows, as illustrated in the diagram. It would be too difficult to diagram a complete area built up in this manner, but it makes a very interesting filling, particularly when the threads are varied to some extent.

The left-hander works the chain in the usual manner, so that the rows go in the opposite direction.

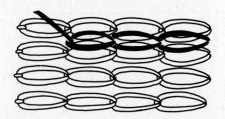

(DOUBLE RUNNING STITCH, LINE SQUARE, STROKE STITCH,
TWO SIDED LINE STITCH, TWO SIDED STROKE STITCH)

The Holbein Stitch is really just a double Running Stitch worked in designs. It is referred to by this name because it appears in some of Holbein's paintings in great detail. The famous "Madonna of Mercy" and the "Mayor Meyer family" illustrate this strikingly. Your observation of them might give you some ideas for use of this stitch in present-day embroidery.

It is also used as a line stitch in conjunction with other types of stitchery around the outside edge of Cross Stitches and other even-weave work. The diagrams illustrate the way that it is worked, both by means of a single Satin Stitch.

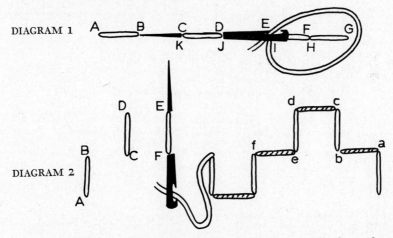

Work a Running Stitch in one direction, and when the end of the line or area is reached, turn around and come back, covering the spaces that have been left on the first journey (DIAGRAM 1). If you are making little stitches off to the side in a pattern, it is best to do this as you are working on your first row. This could be done by means of a single Satin Stitch.

The Holbein Stitch is useful too on sheer fabrics and for items such as room dividers, as it is the same on both sides, particularly if the extra stitches are made with the Satin Stitch.

There are no special directions for left-handers for this stitch is worked in both directions.

215 · HOLLIE STITCH

(HOLY POINT, HOLY STITCH)

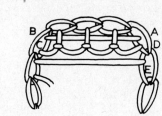 This attractive textured stitch was once famous as Hollie or Holy Point Lace. However it works up very nicely into a surface stitch for regular embroidery. It was widely used in the seventeenth century and can be seen on some of the English samplers of that period, and on any pieces of work that might have survived. When worked for lace, pattern effects were achieved by leaving spaces void in working it up. However this is more suitable in lace work than in embroidery.

The shape is outlined by either a small Chain Stitch or Back Stitch. The former is more effective, since it gives a more finished edge to the shape. However, if it is going to be outlined in some other manner, it doesn't matter. DIAGRAM 1 shows the outline worked and the original thread laid across the work from A to B. The needle is then inserted in the fabric and brought out below at C on the same side of the design.

DIAGRAM 1

DIAGRAM 2

The next stitches do not go through the fabric. The working thread is held with the left thumb as in a Buttonhole Stitch. The needle is inserted *under* the loop left above and *under* the thread just laid. Before it is pulled through, the working thread is twisted around the left thumb, from right to left, and the needle is inserted on top of the thumb, *under* that thread as shown in DIAGRAM 2. After having pulled the needle and thread on through, give a little tug to tighten up the knot, and you are ready to proceed to the next stitch.

These rows are alternated. When you reach the end of the knotted stitches, the needle is again inserted into the fabric, at D, and brought out below at E, ready to carry the thread back to the left again. On the lower edge of this stitch, particularly if you have a wide area to cover, the final stitches of the loop will also be carried down through the chain loop on the lower edge, to pull the work down neatly and give it a tidy, finished appearance.

Left-handers simply reverse the procedure; the Chain Stitches on the outline are made as usual, and the original thread is laid from left to right. The knotted-stitch work begins from the right-hand side, and other directions are reversed. The back side shows only the stitches made in forming the outline of the chain and the little stitches around the outline where the thread is carried from one working row to the next.

216 · HONEYCOMB FILLING STITCH

This attractive little stitch is a type of laid work and most effective when done with three different colors or weights of thread. It is absolutely essential to work this on an embroidery frame. As with most of the laid stitches, it will have to be outlined in some manner so you will end up with a smooth edge.

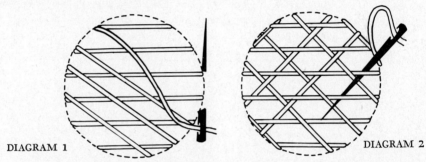

DIAGRAM 1   DIAGRAM 2

The work is begun by laying horizontal stitches right across the space to be filled, keeping the spaces even. The next layer is another series of laid stitches, but these are laid diagonally across from the upper left to the lower right-hand side of your motif (DIA-GRAM 1). These are *not* woven; the horizontal stitches are merely laid over them. The third layer of stitches involves the interlacing, which is to hold the stitch together, and is started from the upper right, down toward the lower left. The needle and working thread are passed over and under the stitches laid in the previous two layers. The needle shows the working of this in DIAGRAM 2, with the needle going under the horizontal thread and over the diagonal thread, for you are working diagonally. This forms an interlocking design over all the area.

The left-hander does this in the same manner. The horizontal area is the same, but you might want to start your first layer of diagonal stitches from the left side which will be a little easier to execute. The back merely shows the stitches on the edge of the outline, where the thread passes from row to row.

231

This Honeycomb Filling is not often used these days, but it does give a very raised trellis, almost a knotty effect. There are several layers of whipping; therefore, it should be worked with a very fine thread. The work is begun by making a laid trellis of the required size, as shown in DIAGRAM 1. The next step is an overcasting of this foundation trellis, covering first all the vertical and then all the horizontal stitches. This is shown in progress in DIAGRAM 1.

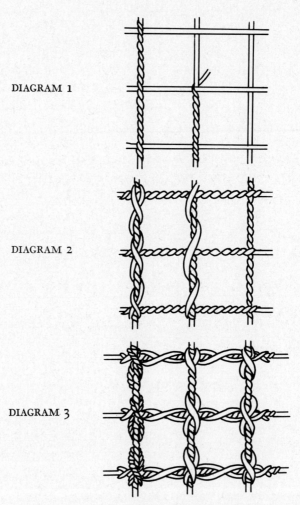

DIAGRAM 1

DIAGRAM 2

DIAGRAM 3

Next a thread is laced around the threads that have just been worked in a whipping action, as shown in the second vertical line in DIAGRAM 2. The work is then reversed and comes down with the same action as shown in the first vertical line in DIAGRAM 2. When this step has been completed both vertically and horizontally, your final step is begun as shown in DIAGRAM 3. The left-hand spiral has been overcast and drawn tight, with a twisted thread over all the spirals that were previously worked. This makes an excellent filling for certain types of work.

The left-hander does the whipping stitches in the direction that is most comfortable.

218 · INSERTION STITCH—BAR
(BULLION BAR STITCH)

An Insertion Stitch is a stitch worked to join two pieces of fabric together, which have the edges turned under to form a hem. There are many decorative stitches for doing this, and they can be useful in embroidery as well as on clothing. As a rule and to help regulate the size of your stitches, it is a good idea to baste the two pieces of fabric onto a piece of heavy paper, such as brown wrapping paper, which has been marked for the width of the insertion. Doing this before the work is begun will help to keep the stitches regular and will give you something to pull against. Most of these stitches should be worked with a good firm thread, partly for effect and partly for holding up under strain.

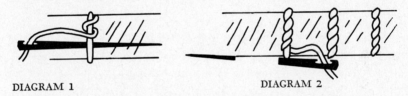

DIAGRAM 1   DIAGRAM 2

The Bar Insertion is begun by bringing out the thread on one edge, usually the lower or left edge, depending on which way your piece of fabric is facing, and carrying it up to the upper level. On the upper level the needle is inserted from just inside the edge of the fabric, straight through, and pulled on to the back of the fabric. With the help of your left thumb, form a little twist with your needle and the stitch just laid, between the pieces of fabric. The needle is then pulled on through, and one more little twist is made by passing the thread over the bar without going through the fabric (DIAGRAM 1). The needle is pulled around and inserted into the back of the fabric, the distance along the edge where the next bar will be required (DIAGRAM 2). Repeat this process down the complete area of the insertion.

219 • INSERTION STITCH—BUTTONHOLE

The Buttonhole Stitch is the basis for a number of Insertion Stitches. However this particular one is worked with the Buttonhole Stitch *only*. The two pieces of material should be mounted on heavy paper before work is begun. The diagram shows quite well the action of the needle and thread. You simply work a series—generally four—of Buttonhole Stitches on one edge of the fabric, carry the needle and thread over to the other edge and repeat. Keep the thread tight between the groups or the stitches will lose their shape and become sloppy.

Left-handers start at the opposite end and work the Buttonhole Stitch as usual.

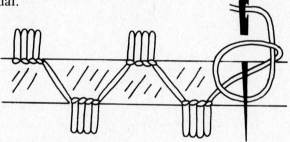

220 • INSERTION STITCH—CRETAN
(FAGGOTING)

This particular stitch would be started in the normal way with an Insertion Stitch. Make sure that your edges are secure for working. The thread is brought out from inside the fold at the left hand, or upper end, of the space to be filled. The action of the needle and thread is the same as the working of the Open Cretan Stitch. However, in this case you are alternating from one edge of the fabric to the other, as illustrated in the diagram.

The left-hander needs no special instructions, because of the alternate nature of the stitch.

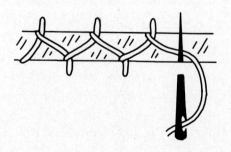

This is a complicated-looking stitch, but quite easy to work if you follow the diagrams carefully. It is by far the richest of all the Insertion Stitches. It is absolutely necessary in this to have your two pieces of fabric securely tacked down to a backing of some type before the work is begun. DIAGRAM 1 shows the original bar being laid to give a firm foundation for beginning this work. The beginning of the insertion work can also be seen in DIAGRAM 1, with the needle in position to start the first group of Buttonhole Stitches. The loop is held with the left thumb, as always in the Buttonhole Stitch, and four stitches are worked side by side. The needle is then carried on over to the left-hand edge, the thread inserted just inside of the edge toward the back, and brought up into the next group of stitches.

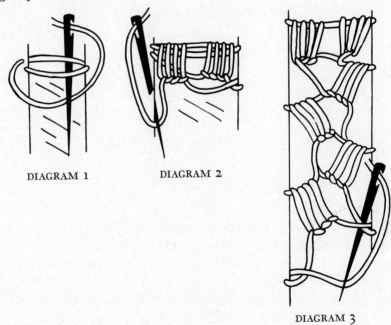

DIAGRAM 1   DIAGRAM 2

DIAGRAM 3

DIAGRAM 2 shows the foundation group of stitches worked and the needle being inserted and brought out preparatory to being carried over. The groups of four Buttonhole Stitches are worked alternately from side to side. DIAGRAM 3 shows a series of these stitches and the action of the needle and thread once your pattern has been established.

The left-hander uses the same method, simply working the Buttonhole Stitches in the manner most comfortable.

The actual working of this stitch is very similar to that of the Antwerp Edging (157) except that the stitches are made alternately on the upper and lower edges of the fabric you are joining together. The two pieces of fabric are tacked onto a backing before this work is begun. The thread is brought out on the left-hand end of the line and carried up to the other edge somewhat to the right, where a single Buttonhole Stitch is made. The second action of the needle and thread is shown in the diagram, with the needle passing under the two threads left by the Buttonhole loop just formed. The needle is carried to the lower edge, and the process is repeated in the opposite direction. These two actions are worked alternately down the edges of the fabric.

The left-hander starts from the other end, and just reverses the direction of the needle.

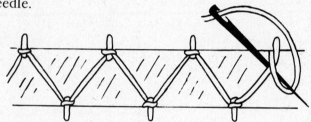

223 • INSERTION STITCH—LAID

This Insertion Stitch consists of a row of Braid Edging Stitch worked along both edges of the material to be joined, and afterward laced together. The needle on the lower line is in process of making one of the Braid Edging Stitches.

After the edgings have been worked on both pieces, the fabric should be tacked to a strong piece of paper or backing in preparation for the lacing. The diagram shows some of these stitches laced together. You will note that the fabric was placed so that the loops are in alternate positions opposite each other to insure proper lacing.

No special instructions are needed for the left-hander.

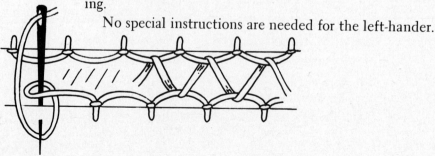

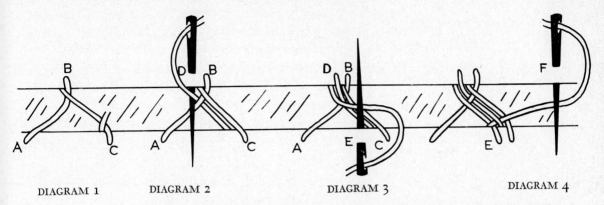

DIAGRAM 1   DIAGRAM 2   DIAGRAM 3   DIAGRAM 4

This is a rather complicated stitch and must be regularly spaced. The fabric is first anchored to a strong backing—and it would be a good idea to mark off the spaces on the backing. There should be no less than three-quarters inch between the two strips, and although the size of the stitches determines somewhat the weight of thread, it should be thick and firm. The diagrams, numbered 1 through 4, show quite clearly the action of the needle and thread. Each time the needle is inserted, it is from *inside* the edge of the fabric *out* to the edge. Note that you go alternately *over* and *under* the working thread as the needle is pulled through. After you reach the fifth step of the movement, as shown in DIAGRAM 5, the stitch repeats from the beginning. Keep in mind that regularity is necessary for this stitch.

The left-hander reverses the directions, starting at the right-hand end of the insertion.

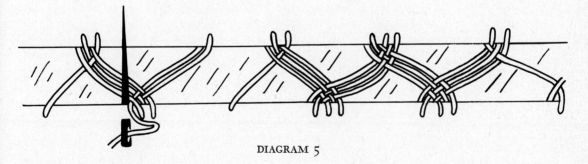

DIAGRAM 5

237

225 · INSERTION STITCH—TWISTED

As with other Insertion Stitches, the fabric should be attached to some sort of backing before work is begun. The diagram demonstrates the action of the working thread and needle. The needle is always brought from *beneath* the material to the surface, and a little twist is made in the working thread. This is easiest done by holding your working thread in your left thumb and forming the twist by slipping it under and around the working thread with the needle. The needle is pulled on through, and the work is begun on the edge of the opposite piece of fabric.

The left-hander reverses these instructions.

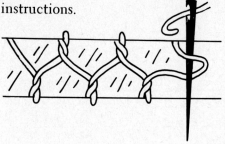

226 · INTERLACING STITCH

This is one of the most beautiful and effective of all embroidery stitches and really repays the trouble and time spent in mastering it. It is used as a border, in motifs, and in patterns. Some thought must be given to the matter of the interlacing of the foundation if the end results are to look their best. If you examine the foundation closely, you will see that it consists of a row of Double Herringbone Stitches, which means that the foundation threads are interlaced.

After the foundation has been established, you start with another thread and a blunt needle, for you will be going over and under threads, not through the fabric. A metallic thread shows up very effectively on this part of the stitch. The arrows on the diagram indicate the direction of the needle as it goes over and under the foundation. The right-hand end shows the first journey completed and the thread twisted *over* and *around* the end crossing of the foundation. The arrow shows the weaving process begun on the return journey. It can be seen on the diagram that the two steps will meet and interlock along the crossed center line, and the needle is shown in the second line of the journey.

This stitch can be used as an Insertion Stitch as well as for a border or pattern, and in that case remember to attach your fabric firmly to a backing before starting work. The interlacing should completely fill and cover the foundation when the work has been completed.

The left-hander simply lays the foundation as he would the Double Herringbone, and since the weaving is done in both directions, its course could be taken right from the diagram.

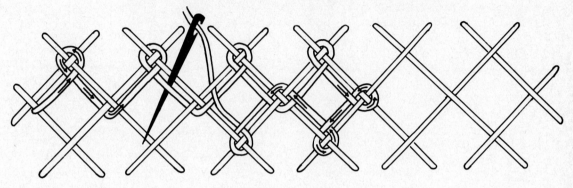

227 · JAPANESE STITCH

This is a stitch that is seldom seen today, but can be found in some old embroidery books. It consists simply of stitches worked in diagonal lines, as seen on some old Japanese screens. The diagram shows the action of the needle and thread, so there you need no detailed explanations.

The left-hander turns the diagram upside down. The back of the work is just a series of slanting lines in the same direction as the motif.

The action of this stitch is very similar to a binding stitch used on rugs and canvas work. However, it is a firm stitch for joining two fabrics. The two actions of the needle are shown in the diagrams.

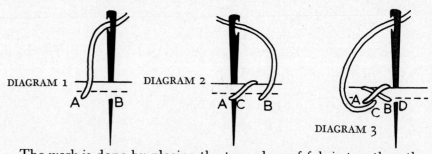

The work is done by placing the two edges of fabric together, the outside edge on the top. It is probably best if these edges are folded in, especially if the weave is somewhat loose, although it is not absolutely necessary. The dotted lines on the diagram indicate this. DIAGRAM 1 shows the thread brought out and the needle carried over to the far side and inserted from back to front, through both pieces of fabric. DIAGRAM 2 shows the needle performing the same action, but in this case it is carried back and put in right beside where the thread originally emerged, as close as possible, at C. Again the needle is brought from the back through both fabrics. DIAGRAM 3 shows the forward action, with the needle worked in the same motion but placed as close as possible to B, emerging at D.

FIGURE 1

FIGURE 2

These two actions are continued on down the seam to be closed. FIGURE 1 shows a series of work completed, and FIGURE 2 shows the two pieces of fabric when they are opened up and how the seam looks when flat.

The left-hander reverses this process and starts from the other end of the line.

229 · LACED EDGE STITCH

This simple and effective edging was devised by the Eskimos and the Aleuts for binding together the seams of their skins and parkas when making them waterproof. It works up very well on fabric, particularly a coarse material such as homespun or heavy linen. The working of the stitch is based on the Running Stitch and Lacing, as can be seen on the diagram.

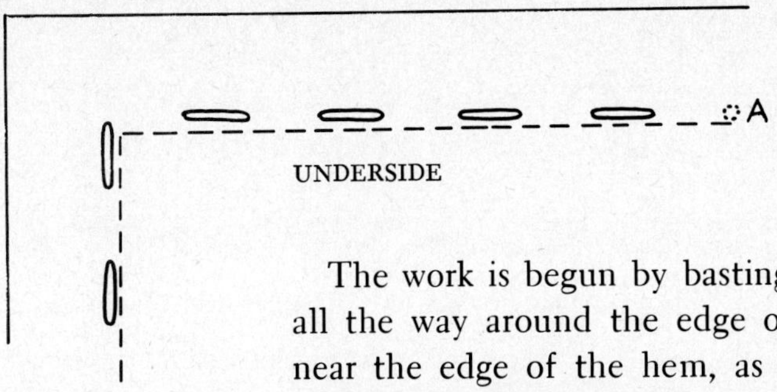

DIAGRAM 1

UNDERSIDE

The work is begun by basting the hem with the Running Stitch all the way around the edge of the article, keeping the stitching near the edge of the hem, as shown in DIAGRAM 1. Start on the wrong side with the knot uppermost. This is most important for the work to come out even; always begin a new length of thread from inside the hem. These stitches should be exactly the same size; the regularity of the stitch is part of the effect. Remember that, once your Running Stitch has been established, your thread does not go through the fabric except to start and finish off.

Now the lacing is started. Go *under* the first Running Stitch without picking up any fabric, as shown in DIAGRAM 2, at the right-hand end. Turn the edge over so that the top side edge is toward you, and again lace *under* the first stitch, this time from the edge in. The next step is indicated by the arrows. You lace to the second stitch *toward* the edge and lace *over* the edge, back again and *under* the first stitch from the edge *inward*. The arrows indicate the correct direction. It may sound a little confusing, but once you start, the lacing effect will fall in place for you.

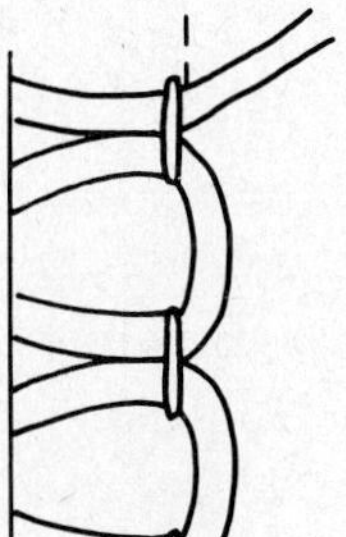

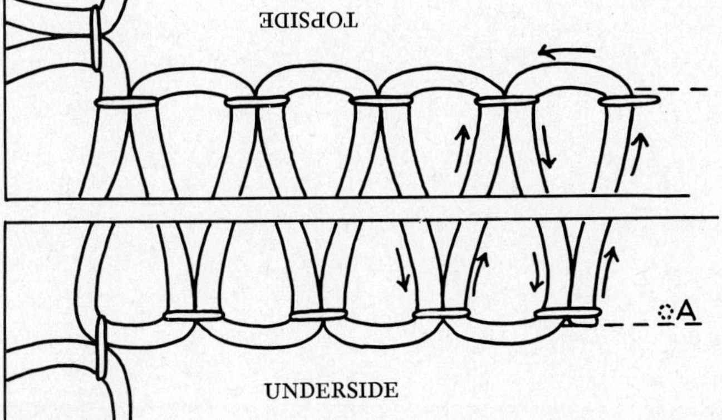

TOPSIDE

DIAGRAM 3

DIAGRAM 2

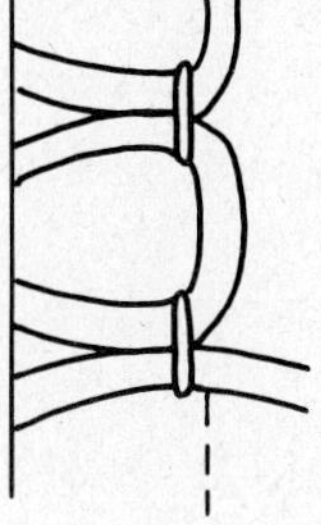

UNDERSIDE

Continue along the base of the hem for the second stitch *toward* the edge and then *over* the edge of the hem to the second stitch on the right side of the fabric. DIAGRAM 3 shows the top side with some of the work done.

The left-hander simply reverses the direction.

230 · LACED KNOT STITCH

This stitch can make an interesting individual knot with a heavy thread. However it is more effective when done in rows. It works up nicely as an outline and takes curves well, but it can also be used as a solid filling, in which case the knots are made in the spaces of the previous row.

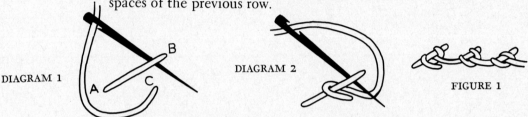

DIAGRAM 1

DIAGRAM 2

FIGURE 1

The thread is brought out at A and a straight stitch taken, slanting upward to the right. The needle is inserted at B and emerges at C down below and somewhat to the left, as shown in DIAGRAM 1. DIAGRAM 1 also shows the needle being passed under the straight slanting stitch just formed without going through the fabric. DIAGRAM 2 shows the next action of the needle and thread. Again the needle is slipped under the straight stitch, above the loop just formed, and the working thread held under so that the needle passes over it as it is pulled on through, forming a chain knot.

FIGURE 1 shows a series of these worked, but the appearance of this stitch can't be appreciated until it is tried. Try packing the knots close together for a closed, textured effect and also varying the length of the stitch as well as the space in between the knots.

The left-hander will probably work best by turning the diagram upside down.

231 · LACE FILLING STITCH

This Lace Stitch is a lovely filling that hasn't been used a great deal in recent years. Yet it works up very well with the new threads on the market. It is worked from left to right and back again, so that you do not have to carry thread across the back. The Lace Filling Stitch is a variety of the Buttonhole Stitch, and you can see by the dotted lines on the diagram that it will have to be outlined by some other stitch, perhaps the Stem or Romanian, to give it a finished look.

Start the work from the right-hand edge of the motif, at AB. A single stitch is laid, and the needle is inserted and brought out lower down on the left-hand side at C. The spacing of these stitches depends on your thread, but in general use a fairly fine thread. The action of the needle on the left-to-right journey is shown by DIAGRAM 2.

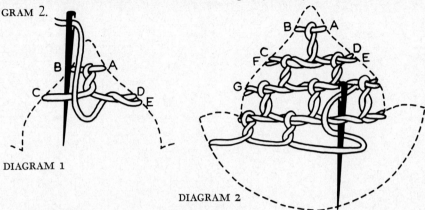

DIAGRAM 1

DIAGRAM 2

On the first row the needle is inserted under the single thread laid across. A reverse twist is formed with the thread, and the needle is pulled on through. The needle is then inserted, and the right-to-left journey is started. DIAGRAM 1 shows the needle being inserted *back* of the threads between the twists and *under* the loop formed on the previous row. The needle is simply slipped under this loop in each space, without going through the fabric, until the left side is reached again. The needle is then inserted right below the previous row—in this case at F under C—and brought out down below at G, which is the same distance as between D and E. These two rows are worked alternately back and forth down the entire area, and on the final line of the return journey, the thread is also passed through the fabric, a small bit being picked up each time, before the next twist is made over the thread. These stitches should be pulled up rather tight to bring out the full effect of this stitch, which anchors down the entire piece of work.

The left-hander starts from the opposite direction, but otherwise the directions are the same.

232 · LADDER STITCH

Most frequently used for the working of straight or border lines, this stitch can vary in width very nicely. It works very well in combination with the Van Dyke Stitch, and it could be called a

Double Van Dyke Stitch, since the working of the two edges is done in the same manner. Mariska Karasz uses these two stitches in combination with great imagination on some of her wall hangings. The diagrams do look a little complicated, but the stitch is not as involved as it seems, once the basic action has been tried. A frame will be helpful when covering large areas.

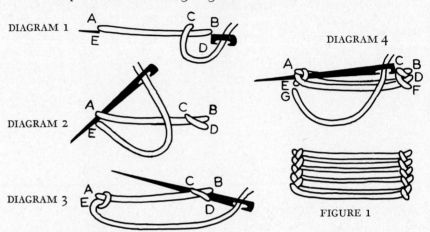

The work is begun by taking the working thread from where it emerges at A directly across the area, inserting it at B, and bringing it out at C. C is just to the left of the end and slightly above. DIA-GRAM 1 shows the needle being inserted at D, directly under B, and carried across the back of the area and brought out at E, just under A, on the left-hand side again. This action causes a loop to be formed over the original line CD. Next the needle is passed under the thread AB near A, from the top down without going through the fabric, and pulled on through. It is next carried over to the right-hand edge of the design, where it is slipped horizontally under the original Cross Stitch there, and pulled through. The needle is inserted below on the right-hand line at F, carried across and brought out on the left at G, which is again directly below the stitch above, E. Now the needle is slipped horizontally under the cross made just above, as shown in DIAGRAM 4, and pulled on through. These alternating motions are continued on down until the area has been finished.

FIGURE 1 shows a group of several of these worked. You can vary the appearance by the spacing. However, it is most effective when worked fairly close together, so that the braid on the outside edges is tight.

The left-hander reverses the directions by starting on the right-hand line and carrying the first stitch over to the left, therefore inserting the needle from the left to the right when slipping it under.

244

This simple stitch is used as foundation for innumerable other stitches, almost always in combination with some other stitch. Any piece of work that is couched has to be laid first. The title describes exactly what is done—filling solid areas or laying a single line on the surface of the fabric and tying it down in some manner. The varieties of laying the work are unending. I have included some as separate stitches, although the basic Laid Work technique, as shown is the diagrams, is much the same.

When doing an area in Laid Work, no matter what size it is (unless it is very tiny, in which case you would be using a Satin Stitch anyway), the work is begun in the center of the motif. The reason for this is to maintain the direction of your stitches, which must always be laid exactly parallel. If the area is any size at all, it would be advisable to mark the fabric in some manner to maintain the direction of your stitches. A hard lead pencil could be used—but lightly, to keep the carbon from getting onto the thread.

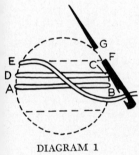

DIAGRAM 1

Diagram 1 shows the work begun on a circle, and the action of the needle and thread is clear. After the thread has been brought out, the needle is carried across the entire shape and inserted on the opposite outline and brought up right above. The space left, which should be the width of your thread, is determined by the weight you are using. The needle emerges on the same edge and is carried back in the other direction to the original edge, inserted at D and brought out above at E, leaving the same space.

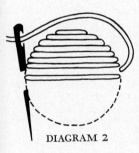

DIAGRAM 2

This work is usually done over a fairly large area, and it is absolutely essential that it be done on a frame of some type, so that the threads are held taut until they are tied down. As can be seen, this stitch is economical in the use of thread and is often substituted for the Satin Stitch. However, you do end up with uneven edges, so it will always have to be outlined in some manner—Stem Stitch or any of the line or border stitches.

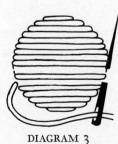

DIAGRAM 3

This back-and-forth action continues to the top of the design. Diagram 2 shows the needle coming down on the return journey. The needle in this case is brought up in the space left on the original journey, so that by the time you reach the middle of your design, the top should be completely filled. Continue on down to the second half of your shape, again leaving spaces between the long threads the width of your thread, and on the third step of this stitch, return and fill in the spaces. Diagram 3 shows the design almost completely covered.

The left-hander needs no special directions, for the work is done alternately from side to side, and the back of the work is simply a series of stitches around the outlines of the design.

234 · LAID WORK—COUCHED

Laid Work is generally used to cover large areas with a solid filling, often in place of the Satin Stitch. One of the reasons for using it, besides the decorative effect of the Couching over the Laid Work, is the fact that too long a stitch will catch on a fingernail or jewelry and pull out. Because there is only a single layer for the thread to go through, instead of the double layer of the Satin Stitch, Laid Work is ideal as a base for decorative Couching. This was done in the old days with gold thread. However, even when done in the same color and thread, the couched effect and pulling down of the threads of the Laid Work can be most effective. ("Couched" and "laid" are almost synonymous, in embroidery, since some sort of tie-down—the Couching part—is always needed for the Laid Work.)

DIAGRAMS 1 and 2 show two designs often used in Couching down Laid Work. Often an entire area is couched down, with a scattering of individual stitches such as Chain, French Knot, or Fly, applied all around a design, but make sure that each laid thread is couched down somewhere in the area. Seed or French Knots worked fairly close over Laid Work give a realistic appearance on a strawberry motif. The Split Stitch is often used for the veins forming a leaf or in an allover design. This can be done in the same color or with contrasting thread.

DIAGRAM 2 shows the Laid Work completed and single threads couched down at intervals to make the veins of a leaf, the outline being worked in Stem Stitch. There are many ways to get different effects with Couching on the surface of Laid Work, and I do hope you will experiment freely.

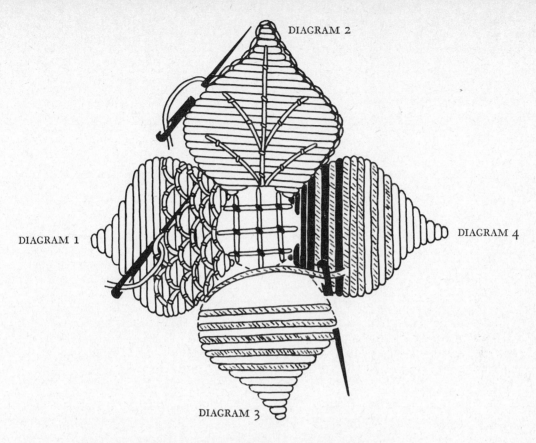

DIAGRAM 2

DIAGRAM 1

DIAGRAM 4

DIAGRAM 3

235 · LAID WORK—COUCHED, SHADED

DIAGRAMS 3 and 4 above show two petals in process of being shaded by Laid Work. The actual execution is done the same as the basic Laid Work, but as can be seen from the diagram, the colors are changed gradually. This is achieved in working the regular Laid Work by going up to the top of the design and coming back down only partway. This gives a solid filling at the top and leaves several spaced threads, the number depending on the size of the design and the number of colors to be used. The next shade is started up toward the top in the first open space. Work down, filling in the spaces left by the first color, and when you reach the open area, continue to work on down, leaving spaces for the gradual change of the following color. Next come back up and fill in the spaces required in the center for this shade. On the last color, by filling in the spaces left by the center color, go on down and complete the design, leaving space when you get to the open area, and then work back up to complete the solid coloring as shown in DIAGRAM 2.

A quick glance will show you that this is a wide-open embroidery field. Whole books have been written on this subject alone. A little imagination and experimentation can bring a whole new area of embroidery with infinite variety. I have tried to include a diagram of each of the basic methods of this type of embroidery work and enough of the needle-and-thread action so you can get the basics.

The type of thread you use will determine to a large degree your spacing and even the type of filling that you might want. However you should try several types on each one of the suggestions given in the diagrams. DIAGRAM 1 shows the basic Laid Work. As the name indicates, on the Open Filling, you are leaving more space than you would with regular Laid Work. The size of these spaces depends on the type of filling you are going to make. If it's to be a simple trellis as shown in DIAGRAM 2, with threads going in just two directions and a simple tie-down stitch, a great deal of space need not be left. If you intend to use your background as part of your design, you will want to leave more showing.

DIAGRAM 2 also indicates the use of some simple stitches as tie-downs. The most common is a small diagonal space stitch across the intersection of the two threads, lines 1 and 2. Line 3 shows small Cross Stitches and line 4 large ones. Line 5 has little French Knots over the intersection, which adds texture as well as a change of color.

DIAGRAM 3 shows the working of a foundation for a number of Open Laid Work Fillings—that is, the upright or regular trellis filling with slightly larger than average spaces left and then a diagonal layer of a different color or weight thread laid directly over this. You will note that the top layer does not bisect *every* intersection of the under foundation, although it crosses only *on* intersections. In this diagram the top layer is simply tied down with a straight stitch across the intersection of the top layer.

DIAGRAM 4 has the same basic Laid Work foundation as DIAGRAM 3; however, the tie-down technique is a little different. Note the needle and thread on the lower part of the diagram. The thread is woven over and under the threads where both layers intersect. In this case, the needle is going under the threads of the first layer and *over* the threads on the second layer, automatically tying down both layers and giving an interesting texture to the filling.

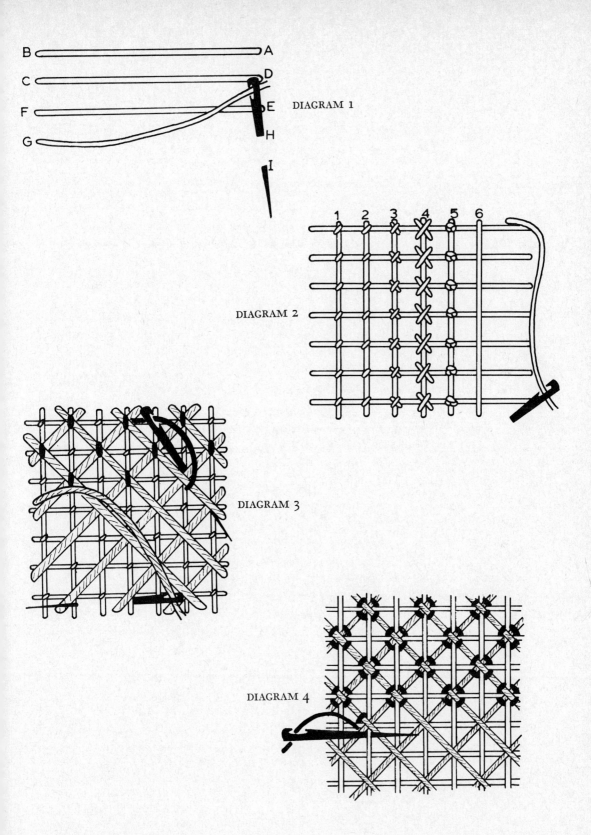

B ———————— A

C ——————— D

F ——————— E

G ——————— H

DIAGRAM 1

I

1 2 3 4 5 6

DIAGRAM 2

DIAGRAM 3

DIAGRAM 4

DIAGRAM 5 shows another technique similar to the previous one. However, the spacing must be larger to accommodate the continued weaving illustrated in this diagram. You wouldn't have to do the entire Laid Work on the second layer; this could be done in the form of Cross Stitches in each square if you wanted to keep them individual. The diagram shows the weaving done in three different colors of thread. Also notice that, on your second and third rounds of weaving, you must carry the thread either *over* or *under* two threads at the beginning of the journey to continue the alternate over-and-under action for the rest of the area.

DIAGRAM 6 is an interesting design, done by varying the tension of the thread and the spot where the second layer of thread is woven over and under. The bottom foundation of Laid Work is done all in the same color, including the tie-down stitches, but the appearance of the drape effect can be varied by weight and color of the thread and also the distance which the thread is carried down.

DIAGRAM 7 is rather an abstract design. Again using the basic foundation—and this one would take a little planning beforehand—threads are couched in various rectangular shapes over the Laid Work in a contrasting color.

DIAGRAM 8 shows that you don't have to follow vertical or horizontal lines in your couching, which can be as varied as you please.

DIAGRAM 9 is often called the Waffle Stitch for obvious reasons. It is simply a matter of three layers of Laid Work, varied either in color or weight of thread. The original foundation on this work must be laid with fairly good-sized spaces, for each succeeding layer is placed inside the previous one. You will also want to allow enough room so that the background will show through, for the fabric helps to give this particular filling a three-dimensional effect. The main thing to remember about this stitch is that all of the horizontal stitches must be laid in the same order—that is, if the main layer has the horizontal threads laid underneath, then the two succeeding layers must have the horizontal threads laid first, and the top layer in each color will be vertical. If you look at the diagram closely, you will see that only the top layer—that is, the fine line on the diagram—is tied down. Whether you are varying weight or only the color of your thread, it is only the top layer which is couched down. This automatically ties down the other two layers and brings their colors up at the intersection for an interesting effect.

DIAGRAM 5

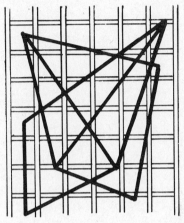

DIAGRAM 8

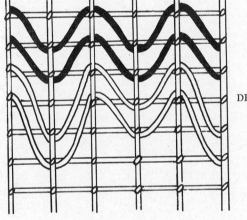

DIAGRAM 6

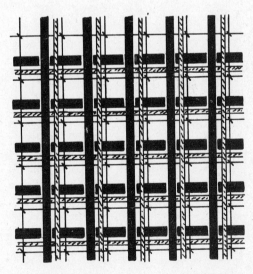

DIAGRAM 9

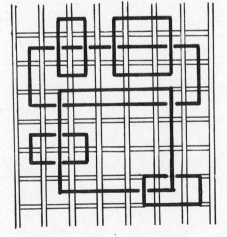

DIAGRAM 7

DIAGRAM 10 has somewhat more detail than the others, so that you can observe both the foundation and the action of the needle in the working. You will note that the second layer of the foundation is carried alternately *over* and *under* the threads of the first layer, instead of lying all on top as in other diagrams. The second step can't be worked properly in this stitch unless the foundation layer is woven thus. The top part of the diagram shows the needle in the first step of the second layer, which is simply carrying a thread down and slipping the needle under the intersection where the threads cross diagonally, and on across the shape. When you reach the end, just pass the needle under the two threads on the outside of the design and continue on with the needle, working from right to left under the intersection. These will be the exact intersections covered on the journey down, as shown by the action of the needle on the lower half of the diagram. The area in the middle indicates that these are most effective when made up in three colors. The second part of the stitch is not worked at every diagonal intersection; one is skipped between each two enriched rows.

DIAGRAM 11 simply shows that Laid Work includes all kinds of stitchery, and that most contemporary stitchery really has a careful plan before it is started. Different lengths and weights of thread in this diagram are couched down to give a nice, overall, balanced filling, which should be very effective as a simple design or incorporated with other work as a filling.

DIAGRAM 12 has been included to show you the possible use of spacing in basic Laid Work and Couching. The wide spaces on DIAGRAM 12 are twice the width of the narrow spaces, and you can see that the middle line in both directions and the outside lines are absolutely straight. The slanted threads in between can give an interesting overall effect without being quite so regular and formal.

DIAGRAMS 13 and 14 show a variation on this method of Couching which gives a three-dimensional effect if you need to employ perspective in a design.

This seems like a large section devoted to this particular type of stitch. But I wanted to give you an idea of some of the possibilities of this very ancient and useful stitch and the wide range of effects to be obtained with it. I hope this brief glimpse will encourage you to experiment with ideas of your own.

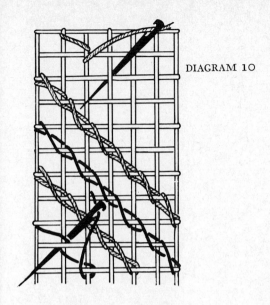

DIAGRAM 10

DIAGRAM 11

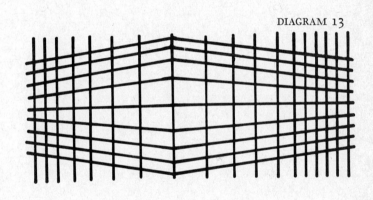

DIAGRAM 13

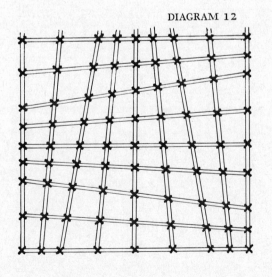

DIAGRAM 12

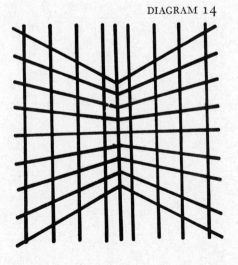

DIAGRAM 14

This type of work is actually a kind of Laid Work. Several people have expanded on this, and done entire projects in this method. As can be seen, when you start following the letters on the diagrams, a series of laid threads, though sewn straight, produce the effect of a pretty curve. These areas can also be overlaid and super-imposed on each other, varied in either color or weight of thread to give some startling three-dimensional effects. A good firm foundation is needed for working this stitch, and you might even do well—if you are going to make an entire project in this stitch—to mount it on some sort of a heavy cardboard and punch holes through both fabric and board with a stiletto before you begin your work. It is a simple matter to lay out the project you have in mind by using graph paper. To get the best effect, your spaces must be equal on any one side of your design.

The original thread is laid from A to B (DIAGRAM 1) and then brought out into the back stitch to C so that you are working back on one side of your work, and forward and up on the other side. Your second thread is carried from C over to D, above A. Continue on in this manner until the entire design is covered and triangles formed.

DIAGRAM 1

These Laid Triangles make useful wings for distant birds, particularly if done in fine thread, or for the sails of a boat, or are lovely simply as an abstract design. This stitch is fun to play with, and something young people enjoy a great deal, particularly if it is done in large scale with the holes punched and numbered on the back of the board for a young child to follow.

FIGURE 1 shows a design completed with fairly wide spacing so you can get an idea of the overlapping of the lines and the curve that is formed.

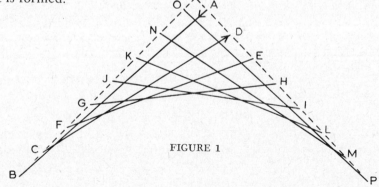

FIGURE 1

238 · LATTICE BAND STITCH

This is an attractive little border stitch worked in two separate steps. The foundation is the Double Herringbone stitch which is shown on the left end of the diagram. If you recall, the second layer of this foundation stitch must be interwoven with the lower, to get the proper effect with the second part of this border. The second step can be worked in the same thread as the foundation or with a change of color for enrichment. If your thread is at all heavy, your foundation shows very little in this stitch (the diagram is drawn somewhat distorted, to show the working). Interlacing is worked in two separate rows, an upper one and a lower one from either direction. The diagram shows the work being started at the right. You will not be going through the background fabric except to start and finish off this lacing; you simply slip your blunt needle under the slanting stitches on the top section of the Double Herringbone. A loose end is shown on the top journey at the left-hand end of the diagram. A second journey is begun at the same end and worked on the lower half of the Double Herringbone, as illustrated in the diagram by the needle and thread.

The left-hander works the foundation in the usual manner, and as the work can be threaded from either direction, that part of the stitch can be sewn in the manner most comfortable.

239 · LATTICE BAND STITCH—TWISTED

This stitch is really an extension of 238, the Lattice Stitch Band. However, this is worked as a filling stitch or can even be used for cutwork. The diagram shows a leaf shape worked with this stitch, the foundation trellis Laid Work. The first set of stitches are laid diagonally across and evenly spaced. The second set of foundation stitches must interlace with the first, so they are darned in and out. Be careful to keep the same regular spacing as on the first set. When the foundation is completed, another thread is put into a blunt needle, and the work is begun at the top of the area at A. The twisted effect of this stitch is achieved by passing the needle under the foundation stitches, as shown in the diagram. The twists must meet each intersection of the foundation trellis. If this stitch is used for filling and cutwork, the foundation stitches are placed much closer together.

255

240 · LEAF STITCH

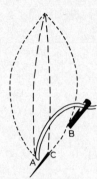

DIAGRAM 1

As the name implies, this is an excellent filling for a leaf shape when a solid one is not required. It also makes a nice light filling for a border. The Leaf Stitch resembles the Open Fishbone somewhat, but it is worked in a quite different manner, and the intersection at the center varies a little.

The work is begun at the base of the design where the needle emerges at A. When practicing this stitch, mark guidelines to follow—other than those for the outline of your design. A pair of lines running up the center of the leaf shape, as shown in DIAGRAM 1, would be helpful. Remember that these must be put on lightly so you won't soil your thread.

After the needle and thread have emerged at the base of the design, the needle is carried up to the right at a sharp upward angle, inserted at B on the outline, brought back down toward the shape, emerging at C on the same outline. This is illustrated in DIAGRAM 1. Then the same type of stitch is taken to the left and brought back down, this time to the center line as from D to E, as illustrated in DIAGRAM 2. These stitches are continued from side to side, the needle always being inserted on the margin of the leaf and brought out again in the center. The diagram shows that this stitch lends itself to an irregular or curving shape, and it can be used to fill either a border or a shape very quickly.

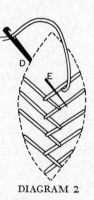

DIAGRAM 2

Left-handers need no special directions, but they might feel less awkward when working with the diagram turned upside down.

241 · LOOP STITCH

This is a nice little line stitch which can be worked in conjunction with other stitches. The diagram shows it worked between two parallel lines. However it will also fill a leaf shape very nicely, in which case the center loops follow the central vein of the leaf, and the legs of the stitch follow the outline.

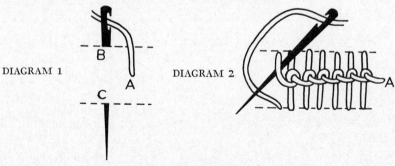

DIAGRAM 1   DIAGRAM 2

Work is begun from the right-hand end, where DIAGRAM 1 shows the thread emerging at A, halfway between the two parallel lines. A little farther to the left, it is inserted on the top line at B and brought out below at C. DIAGRAM 2 shows the second action in this stitch which is the needle being slipped *under* the stitch AB and *over* the working thread, emerging at C. When this is pulled on through, a little loop is formed, as shown by the series of worked stitches in DIAGRAM 2. You then go up to the top line and continue working across in this manner, always inserting the needle on the top line and bringing it out on the lower line before passing it under the stitch just made.

242 · LONG AND SHORT STITCH
(EMBROIDERY STITCH, FEATHER STITCH, PLUMAGE STITCH, SHADING, TAPESTRY SHADING STITCH)

This beautiful stitch can be worked into a variety of designs using the same basic technique. Whole projects can be done by this method, including the background. The effect, like its name, is a gradual shading process. It is one of the oldest stitches and one of the simplest actions, but the most difficult to do well. Many teachers, because the action is so simple, start their students off with this stitch, and have them practice throughout the whole course before allowing them to put it on a project.

There are several musts in this stitch which I will mention before describing the work. Keep them in mind when you start as they really make a great difference in the whole appearance of this stitch. Long and Short work is really a type of Satin Stitch and should be outlined by the Split Stitch before work is begun. This goes completely around the outline, whether it is a straight edge or a curving one. This edging is invaluable as a padding, but mainly it enables you to make a nice sharp edge when doing this stitch. Because you will be pulling tightly against your fabric, it should be in a frame—and make sure it is good and tight before any work is begun.

After your Split Stitch has gone around the entire shape with the same color that you will be using in that area, you are ready to

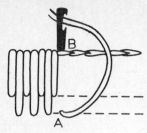

DIAGRAM 1

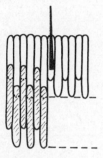

DIAGRAM 2

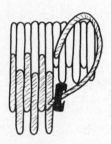

DIAGRAM 3

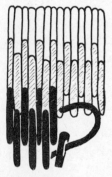

DIAGRAM 4

commence the Long and Short work. Unless you have an exceptionally good eye, it is well to mark lines to follow. The dotted lines in DIAGRAM 1 indicate these guidelines. If you need two lines, one for the long, the other for the short stitch, by all means put them in. Once you become accustomed to this stitch, you will probably need lines only for the longer stitch, as shown in DIAGRAM 2.

The thread is brought out on the lower line, and the needle is then passed up over, as close as you can get, to the Split Stitch around the outline. The same process is done on a short stitch, which emerges on the guideline nearer the Split Stitch, and is in turn also passed over the Split Stitch. You alternate these long and short stitches completely across the area to be covered, keeping each one as close as possible to the last without overlapping and inserting the needle as close as possible to the Split Stitch outline. The long stitches should all be the same length and the short stitches all the same length.

This stitch is sometimes done all in one color, but as a rule it is used as a shading technique. On some of the old pieces a number of shades of one color have been used so gradually and in such fine stitches that you almost cannot see the change from one color to another. When practicing this, however, sharply contrasting colors should be used so you can see the effect of what you are doing.

In the next row, shaded in DIAGRAM 2, all of the stitches are the same length. However, each is begun below the stitches of the row above so the Long and Short effect is continued. On this row the needle comes up and splits the base of the stitch up above, and is carried down and inserted as shown in DIAGRAMS 2 and 3. The little dotted lines on DIAGRAM 2 indicate about where the first row of stitches would be in relation to the stitches just worked over them. If there is any doubt about the length of the stitch in relation to the shape of your design, make it longer rather than shorter. In the second row, you can always go up and split higher on the original stitch, but you can't make it any longer if you didn't carry it down far enough.

The succeeding colors in the shading are worked in the same manner as in DIAGRAMS 2 and 3. DIAGRAM 4 shows a third shade being worked. Your stitches will all be the same length until you reach the final edge. This edge will also have been outlined by Split Stitch, and you simply sew over that edge as you did at the top. This gives your design a nice finished appearance. The stitches should all finish in line with each other.

Instructions vary on the length of the short stitch in relation to the long stitch. I generally do it two thirds to three quarters the length of the long stitch, keeping in mind that I can go higher if I need to shorten the stitch a little.

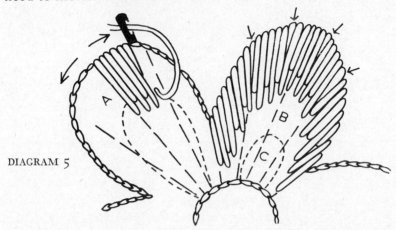

DIAGRAM 5

DIAGRAM 5 shows a design in the working. There are a few difficulties in working a shape that don't appear when you are following a straight line, and I want to bring them to your attention before you attempt a solid area with this stitch. Again you will note that all of the outlines have been worked in a Split Stitch before the work is begun. Section A on the left-hand side of the diagram shows the first row being worked. The arrows at the top indicate the direction the work goes, starting at the center. There are long dotted lines running up and down the length of the petal, as well as the small dotted lines running around the edges. The up-and-down lines are to help you with the *direction* of your stitch, and the others for the *length* of the stitch. When you are doing a curved shape and graduating your stitches, you will be covering more area on the outside line than on the inside line. These long lines will help you to keep your stitches going in the right direction.

To achieve this on a curve, particularly a sharp one, you will have to use little sneak stitches. There is one on the left side of the diagram, beside the needle being inserted. This is done by bringing the needle up, almost under the stitch that has just been worked, about halfway. When the following stitch is pulled up over, the little sneak stitch gets lost in the work, and this gives you a solid filled-in appearance without changing the Long and Short look on the inner circle of your design. The arrows on the right-hand petal show where these little wedge stitches have been inserted in the work. The work is begun in the middle to help the direction of your stitches and the number of your sneak stitches will be determined by the sharpness of your curve. On a long, slightly curved area you might only need one or two, and on a very sharp one, you might need to put one in every few stitches. Knowing this comes only with practice.

The right half of DIAGRAM 5 shows a completed first row worked. You will see that, on a design of this nature, you cannot keep an absolutely regular Long and Short. The stitches must of necessity keep working down toward the lower edge of the design, so that sometimes you will lose a short stitch altogether and will have two stitches that both appear to be long stitches side by side. Skill at working the Long and Short Stitch comes only with experience and practice, so don't be discouraged if your first shading effect doesn't come out as you had hoped.

B and C indicate the next two areas where the colors go. These two rows of Long and Short Stitch are diagrammed in a petal shape so that you can see there would be a very few stitches at the base and that some of those on the outer edge will be very short, just barely going over the Split Stitch. You will find on these various shapes, especially where the area grows smaller as you go down, that there will be times on the inner rows when you will have to skip a stitch to make the work come out smooth. The main objective in Long and Short Stitch is to have a smooth transition from one shade to another as you work down the area.

FIGURES 1 and 2 show two designs you might practice on. The dotted lines indicate which way the stitches should flow. This will vary a bit from design to design. Remember this stitch doesn't have to be used just on floral or leaf work. It lends itself to bird shapes and all kinds of animals as well as ground effects. Remember to keep your fabric especially tight in the frame and use small Split Stitches around the outline.

For a somewhat different appearance on the outside edge of this stitch, after you have become comfortable with the technique of the Long and Short, try doing the outside edge with a Buttonhole Stitch. The Buttonhole Stitch is worked in the regular manner, but the arms are made alternately long and short.

There are no special directions for the left-hander, since this is just an up-and-down stitch and you must work in both directions. You will probably want to start from the right-hand end, however.

FIGURE 1

FIGURE 2

This stitch is actually a variation of the Interlacing Stitch, and it would perhaps be easier if you mastered that first. Having accomplished this, the geometric cross can be tackled with more confidence. One method of laying the foundation for the Maltese Cross, really a type of Herringbone, is illustrated in DIAGRAM 1. The direction for each of the stitches on the over-and-under action is clearly shown. If you choose to make all long lines instead of having the break along the outer edges, carry the thread in the same over-and-under pattern indicated by the arrows. Because of the Laid Work, this stitch must be worked on a frame to keep the foundation in place for the interlacing that follows.

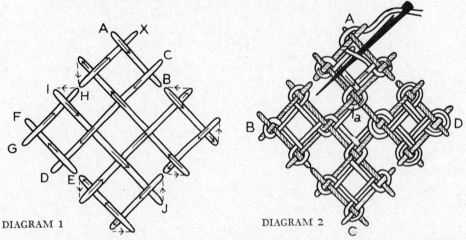

DIAGRAM 1   DIAGRAM 2

The small *a* on the diagram indicates the beginning of the interlacing on the lower two squares—that is, B and C. Area D is the same stitch gone around twice, which gives a more important appearance to the design. Whether to interlace once or twice is partly determined by the weight of the thread you are using.

Maltese Cross Stitch can make a bold, dramatic motif, whether it is done with single or double worked thread, and it is really well worth the time spent mastering the over-and-under steps required to complete this stitch. The top square, A, shows the action of the needle and thread if you are working individual squares, which is sometimes done before proceeding to the next one.

The left-hander will find it easier to turn the diagram upside down and simply follow the over-and-under action of the thread. As most of this stitch is done on the surface, the back view simply shows the little stitches from one spot to another where the next thread is laid.

This stitch was originally used in the weaving together of thread in Drawn Thread Work. The appearance of this work is shown in FIGURE 1 with the threads having been drawn and the weaving in progress, pulling groups of threads together. It's a nice little stitch for surface work and works up quite quickly. DIAGRAM 1 shows a straight stitch having been taken the length of the area to be covered. The thread has emerged again out the same hole at A and the needle is being inserted at B also in the same spot. The thread is brought out a third time from the hole at the top, and the Weaving is then begun. A blunt needle is best for this, particularly with wool thread. The two stitches are opened up with a thumb-nail or with the tip of your needle. The needle is then put *over* the first stitch and *under* the second stitch and pulled on through (DIAGRAM 2). From the left-hand side it is again inserted over the thread nearer the needle and under the one on the opposite side (DIAGRAM 3). These two steps are taken alternately down to the bottom of your threads. Keep closing the stitches up with your needle or thumbnail as you proceed down the line, to make sure that you get a good tight braid effect, as shown in FIGURE 2.

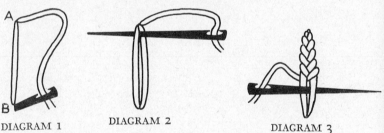

DIAGRAM 1   DIAGRAM 2   DIAGRAM 3

This is a useful stitch for a bud effect and carries well over an area that has already been worked—for instance, a stem or a padded piece of Laid Work of some kind—and stands up nicely on the surface. The tighter your stitches are packed up together, the more raised the effect.

The left-hander needs no special directions, for the Needle Weaving alternates from side to side.

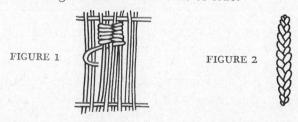

FIGURE 1   FIGURE 2

245 · NEW ENGLAND STITCH
(NEW ENGLAND LAID STITCH)

This is one of the stitches that takes its name from the locality where it was put to use. There was a reason for this stitch coming into being. Due to the shortage of both wool and dyes, the early American embroideries had only about eight stitches. They all were of the type which showed most of the working thread on the surface, such as the Stem, the Chain, etc. This New England Stitch was used a great deal as a substitute for the Satin Stitch because it gave a nice solid filling without wasting thread on the back side of the fabric.

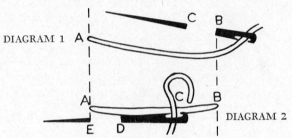

DIAGRAM 1 shows the beginning of this stitch, the thread coming out at A and the needle and thread carried across the area to be covered, inserted at B and brought back toward the center of the shape. It emerges at C, just above the thread AB, about one quarter the width of the entire design. After the needle and thread have been pulled on through, the needle is carried back over and inserted at D, about three quarters of the width of the area. It then emerges at E on the line of the shape and is pulled on through, forming a straight stitch with a long tie-down stitch across the center.

These two steps are repeated on down until the entire area has been solidly filled. This stitch also works well on shapes as well as borders, so that complete areas—leaves, petals, etc.—can be filled in solidly in this manner.

The left-hander reverses the procedure by starting with the thread at A on the right-hand side and carrying it over to the left for the first insertion. The back of the work is just small stitches on the outside edges directly underneath each other.

246 · OVERCAST STITCH

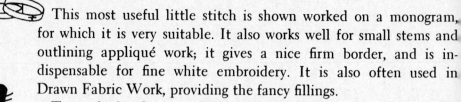

This most useful little stitch is shown worked on a monogram, for which it is very suitable. It also works well for small stems and outlining appliqué work; it gives a nice firm border, and is indispensable for fine white embroidery. It is also often used in Drawn Fabric Work, providing the fancy fillings.

To work the Overcast Stitch, first work the lines in a Running Stitch, as shown in the diagram, picking up as little fabric as possible between the stitches so that they are very close together and given a firm raised line. The action of the needle in making the Overcast Stitch is simply taking close regular stitches, being careful to pick up as little as possible of the material underneath the laid thread, for a round, firm appearance, which is what characterizes this stitch.

The only directions the left-hander will need will be to start from the right end of the line rather than the left for ease of working.

247 · OVERCAST STITCH—DETACHED

This useful stitch is often used in place of the better known Overcast and is really the prettier of the two. The main difference between them is that one is stitched into the background fabric and the other is not—worked instead on the foundation of loosely made Stem Stitches, for a pleasing detached look.

The working of the Stem Stitch foundation is shown in the diagram. It must be worked so loosely that it lies up on the surface and is only picked up on the background at long intervals. It is not practical to work this stitch upon a single Stem Stitch line; two or three are laid down as a rule. The second Stem Stitch is shaded in the diagram to distinguish it from the first, and it should be noted that it crosses over the first line and picks up the background in a different spot from the original row.

The actual working of this stitch is the same as the Overcast in that you are just whipping over the foundation, but in this case the needle does not enter background fabric. The stitches must be absolutely even in tension and very close together. This does take a little practice, but not as much as you would suspect when you first try this stitch.

One of the advantages of this stitch is that it can be worked over an area that has already been worked, such as a fixed stem, and is often used for just that purpose, particularly on little trailing vines. It is also useful where two lines of stems, or something of that nature, must cross each other.

The left-hander follows the same directions, only the work should probably be done from the opposite end to make it less awkward.

248 · OVERLAP STITCH

I found this stitch in an old British publication. It is fun to play with, and although the diagram I have given shows it worked on a circle, it can be done on ovals and oblongs, and with a contrasting texture in the center, it has an interesting appearance. It is a type of Satin Stitch, very similar to the Japanese Stitch, and gives you a curved center.

The needle comes out at A on the outer line of the curve and is inserted at B, diagonally to the right on the inside curve, brought out again at C beside A, and this time inserted on the inside circle again a little above B. This starts the overlapping process. You continue around in this manner.

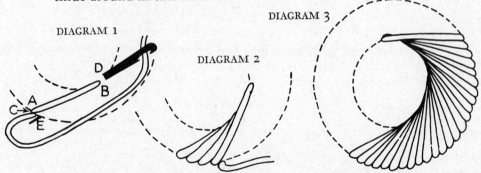

DIAGRAM 1 DIAGRAM 2 DIAGRAM 3

DIAGRAM 3 shows the circle partly worked and the appearance of the stitches as they continue on around the circle. This stitch does not have wide use, but is an interesting one to refer to for certain designs when you want a little variety.

The left-hander simply starts the work in the opposite direction.

249 · PALESTRINA KNOT—REVERSED

 This variation of the Double Knot or Palestrina Stitch is worked from right to left and starts just as the Loop Stitch does. The thread is brought out halfway between the parallel lines, if you are using them to practice, and a slanting line stitch to the left is taken between A and B. The needle emerges down below at C. The needle is slipped under this slanting stitch from above and is pulled on through. Slip it under a second time, this time holding the working thread so the needle passes over, and the loop will gently encircle the first stitch.

You can get different effects with this with different threads and spacing, but it is a lovely stitch that is easy to learn and is worked quickly.

Left-handers turn diagram upside down or use mirror.

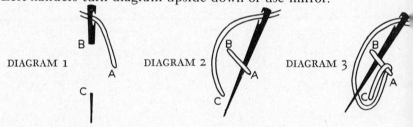

DIAGRAM 1   DIAGRAM 2   DIAGRAM 3

250 · PEARL STITCH

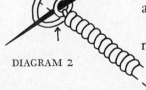 When worked tightly with a fairly coarse thread, this stitch does resemble a row of pearls. This manner of working is probably the most effective. However, it could be spaced out and given more of a Coral Stitch appearance. The work is begun on the right-hand end of the line. The needle takes a small stitch under the line at right angles to it as in DIAGRAM 1. The working thread is not pulled completely through, but a tiny loop is left. Into this loop the needle is slipped, as shown in DIAGRAM 2, and again the working thread is not pulled on through. Take hold of the loop at the spot marked with the arrow and pull the first loop firm and tight. The working thread is then pulled on through firmly, and the first stitch is completed.

This stitch is often used in line work and borders, and is interchangeable with other narrow border and stem stitches, and adds a little dimension to that type of work.

The left-hander starts from the left-hand end and reverses the directions.

DIAGRAM 1

DIAGRAM 2

251 · PEKINESE STITCH

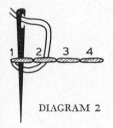

DIAGRAM 1

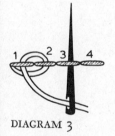

DIAGRAM 2

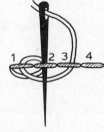

DIAGRAM 3

This stitch is used a great deal in China for executing an entire piece of embroidery, as an alternate to the Chain Stitch. It is very highly thought of, for an embroidery done in Pekinese Stitch brings double the price of one done in Chain. It is used for lines or for filling of flowers and other forms, which it does beautifully. It follows any curving line with ease, and doubling up on the rows makes for a very interesting border. The Chinese work this stitch in silk thread, so finely you almost have to use a magnifying glass to tell what stitch it is.

A foundation row is worked first—a row of Back Stitches, shown in DIAGRAM 1 by the shaded stitches. The contrasting thread, which could be metallic, because this step of the stitch doesn't enter the fabric, is then brought out at the left-hand end of the line. The needle is slipped from the bottom up under Back Stitch number 2 and pulled on through, as in DIAGRAM 1. DIAGRAM 2 shows the needle coming back and passing under the first Back Stitch, over the working thread, and pulled through. DIAGRAM 3 shows the next stitch being begun by passing the needle from the bottom up under Back Stitch number 3. After this has been pulled through, the needle is brought back and inserted from the top down under Back Stitch number 2 and over the working thread. These two actions are worked down to the end of the line.

The diagram shows the stitches rather loose, but in reality the Back Stitches should be quite fine and the Pekinese Stitch pulled up tight, particularly the lower part, for the proper effect of this stitch. Some of the more recent embroideries with heavier threads leave the Interlacing Stitch a little loose, but this is not advisable except on a wall hanging, for it can easily be caught up by a fingernail or a ring if it is on an item that must be handled.

FIGURE 1

FIGURE 2

FIGURE 3

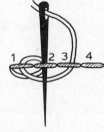

DIAGRAM 4

FIGURE 1 shows a series of these stitches completed, and FIGURE 2 shows two rows side by side for a border effect. FIGURE 3 shows a little variation of the loops laced with another thread to give a richer appearance to the border.

The left-hander follows the directions in reverse and starts bringing his thread under the Back Stitches from the right-hand end and on across the line.

This attractive stitch is really a combination of the Detached Chain or Daisy Stitch and the Stem Stitch. It can be a dainty little pattern in a fine thread, or, when worked in a heavier thread, a bold striking effect. The work is begun toward the right-hand end of the line, the thread brought out at A, some space from the actual end of the row. (The measurement of this space would be determined by the size of the thread and the stitch you are making, but with a medium-weight thread, about one quarter inch in from the end.) The needle is carried back to the right and inserted at the end of the row at B, and brought out at C, halfway between A and B, and pulled on through. This is shown in DIAGRAM 1. DIAGRAM 2 shows the needle being inserted at C again and the Detached Chain Stitch being formed, with the loop from under the needle which has just come out at D. The needle is pulled on through over the working thread. In DIAGRAM 3 the tie-down stitch is in the process of being made at E, with the needle slanting off to the left and coming out on the upper line again at F, half the length of the distance between A and B.

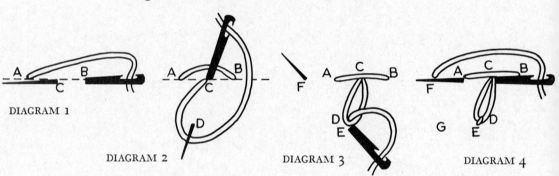

DIAGRAM 1   DIAGRAM 2   DIAGRAM 3   DIAGRAM 4

Now the needle is carried back and inserted at C again and brought out at A, preparatory to forming another Chain Stitch. You will note that the Chain Stitches are not directly down from the upper line. The line slants a bit to the left and gives a flowing petal effect. As the name suggests, when worked in a circle, this stitch gives a floral appearance. When worked with a heavy thread in a circle, the Petal Stitch makes effective sunflowers.

The left-hander simply reverses the directions of the steps.

This stitch, which forms a wide raised border, should be worked with a firm thread to get the best results. The foundation of this work is a series of laid stitches about one-eighth inch apart. The second part of the work is begun over the two lower bars in this stitch, where a series of Satin Stitches is worked side by side without entering the fabric. When these have been completed, the needle enters the fabric and is brought out beside the left-hand stitch and under the second bar at the point indicated by the arrow. Now two Satin Stitches are worked over the second and third laid threads, and then a small stitch is worked over the third one, as in DIAGRAM 2—that is, slipping the needle under the bar and under the working thread. The needle is now in position to work on up over the third and fourth bars.

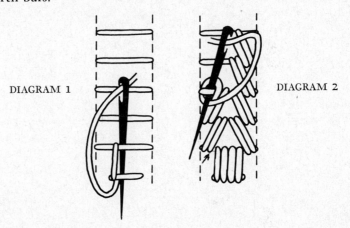

DIAGRAM 1   DIAGRAM 2

This work is continued until the top of the border is reached, and then the entire piece of work is turned around, and the other side worked to match. This time, instead of taking the stitches outside toward the center, take them from the center toward the outside, making the groups of Satin Stitches meet in the middle instead of lying parallel. FIGURE 1 shows a border completed in this manner.

The left-hander will want to reverse this procedure.

FIGURE 1

254 · RAISED KNOT STITCH
(SQUARE BOSS STITCH)

DIAGRAM 1

DIAGRAM 2

DIAGRAM 3

DIAGRAM 4

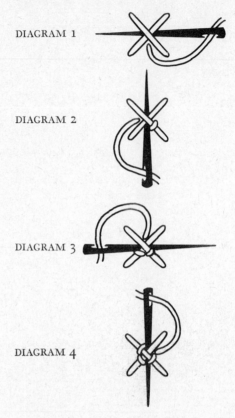

This little detached stitch, when used with a heavy thread, is useful for a point of interest, but with the lighter weight thread works up very nicely for a textured, overall filling as a scattered stitch. The diagrams show quite clearly the action of the needle and thread, which is begun with a regular Cross Stitch. The needle is brought out, as in DIAGRAM 1, just below the intersection of the lower arms of the Cross Stitch. It is then carried up and put under the cross intersection, forming a loop over that leg. DIAGRAM 2 shows the needle being inserted from the bottom up, under the cross intersection, forming a Back Stitch on the other lower leg and emerging at the top of the cross. The needle is slipped under horizontally again, this time from left to right, and the Back Stitch is formed over the upper left leg. The final Back Stitch is formed by inserting the needle from the top down, again under the cross, and carrying it to the back of the fabric.

The left-hander works the Cross Stitch in the usual manner and probably reverses the directions for making the Back Stitches.

This delightful variation of the Romanian Stitch is used in the embroideries of Switzerland, usually white on white. It also makes an interesting decorative band or a scattered filling stitch when worked in color. For best results use a tightly twisted thread. Much of the beauty of this stitch lies in its regularity, and it looks best when worked over counted thread.

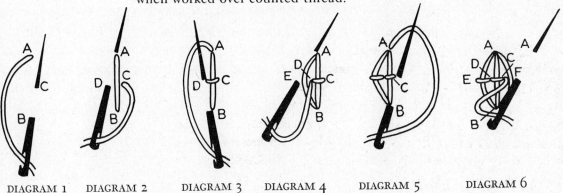

DIAGRAM 1   DIAGRAM 2   DIAGRAM 3   DIAGRAM 4   DIAGRAM 5   DIAGRAM 6

DIAGRAM 1 shows the needle having been brought out at A and inserted at B directly below, emerging at C, halfway between A and B. (C is just to the right of the line AB.) The needle is inserted at D on the other side of line AB, as shown in DIAGRAM 2, and emerges again at A. Next the thread is carried down below again and inserted at B, emerging at D, as in DIAGRAM 3. DIAGRAM 4 shows the tie-down stitch DE in the process of being made, with the needle going in at E and emerging again at A. The last of the vertical stitches is shown in DIAGRAM 5, with the needle going into the fabric at B and emerging at C, to the right of the center line, where the needle goes over the working thread. To complete this stitch, with the needle in position for the next stitch when doing a row, put the needle into the fabric at F, to the right of the line just formed, for the tie-down stitch. It emerges to the right at A in DIAGRAM 6. FIGURE 1 shows one group of these stitches worked in a horizontal line, the lower grouping scattered a bit.

The left-hander simply reverses the direction of the stitches and starts the work from the right-hand side.

FIGURE 1

The action of the needle and thread on this stitch is exactly the same as on the Narrow, except that you are working between two parallel lines and the slant of the needle is different. It is used for heavy stems as a rule but also could be worked in rows of solid filling for certain effects. It does resemble heavy rope. This stitch is most effective when worked with heavy thread or threads that show up to best advantage on a curved line.

The thread is brought out at the top of the right-hand line at A, and the needle is inserted at B, directly under, and slanting over at about a 45-degree angle to the left line where it emerges at C. The thread is looped over the front of the fabric and carried under the needle as shown in DIAGRAM 1. Tighten up the thread and pull the needle on through the loop formed. Another stitch is worked directly under this, as close as you can get it without overlapping, as shown in DIAGRAM 2.

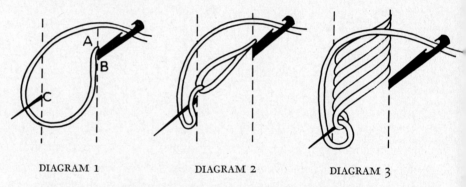

DIAGRAM 1   DIAGRAM 2   DIAGRAM 3

DIAGRAM 3 shows a series of these stitches worked. You will note that the little twist at the end of the stitch is really a kind of reverse Buttonhole Stitch, which gives the raised effect on that side of the stitch. It is easy to lose the slant on this stitch, so make sure that you come up tightly under your previous stitch when inserting the needle, and leave a slight space at the side of the stitch where the needle emerges to keep the loop lying smooth.

The Broad Rope is really a very effective stitch for a heavy stem. The width of the stitches can be varied in the working of a single band, so that for some of the more abstract designs, it lends itself to a line of varying widths.

The left-hander simply reverses the direction of the slant and the twist of the thread over the needle, working from the left over to the right line. The back of the work will be a series of slanting lines across the width of the area being filled.

This stitch can be used for an outline or a heavy solid filling if the lines are worked close together in the same direction. It takes a little practice to get a smooth appearance in this, but if the stitches are fairly long and made with very heavy thread or with several threads of wool, it can work up very nicely.

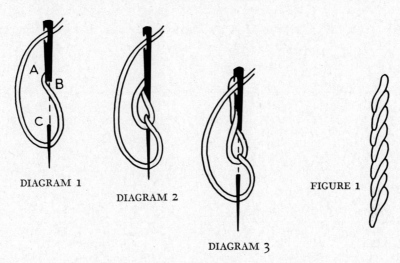

DIAGRAM 1

DIAGRAM 2

DIAGRAM 3

FIGURE 1

DIAGRAM 1 shows the beginning of the work on the line. The thread is brought out at A, and the needle is inserted on the same line just below A and brought out down below at C, the thread being twisted over the surface of the fabric, and carried back under C. When the needle is pulled on through, you have formed a kind of twisted Chain Stitch. The needle is again inserted on the line below the emerging of the thread for the previous stitch, which would be a little under the top of the loop just formed, as seen in DIAGRAM 2. Then it is pulled on through. DIAGRAM 3 shows the third stitch in this series being worked. FIGURE 1 shows a series of these stitches finished, which has the effect of a heavy Satin Stitch.

The left-hander works the twists in the opposite direction and goes right on down the line in the same manner.

(ORIENTAL STITCH, ANTIQUE STITCH,
INDIAN FILLING STITCH)

This stitch is excellent as both filling and border stitch. FIGURES 1 and 2 show that it can be worked in a solid line, or in shapes of varying widths. In either case the tie-down stitches in the center must be kept even and always directly below one another. The appearance of this stitch is varied in some embroideries by the width of the tie-down stitch in the center, and it is sometimes slanted slightly down toward the center, almost in the manner of the Fly Stitch. Whatever the method, the stitches are still packed tightly together, and the center tie-down stitch is kept very close.

If the thread you are using is very thick and the stitches have to be close together, it is sometimes a good idea to bring the needle, when commencing the action of the tie-down stitch, up through the previous tie-down stitch. This gives you a neatly chained line down the center (the heavy thread might distort the shape of your work).

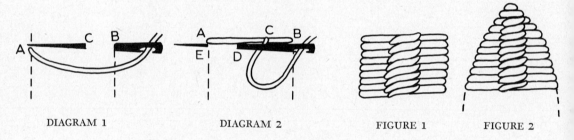

DIAGRAM 1   DIAGRAM 2   FIGURE 1   FIGURE 2

The work is begun with the thread emerging on the left-hand line and carried clear across the shape and inserted at B. DIAGRAM 1 shows the needle emerging at C, about one third of the way back, and with the working thread being held below so that it will come out above the stitch just laid. The needle is then inserted over to the left again at D, about two thirds across the design, and brought out at E. These two actions are repeated on down the row. Keep in mind that, if the width of your area is varied, you change the size of your outline but *not* the size of your center stitch, as illustrated in FIGURE 2.

The left-hander just reverses the directions—that is, brings the thread out on the right-hand line and carries it over to the left for the first half of this stich, proceeding from there. The back of the work shows a series of small, horizontal lines directly under one another.

259 · RUNNING STITCH

The name is very descriptive. The main difference between this stitch and the Darning Stitch is the size of the stitches taken over and under. The Running Stitch is a regular stitch, the stitch on top exactly the same size as the stitch taken on the back side, as illustrated in the diagram. In the Darning Stitch, the surface stitch is much longer than the tiny back-side stitch. The Running Stitch is a simple action but not always easy to perform with regularity. You might do well to practice it at first on heavy cotton with threads that you can count. As with the Darning Stitch, borders can be built up by making rows of this stitch closely together and designs worked out by varying the original placement of the rows. As mentioned, this is the basis for the Holbein Stitch and for some other types of embroidery, such as Black Work.

The left-hander simply starts from the left-hand end. It will be easier for you to see the action of the needle and thread if the diagram is turned upside down.

260 · RUNNING STITCH—THREADED

The foundation for this stitch is made of Running Stitches in the regular manner. Then with a second thread, which can be of contrasting color or weight, the threading process is begun. For a single threading simply slide the needle under the stitches worked, first from the top down and then from the bottom up. Do not pull the thread too tightly, or there will be a waved effect. Double threading reverses this process, so that the needle, which should be blunt, goes down *under* the Running Stitch where it previously went *up*, forming a series of little loops. The diagram clearly shows the action of the needle and thread in this stitch.

This can be worked from either direction so there should be no problem for the left-hander.

261 · RUNNING STITCH—WHIPPED
(CORDONNET STITCH)

Again this title is a descriptive one, and the diagram clearly shows the action of the needle and thread. After the foundation of Running Stitches has been worked, the needle is inserted at the end of the line, from the top down, into each Running Stitch. This will form an almost solid zigzag line, which should not be pulled too tight.

The left-hander just reverses the direction of the work.

262 · SATIN STITCH

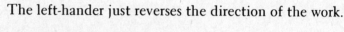 This lovely smooth stitch appears to be one of the simplest embroidery stitches, but it is one of the most difficult to work well. Because of the nature of the stitch, it should be worked over fairly small areas. If you want to work a large area, it should be broken up into smaller sections, or one of the other stitches—such as the Romanian or New England Stitch, which incorporate a tie-down stitch—substituted for it.

One of the main effects of this stitch is the smooth, neat appearance, which means it must have a sharp edge. Therefore, unless the work is a very small design, it should always have a foundation of Split Stitch, or perhaps a small Chain Stitch, worked around the outline first. When you are working on small designs, the stitches can be begun on one end and worked right on down, horizontally. However it is easiest to maintain the proper appearance of this stitch by working on a slant, as illustrated in the diagrams.

The work is begun in the middle of the area, and if necessary to maintain the proper slant, lines are marked with a hard pencil on the inside of the area to be covered, to help keep the direction of the stitches uniform. This stitch must be worked very firmly, with a good tight pull to each stitch as it is formed, so the background must be mounted in a frame of some type.

DIAGRAM 1 shows the Split Stitch being worked on the outside of this shape. The arrows at top and bottom indicate something to remember, in this stitch in particular. With all stitches, it is best to exaggerate the corner stitch when coming to a point, for the fabric, no matter how tightly woven, will tend to give when pulled against. To exaggerate the Satin Stitch, exaggerate the foundation to begin with. In the diagram, the Split Stitch at each point has gone *beyond* the outline.

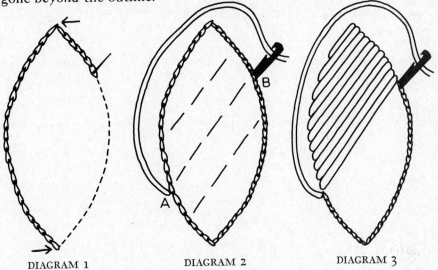

DIAGRAM 1   DIAGRAM 2   DIAGRAM 3

DIAGRAM 2 shows the work being started. The thread has emerged on the left-hand side at A, and the needle is being inserted at B on the right-hand side. You can see that this stitch is bisecting the design diagonally. Continue these stitches, keeping the same slant by using your guidelines, as illustrated, for one half the shape. (The half that you work is optional. I prefer to work down when doing this stitch, because it seems to me that I can get the stitches closer together that way, without overlapping, which is the idea of this stitch. However, if you find it easier to work the stitches up, do so.) After you have finished one half the work, reverse your fabric, and go down and finish the other half, as illustrated in DIAGRAM 3.

The tension is important to remember in this stitch, and this is directly related to rhythm. It will help to practice a bit on an extra piece of cloth before beginning this stitch on an important project, for, once you establish your rhythm, your tension will automatically become regular.

The left-hander simply reverses the direction of carrying the thread—that is, right to left rather than left to right—and again should practice before putting the Satin Stitch on a final project. The back of the work looks almost the same as the front, for you are carrying your threads directly across the back.

263 · SATIN STITCH—COUNTED

This is one exception to the rule that foundation stitching is needed in the Satin Stitch. As can be seen in the diagram, the Counted Satin is generally worked on an evenweave fabric. The effect of the stitch is influenced by the weave of the background material.

The method of working this stitch is exactly the same as for the regular Satin. However, it is seldom slanted. The upper left-hand corner of the diagram shows the needle and thread in action, and the rest shows units worked up to give you an idea of what can be done with this stitch. The upper-right corner shows small motifs with the center of the fabric cut away as would be done in Hardanger Work or other openwork embroidery.

264 · SATIN STITCH—ENCROACHING
(BLOCK SHADING STITCH)

This method of shading a shape gives a more pronounced line between the various shades than the Long and Short Stitch. It is worked by going up *between* the stitches of the previous row so that you have no background fabric showing.

The shape is first outlined with the Split Stitch, as shown in the diagram, before the surface work is commenced. It is also wise to have a line to follow both horizontally and vertically, because it is easy to lose the direction of your stitch and also because it keeps the lengths regular, which is part of the beauty of this stitch.

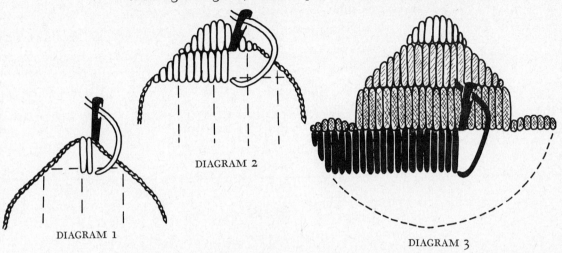

DIAGRAM 1

DIAGRAM 2

DIAGRAM 3

Work is begun at the top of the motif with the needle brought out in the center of the design and carried out over the Split Stitch at the outside edge, as shown in DIAGRAM 1. As with all stitches that cover areas of any size, the work should be begun in the middle and worked in both directions from there to help maintain the angle of the stitch.

DIAGRAM 1 shows the beginning of the top row, worked from the right out toward the edge. DIAGRAM 2 shows the working of the second row of this stitch, and as can be seen, the action of the needle and thread is exactly the same as for the first row, except that the needle and thread are carefully inserted between the stitches of the previous row and do not split any of the thread. Again lines made with a hard lead pencil will be helpful in keeping the size of the stitches regular and maintaining the direction of the stitch. DIAGRAM 3 shows several shades having been worked, all in the same manner, the color being graduated as the work progresses.

To work around a curve, the method for covering both the outside and inside edges properly is the same as that used in the Long and Short—that is, a sneak stitch. If it is a sharply curving shape and you are using several colors, you will probably have to incorporate this short stitch in your outer line in each color. The sneak stitches should be inserted carefully so that they are not really visible except under very close inspection.

There are no special directions for the left-hander, for this simple stitch is done the same whether from right or left, and is kept taut by the use of a frame.

279

265 · SATIN STITCH—PADDED

Your Padded Satin Stitch is exactly that—the motif is padded in some fashion before the Satin Stitch is begun. The padding used will depend on the final effect you desire. For a slightly raised effect, rows of Running Stitches can be worked over the entire surface, and then the Satin Stitch worked on top. (Always remember to keep your fabric taut in a frame and your needle slanting.) A somewhat heavier effect can be obtained by using Chain Stitches underneath, or closely packed Satin Stitches. However, the best method for a heavy pad is a series of layers of Satin Stitch that have been tied down. The number of layers would depend on the height of padding needed.

DIAGRAM 1

DIAGRAM 2

Diagram 2 shows one row of Satin Stitches laid lengthwise and tied down with horizontal stitches. These padding stitches should lie in the opposite direction from the final direction of the top Satin Stitch to be worked. In Diagram 2 the Satin Stitch is worked in much the same manner as the regular Cross Stitch—that is, crossing the tie-down stitches at right angles—except that the needle is tucked in close beside the padding.

No special directions are needed for the left-hander.

266 · SATIN STITCH—SURFACE

This is really a combination of the Satin Stitch and Laid Work, as can be seen in the diagram. It is a thread saver, but it is difficult to keep smooth and regular. It almost has to be worked on a tightly woven fabric to keep the stitches taut.

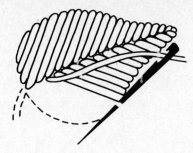

The diagram shows the action of the needle and thread. After the needle has emerged, it is taken to one side and, picking up as few threads as possible, brought right out on the same outline, carried back to the other side of the design and the action repeated. Because of picking up the fabric, this really is not a very satisfactory stitch, although it saves a little thread; you would probably do well to use the regular Laid Work as a substitute for this if you are filling in an area of any size.

267 · SATIN STITCH–TWISTED

As the name suggests, this is a variation on the Satin Stitch and does not have the smooth appearance of the regular Satin Stitch. It can be used as an individual stitch with spacing or in groups worked closely together.

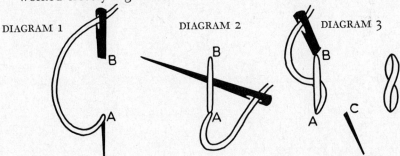

DIAGRAM 1   DIAGRAM 2   DIAGRAM 3

DIAGRAM 1 shows the original Satin Stitch being made with the needle emerging from the same spot where the thread started its work at A. The needle is then slipped under the straight stitch just made, without going through the fabric, and pulled on through. It is inserted in the same hole at the top of the stitch at B and, as shown in DIAGRAM 3, carried on down. It emerges at C to be in position for starting the next stitch.

268 · SATIN STITCH–WHIPPED

The diagram clearly indicates the working of this stitch, which gives you a raised and corded effect. A line or filling of ordinary Satin Stitch is worked, and then a whipping, slanting in the opposite direction, is carried over the base. It is usually worked in the same color of thread. It gives a heavy, important look to the regular Satin Stitch.

269 · SCROLL STITCH
(SINGLE KNOTTED LINE STITCH)

This stitch lends itself to many imaginative uses. It is suitable for outlines and, with proper spacing, for borders and fillings. The various effects can be obtained by the spacing of the knots and the distance of the rows between. Of course the type of thread used will vary the appearance. A good tight twist works the best; however, a single-stranded thread such as a soft cotton gives an interesting texture, too. Stranded cottons do not work well, but a fairly heavy wool is most interesting. As can be seen from FIGURE 2, when worked in rows and the spaces knotted alternately, this stitch gives the feeling of motion, useful when a water effect is needed for a conventional picture.

DIAGRAM 1

FIGURE 1

FIGURE 2

The work is begun at the left-hand end of the line. After the thread has emerged, it is held along the line and slightly above, a loop being allowed to drop below. The needle is inserted just above and emerges just below the line, as shown in DIAGRAM 1, and at both B and C will be over the working thread. The thread is tightened up and the needle pulled through. These stitches should be taken at intervals which will be determined by the space or line that you are filling. FIGURE 1 shows one completed stitch, with the thread in position for the next one.

The left-hander starts from the right-hand end and reverses the directions.

270 · SEED STITCH
(SEED FILLING STITCH, SPECKLING STITCH, DOT STITCH)

This is a series of little double stitches taken at all angles and in any direction but of an equal size, and they produce a surprisingly effective filling. FIGURE 1 shows how these can give an interesting effect simply by their spacing, which effect could be further enhanced by the change of color from dark to light. The diagrams are greatly enlarged to show the action of the stitch, and the fabric must be kept taut on a hoop.

DIAGRAM 1

DIAGRAM 2

FIGURE 1

DIAGRAM 1 shows the thread having been brought out at A and inserted at B just a fraction away. Draw the thread through but not too tightly. The needle is again brought out at A, and this time is inserted just inside B at C and pulled on through. The finished result should be a tiny stitch that does not actually show the individual two stitches but gives you the fat, heavy effect of a raised knob.

The Seed Stitch can be used interchangeably with the French Knot when the effect does not require the textured look produced by the knot stitch. It takes a little practice to keep the stitches tiny and get the fat effect desirable in this stitch.

The left-hander simply works the stitch from the opposite direction, but the action of needle is the same as for the right-hander.

As can be seen by the end result in FIGURE 1, this somewhat complicated stitch makes a handsome and unusual border. Actually, to get the full effect of this stitch's dramatic, bold look, you must work it. It is well worth mastering. The best results are obtained by having the background fabric firmly secured in a frame and by working with a stiff thread on all four stages required for this stitch.

The foundation is formed by a series of transverse threads laid in pairs up the full length of the border, each pair spaced evenly according to the length of the sheafs required. DIAGRAM 1 shows these threads laid and the second action of this stitch beginning. The working thread is brought through at a point just under the lower set of bars, and work is begun over the first two sets in the form of a Satin Stitch, which does not go through the background fabric. DIAGRAM 1 clearly shows the progress of this work across the rows. It usually takes six or seven stitches to cover the bars completely.

Still without entering the fabric, the needle passes to the next pair of bars, numbers 2 and 3, and again Satin Stitches are worked. This time the needle is of course traveling from left to right, and the needle is inserted between the Satin Stitches worked on the first journey, shown in DIAGRAM 2. This stage continues right on up to the end of the line until all the bars are covered.

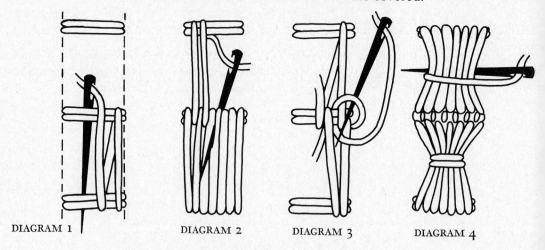

DIAGRAM 1   DIAGRAM 2   DIAGRAM 3   DIAGRAM 4

The third stage of this stitch is now begun at a spot where the Satin Stitches interlock over the second pair of laid stitches. The needle emerges on the right-hand side, as shown in DIAGRAM 3, and passes over the top of the first Satin Stitch, below and over the bottom of the first stitch above. It is slipped downward beneath the bar without entering the fabric. Before the thread is pulled through, the needle is slipped under the loop left by the working thread, as shown in DIAGRAM 3, and pulled tightly through, making a firm knot.

This process is repeated on across the row over each pair of interlocking Satin Stitches until the opposite side of the border is reached. In between the pairs, the final stage is worked. Two Satin Stitches are formed over each group of stitches, and can be done at the same time as your needle and thread travel upward to cinch in to form the sheaves. This step is shown being worked in DIAGRAM 4.

FIGURE 1 shows a series of these stitches completed. They will, with proper placing of the bars, go around curves that are not too sharp, so that it makes a nice circular border.

The left-hander reverses the direction of the tie-down stitches across the bar, but the Satin Stitches are worked back and forth.

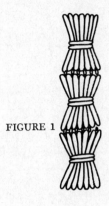

FIGURE 1

272 · SHEAF STITCH—FILLING
(FAGGOT FILLING STITCH)

This pretty filling stitch consists of three vertical Satin Stitches tied horizontally around the middle with two Overcast Stitches. The working of a single one of these is shown in DIAGRAM 1. After the three Satin Stitches have been formed, the needle emerges from beneath them on the left, and the needle makes two Overcast Stitches over the sheaf without entering the fabric at all until it passes on to the next sheaf. These tied sheaves may be set in alternate rows, as in FIGURE 1, or in close horizontal rows directly beneath each other.

The left-hander will do the Satin Stitches normally and will probably want to apply the Overcast Stitches from the other direction.

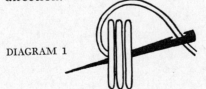

DIAGRAM 1

FIGURE 1

This Sheaf Stitch is worked in a different manner from the others, in that you are working individual teepees in opposite directions with a series of Back Stitches in between. Many bold designs can be worked in this way for a dramatic effect, even by varying the different size or shape of the sheaves..

In DIAGRAM 1, the work is shown begun, with the thread emerging at A, carried up to the right, and inserted at B. The needle is brought out again below, on the same level as A, at C, with a little space left between. A series of these slanting stitches is made in groups of four, as shown in DIAGRAMS 2 and 3, with equal spacing between pairs.

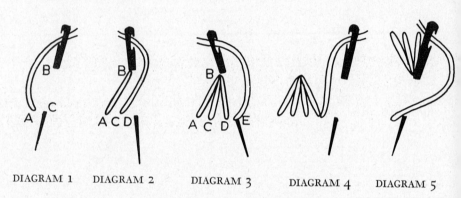

DIAGRAM 1   DIAGRAM 2   DIAGRAM 3   DIAGRAM 4   DIAGRAM 5

DIAGRAM 4 shows one group being completed, with the thread emerging at the base of the last stitch and the needle being inserted to form the beginning of the next one. When a row of these has been completed, or an individual one if you are using this as an isolated stitch, then your fabric is turned upside down and a like group of stitches is worked in the opposite direction with the apexes meeting.

DIAGRAM 6

DIAGRAM 6 shows a series of these stitches with the Back Stitch in the process of being worked across the group. As can be seen, one Back Stitch completes the stitch where the tops meet and another is formed in between the groups. The next one is again at the tip of the next group.

A left-hander works this by reversing the direction.

This stitch, a specialty of the Italian village of Sorbello, is rarely described or used outside Italy. It is very decorative and works up quickly and differently from any other stitch. In Italy it is usually done with a heavy white cotton on a colored linen or with a brown cotton on a white fabric. It is a versatile stitch, which looks good in straight or curved lines and like the Cross Stitch can also be used to fill geometric designs. A textured stitch, it is easily adapted to candlewick or Cross Stitch patterns. Worked up in heavy thread, it makes a striking bedspread. Because of its relaxed tension, a heavy, tightly twisted thread works best in Sorbello Stitch. Do give this stitch a try, for it is well worth adding to your repertoire.

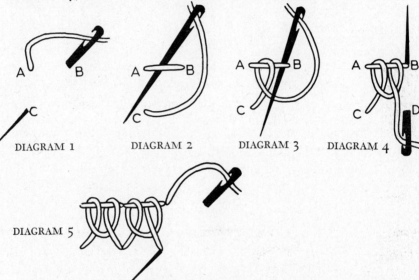

DIAGRAM 1   DIAGRAM 2   DIAGRAM 3   DIAGRAM 4

DIAGRAM 5

The thread is brought out at A, and the needle is inserted to the right at B. It is brought down underneath the fabric, at a 45-degree angle, to emerge at C, AC being the same length as AB. Slip the needle under AB from above without picking up any fabric, and come out toward the left. Hold the thread with your left thumb and slide the needle again under the top line, this time pulling it over the thread being held. This thread now goes under the point of the needle from left to right, making a Buttonhole Stitch as the needle is eased through. Insert at D (this completes your stitch) and come out at B. When the needle is pulled through, the first stitch is completed, and your thread is in position to start the next stitch.

The left-hander reverses the direction, starting at the right-hand end of the line.

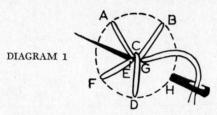 There are several ways of working this stitch, and several methods for laying the foundation as well. I have covered all foundations in this one section; you can make your choice. This stitch is really much more versatile than the diagrams would indicate, and many different effects can be achieved with a variety of threads and foundation spacings. Although there is no diagram to indicate it, it can be worked up into a square and, surprisingly enough, works up very well on needlepoint canvas.

DIAGRAM 1

DIAGRAM 1 shows a simple method of laying a foundation, particularly when doing a small Spider Web. It is a good idea to mark out the circle on your fabric before starting. If you have any doubt as to whether you'll be able to divide your circle evenly, by all means mark off the spots where the threads are to be laid. One thing in particular to remember on this stitch is that it must be done on a frame. As the foundation stitches are laid, they should be inserted beyond the outline that you have made. As the working of the web goes along, your foundation threads will pull in, and your outline will show, or you will not have as large a motif as you intended.

To lay the foundation as shown in DIAGRAM 1, first form a Fly Stitch with a long tail. The thread is brought out at A, and the needle is inserted at B, brought out in the center of the circle at C and pulled on through. The needle is then inserted at D and brought near the center again just under the threads at E. After the needle is pulled through there, it is carried over and inserted at F to complete that spoke. Again the needle emerges near the center of the circle at G and goes out to the outside edge at H, giving you five spokes, equally divided.

The diagram shows the needle entering the fabric again at the center of the circle, which is done to bring it out again in preparation for the surface work. The foundation threads may be laid with a sharp needle, but the surface work must all be done with a blunt needle so that you don't split the thread. DIAGRAM 2 shows a circle being divided by three diagonal lines, which cross each other in the center and give you six spokes; these can be used for the Raised or

Whipped Spider Web, but wouldn't do for the Woven, because you must have an even number of spokes on your foundation. The process of laying this foundation can easily be seen by following the letters on the diagrams.

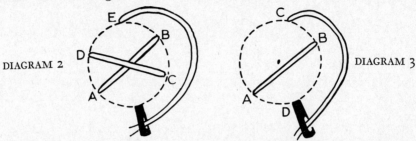

DIAGRAM 2   DIAGRAM 3

DIAGRAM 3 shows the start of laying a foundation of seven spokes to obtain the uneven foundation which can be used for the Woven Spider Web. (An uneven number of spokes *may* be used on other types of Spider Webs if that is the effect you want, but you *must* have an uneven number for the Woven.) As can be seen in DIAGRAM 3, AB does not bisect the circle directly; one half is larger than the other. The lower half of the circle will be divided into three spaces and the upper half into four, and until you get to where you can do this by eye, you should mark off the spacing on the circumference line.

AB is laid, and the needle is brought out in the wider half of the circle at C, about one quarter of the way around. After the thread emerges at C, it is carried across the circle and inserted at D, about one third of the way around the curved line between A and B. The needle is brought up on the same section of the circle at E, about halfway between D and B, which will have divided the lower half of the circle into thirds. The thread is then carried across the circle to F, about halfway between A and B in the larger half of the circle, and brought out at G. This will give you the extra spoke and complete the division of your circle.

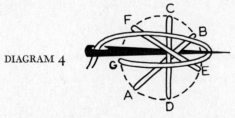

DIAGRAM 4

The thread that emerges from G is laid across the center of the circle. The needle is slipped under, where all three spokes cross, without going through the fabric, and the working thread is passed under the pointed end, as shown in DIAGRAM 4. The needle is pulled on through, a loop being formed in the center of all the stitches, which you can shift around until it is over the center of your circle, as shown in DIAGRAM 5.

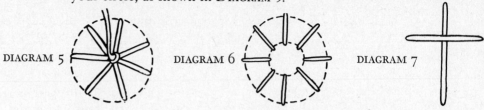

DIAGRAM 5   DIAGRAM 6   DIAGRAM 7

DIAGRAM 6 shows the foundation for Ring Spider Webs, and this simply means that the spokes do not go completely to the center. You are forming an outside ring, and the center may be filled or left void. The spokes are worked like Satin Stitches around the circle that has been marked off into even spaces.

DIAGRAM 7 shows the base for the Lozenge, or God's Eye, Spider Web, which is a simple Cross Stitch with the lower leg longer than the other three.

276 · SPIDER WEB–LOZENGE
(GOD'S EYE)

This is the simplest of the Spider Web Stitches and is most popular in Mexico, especially when done in bright colors and with heavy threads around sticks which have been whipped together. Lozenge Spider Webs are used singly or in groups for lively decorations.

Lay the foundation as in DIAGRAM 7 of 275 and bring a blunt needle out near the intersection of the crosses. Either the Whipped or Raised method of working the Spider Web can be applied to this, and if you are making a large one, you may occasionally need to pick up a thread or two of your background fabric to keep the shape from distorting.

The left-hander works this in the direction most comfortable.

277 · SPIDER WEB–RAISED

There are two ways of whipping the spokes to form a Spider Web, and this one is not as commonly used as the other. The two methods give entirely different results, so be sure to try both of them. After your foundation has been laid by any of the methods described in 275, the working thread is at the center of the circle, preferably in a blunt needle. Be sure, before starting this stitch, that you have a long thread. You can finish off and start a new thread by slipping your needle back under the worked area, but it does spoil the effect sometimes.

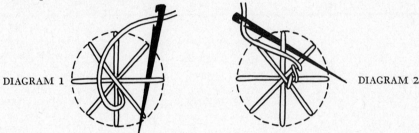

DIAGRAM 1   DIAGRAM 2

The working thread is shown coming out between a pair of spokes in DIAGRAM 1. The needle is carried back so that the working thread lies over two spokes. The needle is then slipped from the left under one of these spokes. Continue around in this manner, carrying the thread to the left, *over* two spokes but *under* only one, as shown in DIAGRAM 2.

278 · SPIDER WEB–RINGED

The foundation for this stitch is shown in DIAGRAM 6 of 275. I have not shown a working diagram of this stitch, merely how it will look when finished. It may be worked in either the Raised or Whipped Stitch. This stitch also shows up effectively when done with the raised Stem Stitch and creates a feeling of depth especially if a heavy thread is used.

279 · SPIDER WEB—WHIPPED
(RIBBED)

The foundation layer for this stitch can be any of those given in 275, for the work is done individually around the spokes, and an uneven number of spokes is consequently not necessary.

DIAGRAM 1 shows the foundation laid and the working thread emerging in the center of the diagram between two of the laid threads. This stitch is worked somewhat differently from the other Spider Webs. The working thread lies back over the thread to the right, so that the needle is inserted under that thread, as well as under the spoke to the left. When it is pulled on through, the working thread is between the next pair of spokes to the left. This process is repeated. Again the needle is carried *under* the spoke to the right of the working thread and from right to left *under* the spoke on the left of the working thread. This step is worked continuously, forming loops around the spokes until the shape is filled.

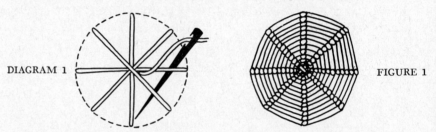

DIAGRAM 1

FIGURE 1

FIGURE 1 shows the appearance of the completed stitch, little ribbed rows with the threads lying between. If these are worked very close together, they resemble a series of little Bullion Knots emerging from the center.

Left-handers reverse the directions.

280 · SPIDER WEB—WOVEN

The foundation for this Spider Web must be like DIAGRAMS 1 and 5 in 275. An uneven number of spokes is absolutely essential for this Spider Web, because the action is a weaving in and out of the spokes in a continuous thread, and you must go *over* the spokes you went *under* on the previous journey.

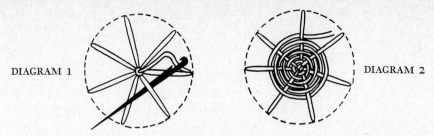

DIAGRAM 1   DIAGRAM 2

DIAGRAM 1 shows the threads having been laid and the needle slipping over one spoke and under the next one to begin the work. DIAGRAM 2 shows a circle partially worked. Keep the working thread up tight against the center as the weaving is begun, but loosen the tension a little as you work out.

I have on occasion, while working over a very large area, added spokes out near the circumference, in between the threads already laid; this is done when the distance between the spokes gets too long or sloppy looking. If you plan to do this, however, remember you still must keep an uneven number of spokes for the foundation, so it is best to add them in pairs—that is, two spokes between two spokes.

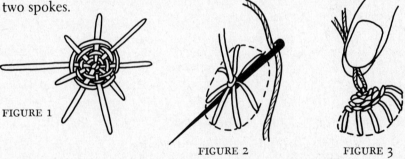

FIGURE 1   FIGURE 2   FIGURE 3

FIGURE 1 shows a Spider Web made with the foundation spokes of varying lengths which you may want to try sometime, for a certain effect. Of course you don't work completely out to the edge of the foundation in this stitch—it is not necessary to work to the edge on any of your designs if the result you want doesn't call for it.

FIGURES 2 and 3 show a method of raising up the Spider Web to get a high, three-dimensional appearance. A separate thread is slipped under the center, where all the threads have intersected, and the needle pulled on through. The thread is held with the left hand while the surface work is being done. With wool in particular, which has more elasticity than other threads, this works most effectively. A thin wire, such as a fine hairpin or an opened-up paper clip, can also be used for this hooking-up purpose and gives something a little firmer to grip.

The left-hander simply works in the opposite direction.

281 · SPLIT STITCH
(KENSINGTON OUTLINE STITCH)

This dainty little stitch is more widely used than one would suspect when first doing it. It was used a great deal in medieval days on the faces of figures, to show contours, also for drapes of fabrics and for solid fillings, with the shading beautifully executed. It works up well and goes around curves nicely for line work, but is also a very successful solid filling, resembling fine Chain Stitch.

The name is very descriptive. The working thread is brought to the surface of the fabric, and it is split by the needle, which has been inserted and comes out to the left a bit. Split Stitch must be worked in a soft thread of some sort, for a hard twist is difficult to split.

This stitch can be worked either in a frame or in the hand, but comes out smoother and more uniform when done on a frame. It is always used as a base under Satin Stitch, and as the Satin Stitch is worked on a frame, it is obviously easier to mount the work for both processes.

The left-hander simply starts from the right-hand end and follows the rest of the directions in reverse.

282 · SPLIT STITCH—SWEDISH
(ANUNDSJÖ)

This little stitch is actually a combination of a Split Stitch and Romanian Stitch, and is used as a leaf filling in Swedish folk embroidery. When it is used for solid fillings, it is arranged in alternate rows so it resembles the Long and Short Stitch. It is generally worked with two threads in the needle, for ease of splitting, and the tie-down effect on this is part of the charm of the stitch. It is not much used in this country, but it is worthwhile adding to your vocabulary.

The left-hander reverses the direction when working the stitches and starts from the right-hand end.

DIAGRAM 1 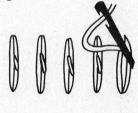 DIAGRAM 2

This stitch is used chiefly in the tailoring of garments, to anchor points of stress. However it also makes an unusual effect in surface embroidery, and works up best in a tightly twisted thread, fine or heavy.

Before the stitching is begun, an equilateral triangle is marked on the fabric in some manner. The work is started at the lower left-hand corner, as shown in DIAGRAM 1. After the thread has emerged at A, the needle is taken up to the point at the top and inserted from right to left, picking up only a couple of threads of the material. The needle is pulled through to make a firm stitch and brought down to the lower level again. Now insert the needle on the right-hand corner at D and bring out on the left-hand corner at E. E is just to the right of A, as close as possible. The needle again is pulled through, carried to the top of the triangle and inserted directly across, just under the stitches already formed at the apex.

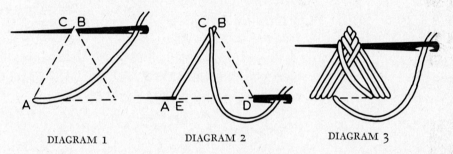

DIAGRAM 1   DIAGRAM 2   DIAGRAM 3

DIAGRAM 3 shows this action in progress after several stitches have been worked. As can be seen from the diagram, you alternate one stitch on the top level and one stitch on the lower level. On the top level, the needle is inserted just under the stitches previously worked, and on the lower level it is inserted inside the stitch on the right, emerging just inside the stitch on the left. FIGURE 1 shows a completed stitch.

The left-hander works it exactly the same as the right-hander but will probably find it less awkward starting on the lower right.

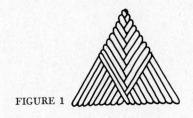

FIGURE 1

284 · STAR STITCH

This simple little stitch is generally used as a powdered filling stitch. The working can be easily seen by the diagrams. Diagram 1 shows an upright Cross Stitch already completed and the thread emerging at E. The thread is then carried diagonally up over the cross already formed and, as Diagram 1 shows, the needle is inserted at F. It emerges at G to begin the second half of the diagonal cross.

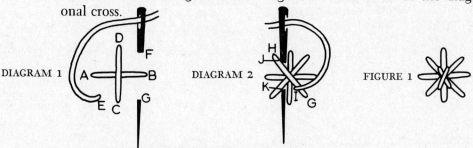

DIAGRAM 1   DIAGRAM 2   FIGURE 1

Diagram 2 shows the first two crosses completed and the thread brought out again, in preparation for forming the last Cross Stitch in this series, which is an oblong cross. The thread has emerged at I, and the needle is inserted on the upper level, between the spokes of the two crosses already formed, and emerges vertically below at K. Figure 1 shows the completed stitch, and Figure 2 shows its effect as a filling stitch.

The left-hander simply reverses the direction of the crosses.

FIGURE 2

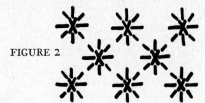

285 · STEM STITCH
(CREWEL STITCH, OUTLINE STITCH, STALK STITCH)

This simple little stitch is the basis of much hand embroidery. It is used as an outline or as a solid filling, and can be varied some by the working method, for the appearance changes with the angle of the needle. (If the angle changes sharply enough, it becomes a Satin Stitch.) The rhythm is important in working this stitch, but it is very easy to acquire, and this stitch looks good when worked with any kind of thread.

In the older embroidery books, the Stem Stitch and the Outline Stitch are considered two quite different stitches. The Outline Stitch is worked with the thread held to the left or above the line, as illustrated in DIAGRAMS 1 and 2, whereas in the Stem Stitch the working thread is held to the right or below the line being worked. As mentioned earlier, work your stitches in the way that is most comfortable for you. The diagram shows this stitch being worked from left to right, but if you are more comfortable working it from the bottom up, by all means do so.

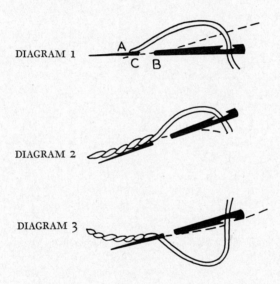

DIAGRAM 1

DIAGRAM 2

DIAGRAM 3

The thread emerges at the left-hand end of the line, and the needle is inserted a short distance to the right and emerges back to the left, almost at A but not quite. DIAGRAM 1 shows the needle in the process of making this stitch, and DIAGRAM 2 shows several stitches worked and the needle performing the same action. DIAGRAM 3 shows the working of the Stem Stitch also, but with the thread held below the line. In most cases it doesn't matter whether you use the underhand method or the overhand in working the Stem Stitch, but whichever method you decide upon, it must be continued to the end, or you will have a sloppy-looking line.

The left-hander simply works in the opposite direction, and the diagrams turned upside down will show clearly how this stitch is executed.

In this stitch the action of the needle is the same as for the regular Stem Stitch and is worked from left to right. But instead of holding the thread in the same position for each stitch, it is held alternately up and down.

DIAGRAM 1

DIAGRAM 2

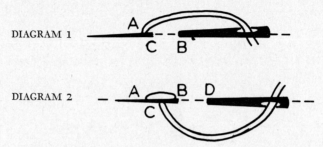

DIAGRAM 1 shows the first stitch in the process of being worked, with the thread brought out at the left-hand end and held above the line, the needle going in at B and out at C, halfway back to A. DIAGRAM 2 shows that the needle action is the same but the placing of the in-and-out varies slightly. Your stitch AB has been formed, and as can be seen by the diagram, the thread is emerging from C, which is about halfway down the stitch. The needle is inserted to the right again, forming a stitch the same size as the stitch AB and emerging at B, with the thread held below the line. After this has been pulled through, your thread is flipped up to the top of the line and the same size of stitch made. Continue in this manner, alternating with the thread above the line and below the line until the end of the line has been reached.

FIGURE 1

FIGURE 1 shows a section of this stitch being completed and also a second row worked directly underneath. As can be seen, the working of these two rows close together gives the effect of four rows of stitching, and if it is done in a heavy thread, it makes an interesting border which works up very quickly.

The left-hander turns the diagram upside down and starts the work at the right-hand end of the line.

287 · STEM STITCH—FILLING, FRENCH

This stitch is actually a combination of stitches. It makes a very effective filling that goes quickly. DIAGRAM 1 shows a row of Stem Stitches worked and the needle brought out directly below, at the end where the Stem Stitch has been finished. The return journey is done in a Running Stitch. When you reach the left-hand end of your design, the needle is again brought out directly below, and another row of Stem Stitch is worked.

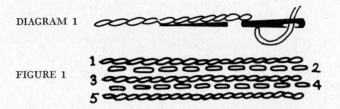

DIAGRAM 1

FIGURE 1

A section of this combination is shown in FIGURE 1. Rows 1, 3, and 5 are the Stem Stitches, and 2 and 4 are the Running Stitches. If these are worked quite close together, you can get an interesting filling, and it goes quickly because you can just work back and forth.

The left-hander turns the diagram upside down.

288 · STEM STITCH—FILLING, SHADED

The Stem Stitch is useful for shading entire designs. The method of working is exactly the same as for the Stem Stitch Solid Filling, number 289. The diagram shows the rows worked in much the same manner, the shading indicated on the diagram. The values can be graduated very nicely in this stitch, which is found in many old embroideries of China and India.

289 · STEM STITCH—FILLING, SOLID

This method of using the Stem Stitch gives a woven appearance to the design being filled and lends itself to solid fillings very nicely. One suggestion: as a rule, when filling a design with solid rows of Stem Stitch, hold the thread below the work when the stitch is being worked. Another suggestion: do the outside outline first.

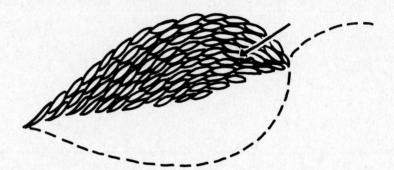

The diagram shows half a leaf shape filled with Stem Stitch, and there is an arrow going to the first adjusting, or short, row. You will find, when you are working designs that are not rectangular, that you must make adjustments to get a smooth, solid appearance to your filling. This will occasionally require you to vary the length of your rows. In the diagram, most of the rows below the arrow are of varying lengths, which means they are started other than at the end of the design. You will have short rows sandwiched between rows that go completely across. These do not show once your design is solidly filled in. Try to work the Stem Stitch so that the center of each stitch falls under the end of a stitch in the row above, brick-fashion, so they blend together.

The entire piece is worked in the regular Stem Stitch, so the left-hander uses the method most comfortable for that stitch.

290 · STEM STITCH—LONG

This stitch is used a great deal in France, partly because of its interesting texture, partly because it is economical of thread. The French like the Stem Stitch particularly for filling shapes and doing solid areas.

Stagger the stitches so that they fill in the spaces solidly and none of the background is showing. All of them move in the same direction, and when the shape is completely filled, it is outlined with a closely worked Stem Stitch.

DIAGRAM 1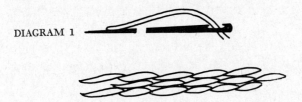

The diagram shows a stitch being made, and as can be seen, the needle emerges well down the line from the spot where the working thread starts. Very little fabric is picked up in this stitch, but the stitches themselves are considerably longer than the regular Stem Stitch, the actual length varying with the weight of thread.

As with the other Stem Stitches, the left-hander simply turns the diagram upside down.

291 • STEM STITCH—PORTUGUESE

The Portuguese Stem Stitch has a nice rugged texture and a knotted look and creates unusual sturdy lines, giving the effect of a couched cord. It is often used, when made with fine thread, to outline drawnwork, for it gives a firm outline with a bit of texture. The diagrams look rather complicated but the stitch isn't too difficult to work. The effect is rather like a knotted rope and should be tried on heavy thread with a tight twist.

The action of the needle and thread at the beginning of the stitch is very similar to the regular Stem Stitch, and the diagram shows it being worked upward, since it is easier to do the following steps with the work held in that position. It is a good idea to use a blunt needle on this stitch, for you are going under threads a good deal.

301

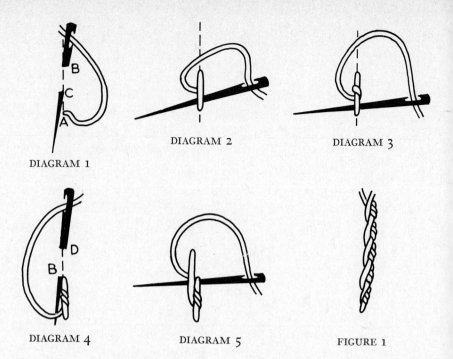

DIAGRAM 1

DIAGRAM 2

DIAGRAM 3

DIAGRAM 4

DIAGRAM 5

FIGURE 1

The thread is brought out at A, and the needle is then inserted farther along the line at B and back toward A, at C. C is at about half of the distance between A and B (DIAGRAM 1). DIAGRAM 2 shows the needle being slipped under the first stitch, made from right to left, with the working thread held above the needle. The needle is pulled on through and again inserted under the same stitch, with the working thread held in the same position, as illustrated in DIAGRAM 3.

The next step is shown in DIAGRAM 4. The needle is inserted in the fabric again at D and brought out at B, with the working thread held out of the way so that no loop is formed while the Straight Stitch is being made. DIAGRAM 4 shows the needle being slipped under again, this time passing under two threads. The lower part of the last stitch is made and the top of the first one. Then the needle is slipped on through. Tighten up the coil just made and make another directly below in the same manner (DIAGRAM 3), again passing under both threads.

Continue working in this manner. With each succeeding Stem Stitch, the thread is held down and to the right. All the loops around the thread should be very close together and executed with the thread held up and to the left. FIGURE 1 shows a series of these stitches worked.

The left-hander will find this stitch easy to work by reversing the directions and even easier if the diagrams are turned upside down.

292 · STEM STITCH—WHIPPED

The Whipped Stem Stitch comes in handy if a bold line or something a little more dramatic than the ordinary Stem Stitch is required. The whipping process can be worked with the same thread as the stem or with a contrasting one. The thread is simply laced around a foundation of Stem Stitches, the needle not entering the fabric at all, as shown in the diagram. For this stitch to be most effective, the whipping should be done at regular intervals preferably slipped under each Stem Stitch.

The left-hander works the Stem Stitch in the regular manner and the whipping from the direction most comfortable.

293 · STEP STITCH

A very decorative band of stitching, suitable for formal design, can be made with this stitch. It is worked in a series of three steps. First, two perpendicular lines of Chain Stitch are made about half an inch apart. Secondly, parallel lines are laid between the Chain Stitch one-eighth inch apart. The procedure is clearly shown in DIAGRAM 1.

DIAGRAM 1

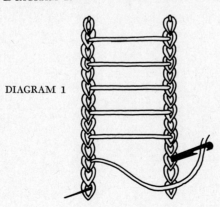

When this step has been completed, your needle is brought out on the upper level just underneath the top bar on the left-hand edge. This step of the stitch will be easier to work with a blunt needle, since you are no longer going through the fabric. The needle is slipped under the bar, from five to seven times, working across toward the center.

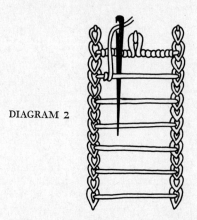

DIAGRAM 2

When you have reached the center, which could be marked by a line when practicing, a different type of stitch is taken. The thread is taken up a little above the line, and a couple of threads of background material are picked up. In another method you can pass the needle through to the back of the material, about one-eighth inch above the bar, and then bring the thread to the surface again below the bar. Slip the thread under this stitch, forming a little loop. Continue passing the working thread over the horizontal bar to the end of the row, this time with the needle passing under the bar from the bottom up, as shown in DIAGRAM 3.

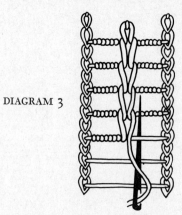

DIAGRAM 3

All the succeeding rows are worked in a similar fashion, except that, when the center is reached, the working thread is slipped behind the legs of the center stitch on the row above, forming a kind of large Chain Stitch, as illustrated in Diagram 3.

Remember that regularity is part of the beauty of this stitch, so you should always have an equal number of loops on each side of your center stitch. Diagram 3 also shows several rows of this stitch, to give you an idea of the completed work.

The left-hander does the basic work the same and simply starts the whipping process from the right-hand side instead of the left.

294 · STRAIGHT STITCH
(STROKE STITCH)

The Straight Stitch is exactly that—an isolated Straight Stitch of any desired length and worked in any required direction. The diagram shows them as random stitches worked in various directions, which can be used for grasses, small leaves, or just for an overall effect. This stitch also works up very nicely in a geometric pattern with stitches of regular size for solid fillings of various types.

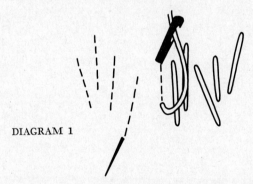

DIAGRAM 1

FIGURE 1 shows a very simple combination of these stitches, which can be used as a border. You might try working them around a small circle to give the effect of a flower. Many other stitches are formed of the Straight Stitch in combination with another stitch.

FIGURE 1

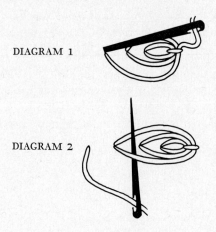

DIAGRAM 1

DIAGRAM 2

The Surprise Chain is a variation on the working of the Broad Chain. It has a somewhat different movement and gives an unusual result when completed. DIAGRAM 1 shows the Broad Chain action being done on the first stitch. A Straight Stitch is taken and the working thread passed under it to form the Broad Chain. In this case three chains are made. When the first group of stitches is complete, the needle is passed down along the line, the length of the stitch desired, for the second small chain. The needle then passes under the lower leg of the previous chain, or the upper, depending on how you are holding your work. Insert your needle back in the same hole, carry it down the line for the next stitch, and repeat twice more, making each stitch a trifle longer than the one before, as FIGURE 1 shows. All are passed under the same leg of the Chain Stitch.

FIGURE 1

When working this stitch, pull the thread firmly, so your stitch does not have a lopsided look. The end result is most unusual. A heavy thread shows this stitch off best, although it does have an interesting delicate look, too, when worked with fine thread.

The left-hander turns the diagrams upside down.

This little stitch can be used in several ways as a powdering pattern, which is most common, to soften the hard edge of a leaf outline, or as a sort of cresting edge on a stitch. The Sword Edge can be used effectively as a line stitch also.

The thread emerges originally from the right-hand end of the line. A diagonal upright stitch is taken, as shown in DIAGRAM 1, from A to B, the needle emerging at C, diagonally down. The distance between B and C should be equal to that between A and B. This line is worked from right to left, with A just to the left-hand end of the line.

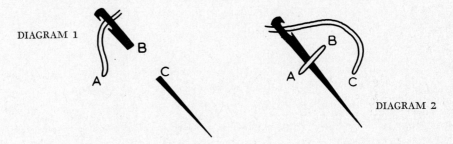

DIAGRAM 1

DIAGRAM 2

Step 2 is shown in DIAGRAM 2, with the needle being passed up under the diagonal stitch between A and B and pulled on through to form a little twist. DIAGRAM 3 shows the needle carried down below and inserted at D and carried on to the left, emerging at E, in position to start the next stitch.

DIAGRAM 3

FIGURE 1

Note that the little tail which ends at D on the lower half of this stitch is somewhat longer than the distance between the other points of the upper edge of the stitch. FIGURE 1 shows a little series of these stitches worked in a line.

This interesting little stitch can be used as an isolated stitch or, when done in dainty proportion, for powdered filling. The first step is making a small Chain Stitch, as shown in the left-hand section of DIAGRAM 1, then two slanting Straight Stitches for the base as shown in the right-hand half.

DIAGRAM 1

FIGURE 1 shows a group of these little stitches worked to give you an idea of the effect. It is a simple little stitch but sometimes a nice change from the regular filling stitch.

FIGURE 1

298 · THORN STITCH
(BRIER STITCH)

As the name implies, this stitch reproduces the effect of thorns, but it is equally adaptable for depicting ferns, grasses, and stems. It can give a nice flowing effect because of the central line, which is tied down with the Cross Stitches. It is worked in two methods, and DIAGRAM 1 shows the beginning of the first method, in which the laid thread is incorporated as part of the Cross Stitches. The other method is to bring out a separate thread and let it flow along the line while you do the Cross Stitches over it. Both methods of working are done exactly the same, except that in the diagrammed method you are taking that first stitch with part of your working thread.

The needle is inserted at the end of the line and brought out to the left at C, slanting downward a bit (DIAGRAM 1). From C the working thread is carried across the central line, inserted just to the other side, down the length of the Cross Stitch desired, and brought up on the right-hand side of the central line at E, slanting outward to the right. This step is shown in DIAGRAM 2.

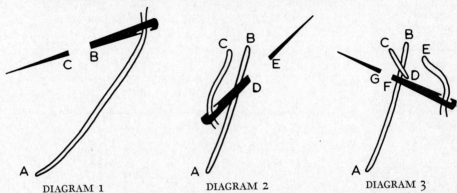

DIAGRAM 1   DIAGRAM 2   DIAGRAM 3

DIAGRAM 3 shows the stitch with the first cross thread in position and the working thread ready to begin the second one. With the thread coming out at E, the needle is inserted at F to the left of the central line and brought out horizontally at G, further left and directly under C.

These alternate steps across the main thread continue on down, forming your thorn appearance. A completed line of these is shown in FIGURE 1.

FIGURE 1

While the left-hander will not need any special directions, it might be more comfortable to work from the other direction. However the crosses do alternate so you could probably do the stitches as diagrammed.

This stitch is not related to Trellis Work resulting from Laid Work. It is an individual stitch, almost unknown these days, and unusually attractive. It seems to be of English origin and was in common use around the sixteenth century, often seen in clothing embroidery of that period. It can also be seen on very early British samplers. It is used only for solid fillings—any design can be filled with the Trellis Stitch.

Trellis Stitch must always be outlined, either with the Chain Stitch or the Back Stitch, for the stitches need an outline foundation to work into. The Back Stitch doesn't give quite as finished an effect as the Chain. When using the Chain Stitch, you enter only the inside loop with the working thread, so that you obtain a finished appearance along the edge formed by the outside loops of the chains. Your choice of stitch for this outline may be governed by your choice of thread. The untwisted thread works to best effect, and it will have little wear, since it is not going in and out of a tightly woven fabric. The Trellis Stitch also works up well in some of the heavier modern threads.

Once the surface work is begun, the needle no longer enters the fabric, so you may use a blunt one. You can start a new thread along the outline if you must, but this is one stitch where it is best to start with a good long thread so that this does not become necessary.

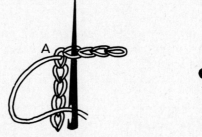

DIAGRAM 1   DIAGRAM 2

DIAGRAM 1 shows the upper left-hand corner of a design to be filled, which has been outlined with the Chain Stitch. The working thread is now emerging from the center of the top chain on the left-hand side. The needle is slipped under only the inside loop of the Chain Stitch and pulled on through, but not too tightly. The needle is then inserted in the loop left by the working thread and at this point is given a pull to tighten up the knot. A knot should be pulled up tight before you go on to the next stitch. You will see that the rows slant in different directions as you work back and forth. The working thread is given a little pull, and a knot is formed in the direction you are working—in this case to the right.

DIAGRAM 2 shows one stitch formed on the first row. The needle is again slipped under the lower leg of the next Chain Stitch and a loop of the working thread is left lying below. The needle is slipped into that loop and the knot again tightened up. Work completely across the row in this manner until the far side of your design is reached. The working thread is then slipped under the inside loop of the upright Chain Stitch at the end of the row and passed under. It is then brought down and slipped from the outside in on the next one.

Work is then begun in the other direction, and DIAGRAM 3 shows the action of the needle and thread going to the left. The direction of inserting the needle in the loop is the opposite of the previous row. The knots are tightened up in the same manner, but this time the working thread is pulled to the left. On all succeeding rows after the first, the needle is slipped under the little loop left between the knots in the previous row, as shown in DIAGRAM 4. (The size of these stitches is exaggerated in the diagram to show you the action of the needle and thread. In the actual working of this stitch, these little knots are close together with practically no fabric showing underneath.)

If you desire, these stitches can all be worked with the knots slanting in the same direction. In such a case, a row must be finished off and a new one started back at the same side each time, before you commence another row.

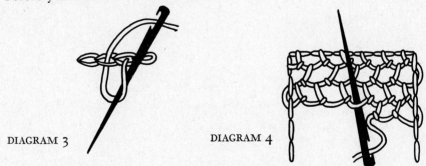

DIAGRAM 3   DIAGRAM 4

Trellis Stitch can be used in this manner very effectively for the center of flowers or any other circular shape, and to do so the innermost circle of knots is fixed into a single Chain Stitch and then the spiral continued on around until the size required is obtained. The appearance of this stitch cannot be properly shown in a diagram, so it should be tried at least once.

Because directions are given for working both right and left, no special instructions are needed for the left-hander.

The Triangle Stitch is really two rows of Bosnia Stitch, worked up and down and facing each other. This can be used to create some interesting patterns, particularly by varying the size of stitches and weights of thread. The Triangle can be further enriched by adding an extra stitch of a Chain Stitch or a French Knot in the center of the triangle, or by bisecting the Triangle with Straight Stitches down the middle.

DIAGRAM 1 shows the first step of this stitch being worked, in which the Straight Stitches are laid at regular intervals down the line, with the needle slanting across the back and into position for the next one. DIAGRAM 2 shows the second step, in which the diagonal stitches are laid between the two upright stitches and worked on down the line. DIAGRAM 3 shows the last part of this same journey being worked in the second group of stitches, which completes the Triangle.

FIGURE 1 shows a row of these stitches completed in varying sizes to give an interesting design, and FIGURE 2 shows the stitches with an added stitch for a little more interest.

There are no special directions for the left-hander because of the up-and-down nature of this stitch.

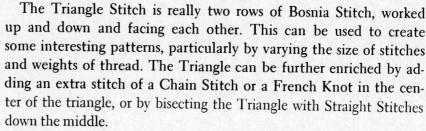

DIAGRAM 1

DIAGRAM 2

DIAGRAM 3

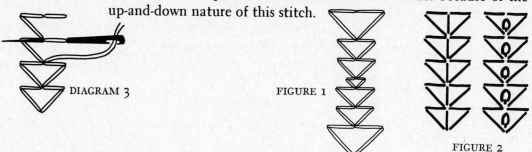

FIGURE 1

FIGURE 2

301 · TURKEY KNOT STITCH
(TURKEY WORK, GHIORDES KNOT STITCH)

From the title you might suspect that this stitch is used in making rugs, and it is. The Oriental and Far Eastern rugs were all made on a fabric ground, and this stitch was used on many. It is in common use in Canvas Embroidery these days. In surface stitchery it is most effective for a tight fuzzy effect, with depth to it. If the stitches are done close enough together and closely trimmed, this stitch gives the effect of a thick velvet.

The working is begun on the front of the piece—it anchors itself down, one of the beauties of this stitch. However, it eats up thread, and you must work in continuous lines without stopping to change thread. In the diagrams in this book the loops are shown worked above, but the loops may be worked so they fall in either direction, either above or below, determined by whether you are filling your shape from the top down or the bottom up. Obviously it will be awkward if the loops are in your way, so that if you are filling your design from the top down, you leave the loop *above* the row, and if you were starting at the bottom, the loops should lie *below* your tie-down stitches. The diagram turned upside down will give you the appearance and the action of the needle and thread as you work your loops below.

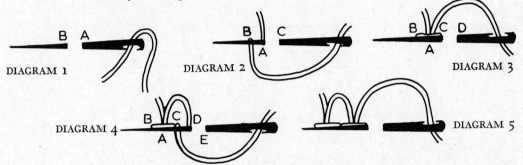

DIAGRAM 1   DIAGRAM 2   DIAGRAM 3   DIAGRAM 4   DIAGRAM 5

DIAGRAM 1 shows the needle inserted at A and emerging at B, a short distance to the left—the distance determined by the weight of thread you are using. The working thread is pulled on through, and the tail end of the thread is left on the front of the fabric. This is shown in DIAGRAM 2, standing up above the line, emerging from A. The working thread then emerges from B, and the needle is inserted at C and brought out to the left at A, forming the same size stitch as AB. This time the working thread is held down below the line, and when the needle is pulled through, it is pulled up tight.

DIAGRAM 3 shows the next stitch in the group being formed, again inserted at the right—being the same size as the other stitches formed—and emerging at C with the thread held above the working line. This time the thread is not pulled up tight—a loop is left. If it helps you to keep these loops uniform, use a knitting needle or a thin straight edge to work the loop over.

DIAGRAM 4, E-to-B shows the loop being left. I have found that, with a little practice, you can leave the loop over the tip of your left thumb while you are forming your next tie-down stitch. This stitch is pulled up tight, anchoring the previous loop. Another stitch of the same size is taken to the right, and again the loop is left above the line (DIAGRAM 5). You continue across the row, making these alternate stitches, first one above the line and then one below, and if your loops are being left above the line, the lower stitches are the ones that will be pulled up tight.

Figure 1 shows a finished row of these stitches worked. You will note, on the right-hand end of Figure 1, the dotted line indicates where the top of the loop has been cut. As a rule, you don't clip your loops until the entire area has been worked. That way you can keep them all an equal length. Sometimes in the clipping, it helps to go along and first cut just through the top of the loop, then clip them off at the top, to keep them level. Figure 2 shows the way to get the tightest effect from your solid work. If you look closely, you will see that the loops of the row in the back have been worked alternately to those of the row in the foreground. The loops in the back row are formed between the stitches that form the tie-down in the front row, so that every space is filled in. When these are clipped—particularly with wool—the top fluffs out and gives a good solid filling, even though you may have left a slight space between the rows when working.

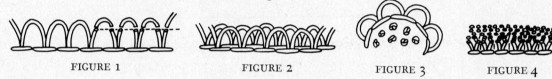

FIGURE 1   FIGURE 2   FIGURE 3   FIGURE 4

Figure 3 shows a way of using this stitch, particularly effective in heavy thread. The stitches are forming loops around a circle to use as petals on a flower. You can even do several rows of this for a layered effect on flowers.

Figure 4 shows an area of stitches that have been clipped. They have been worked tightly and give a nice pile effect. If you enjoy doing animals, this stitch lends itself to fuzzy tails for squirrels, skunks, or bunnies.

The left-hander can follow the directions as given, simply starting work at the other end of the line, the right-hand end.

302 · VAN DYKE STITCH

The Van Dyke Stitch is versatile and fun to experiment with, both as to spacing and threads. Although it is not essential, I find it easiest to work this stitch on a frame, particularly if the pattern is of any size. The action is really quite simple, but a little practice helps to establish the rhythm, which does improve the end result. For beginners, it is best to work between a pair of vertical, parallel guidelines, with the arms all the same length.

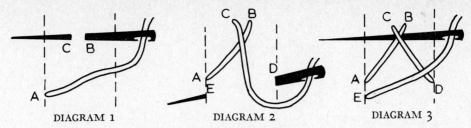

DIAGRAM 1   DIAGRAM 2   DIAGRAM 3

DIAGRAM 1 shows the thread emerging at A on the left line, a short way below the top of the area. This distance will be determined by the weight of your thread and the size of your overall space, but is generally about one-quarter to one-half inch down from the top. The needle emerges at A and is inserted in the center of the shape from right to left, almost like a Back Stitch, between B and C, picking up only a small amount of fabric. It is then carried down and to the right, to be inserted on the right-hand outline at D on the same level as A. The needle is then slanted across the back of the work and emerges at E, just below A.

The next step, shown in DIAGRAM 3, is the needle being carried up and slipped under the cross made by the first stitch, but not going through the fabric. It is then brought down to the right again and inserted just below D at F. Slanting down below the back of the fabric again, it is brought out on the left-hand line below E.

FIGURE 1

FIGURE 2

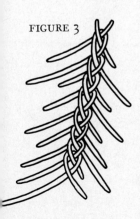

FIGURE 3

The two steps forming the last part of this stitch are repeated right on down the line, resulting in a braid effect down the center, with a little arm coming out to each side. It looks best if the arms have a slant. If you find you are losing this slant, it's a good idea to pick up just a thread or two of fabric underneath the cross as you slide the needle under.

FIGURE 1 shows a series of stitches completed. FIGURE 2 shows the exact same stitch worked with a heavier thread. Shorter arms and stitches directly under each other give a heavy, tight braid effect. FIGURE 3 shows the stitch worked with a little more spacing and arms of irregular length. Thus this stitch, although shown as a band in the working diagram, is useful for shapes of varying widths, lending itself to leaf shapes and flower shapes and working well on contemporary pieces.

Mariska Karasz uses this stitch with great imagination in many of her works. It is a stitch that combines well with the Ladder Stitch and Open Chain Stitch, and her wall hanging "Alchemy" shows this done expertly. By all means experiment with this stitch in all sizes and threads.

A left-hander works by starting on the opposite side of the parallel lines and inserting the needle from left to right under the Cross Stitches.

303 · WAVE STITCH—CLOSED
(LOOPED SHADING STITCH)

This stitch is excellent for allover filling, as well as useful for shading. In the diagram its real effect has been sacrificed to show the working of the needle and thread. When it is actually worked, the stitches should be packed so tightly together that none of the background shows through. When worked with a slight bit of spacing, particularly in wool, the effect is something like knitting.

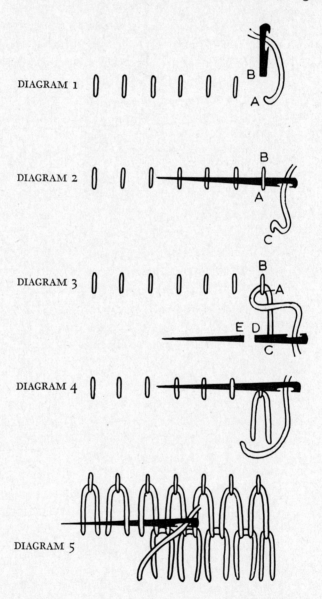

DIAGRAM 1

DIAGRAM 2

DIAGRAM 3

DIAGRAM 4

DIAGRAM 5

316

To start work, first form a row of Straight Stitches, as shown in DIAGRAM 1. Remember that, in the actual working, these should be so close together that they almost touch. When a row of these has been applied to your fabric, your thread is brought out down below, the width of the stitch to be made. The needle is then carried up and slipped under the first stitch without going through the fabric, as shown in DIAGRAM 2. DIAGRAM 3 shows the thread pulled through and the needle back on the level with the stitches being worked. It is inserted at D on the same level with C and emerges a short distance to the left at E. DIAGRAM 4 shows the next loop being formed, the needle again slipped under the straight stitch and not entering the fabric.

Continue across the row, alternating these two movements until you have reached the other end. If you have packed your top row of straight stitches *very* close together, you may want to slip your needle under two of the stitches instead of just one. This will depend on the thread you are using as well as the spacing of your stitches.

DIAGRAM 5 shows the second row being worked. As you can see, the lower action of the stitch is worked the same as the lower action of row 1. However, when the needle is carried up, it is slipped under two legs of two different stitches in the upper row. Note the right end of the diagram. The first stitch is slipped under only the outside leg of the first stitch. This keeps the stitches in order for the rest of the row and also makes it easy to enlarge the area. (If you are trying to make your areas smaller, you simply overlook the first and last legs. However, if you have this in mind, it will be well to insert these outside legs very close to the other legs of the same stitches.)

FIGURE 1

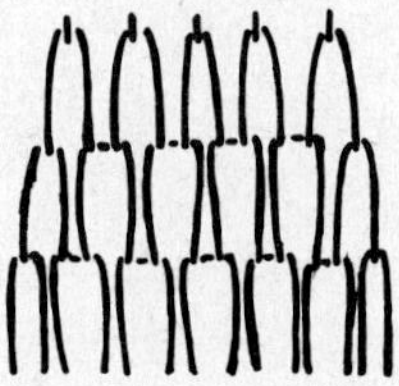

FIGURE 1 shows a group of these stitches worked. Look at the working and try this stitch out, and you will see how convenient it can be for shading purposes.

Left-handers should reverse the direction of working.

317

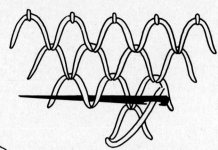

A look at the diagram on this stitch will show you that the actual working is done exactly the same as 303, the Closed Wave Stitch. The main difference is the spacing of the Straight Stitches and the subsequent rows, which are all worked quite openly, to produce a lacy filling. Your Closed Wave Stitch, when it is so tightly packed, can easily be used without an outline of any kind, but the Open Wave Stitch requires some sort of edging to give it a finished look.

Left-handers reverse the direction of working.

305 · WEAVING STITCH
(DARNING, SURFACE DARNING)

This really is just the basic Darning Stitch used in the old days when people still mended socks. In darning you use an egg, but for embroidery, this work is best done on a frame.

The foundation for this stitch is Laid Work, which the diagram shows done vertically, to make the working of the second step a little easier. You can tell by the letters the direction the laid stitches follow. Weaving Stitch shows up best in a fairly heavy thread or with several threads in the needle at the same time. It gives a nice textured effect when done all in the same color. However you can also get a delightful woven or seeded effect when you use a contrasting color for the weaving step.

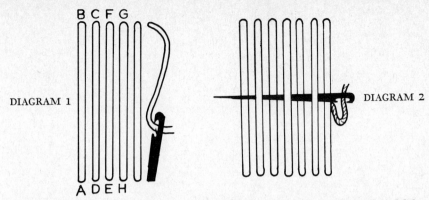

DIAGRAM 1

DIAGRAM 2

DIAGRAM 2 shows the beginning of the weaving, which should be done with a blunt needle as you are going continually in and out of the laid threads. The over-and-under action of the needle shows up clearly in DIAGRAM 2, which also shows where the weaving is begun. As with many of the stitches that cover a long area, there could be a chance of losing your direction. It is best to start this stitch, unless your design is very small, in the center. After the needle has passed over and under the thread, it is pulled on through and inserted in the fabric at the edge where the thread has just emerged, but right next to the laid threads.

Don't pull your working thread tight. You want a firm appearance, but if you give too tight a tug, you will simply draw in the laid threads like a waist, and the overall effect will be most unpleasing. Come up right above where the needle has been inserted, and work back in the other direction, going over threads you previously went under and under threads you previously went over. The needle is again inserted into the fabric when you reach the right-hand edge and brought up just above.

These two journeys are continued until the top of the area is reached. Then the needle is again brought out at the center of the material, and the bottom half of the design is filled.

There are no special directions for the left-hander, for this stitch alternates naturally.

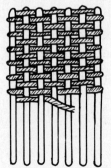

This stitch is a little more versatile than it would at first appear. You can create interesting lines and borders with it and can use it in combination with other stitches for unusual effects. Of course, as the name implies, it makes very realistic ears of wheat. It is also exactly the right shape for the head of a bunny made with line stitches—work a large Chain Stitch at the bottom, and you have it.

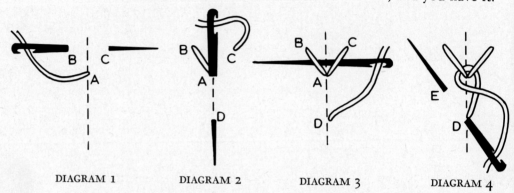

DIAGRAM 1   DIAGRAM 2   DIAGRAM 3   DIAGRAM 4

DIAGRAM 1 shows the beginning of this work at the top of the line. Working from the top down is a must in this stitch. The thread is brought out below the top at A, on the line to be followed. The needle is carried up and to the left of the line and inserted at B. It emerges at C on a level with B, the same distance from the middle line as A (DIAGRAM 1). DIAGRAM 2 shows the slanting stitch formed between A and B, the thread emerging at C and the needle inserted back on the line at A. It is brought out below at D, and the next step is shown in DIAGRAM 3. The needle is passed horizontally under the two slanting stitches just formed, pulled on through, carried down, and again inserted at D. It is brought out to the left at E, directly below B, where the thread is in position to repeat the four steps just taken.

FIGURE 1 shows a row of these stitches worked. Try them as a curved border, remembering to keep the inside slanting stitches a little closer together than the outside ones.

The left-hander reverses the directions but, because of the from-the-top-down nature of this stitch, you still start the same as the right-hander.

FIGURE 1

307 · WHEAT EAR STITCH—DETACHED

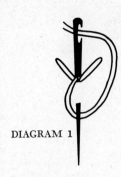

DIAGRAM 1

The Detached Wheat Ear Stitch makes an interesting powdered filling and can be used for small detached stitches. The working of this stitch is completely different from that of the regular Wheat Ear. The two straight stitches are set at right angles, as they are for the ordinary Wheat Ear, but over the base of these two stitches the Detached Chain Stitch is worked (DIAGRAM 1). FIGURE 1 shows an area with these little stitches scattered around as a filling.

The left-hander needs no special directions, for the Chain Stitch is worked in the usual manner.

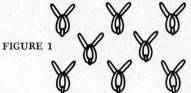

FIGURE 1

308 · WHEAT EAR STITCH—PLAITED

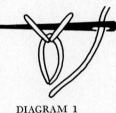

DIAGRAM 1

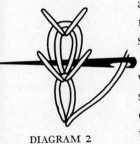

DIAGRAM 2

The Plaited Wheat Ear gives a more interesting effect than actually appears in the diagram. If you want to use the Wheat Ear but give it a more important appearance, do try this stitch. It makes a quite dramatic border when used with a heavier thread.

DIAGRAM 1 shows the work begun in the same manner as for the ordinary Wheat Stitch. However, after the first one is completed, the thread is brought out right below rather than to the side. DIAGRAM 1 shows the needle passing under the Straight Stitches without going through the fabric. The needle is then brought down, and the Straight Stitches out to the side are made in the usual manner. The needle is then carried down, to put the thread in position to form the first loop of the second stitch.

The second stitch is made in the usual manner by slipping the working thread under the straight lines of the base of the previous stitch. When that loop has been completed, the needle is brought out directly below, as shown in DIAGRAM 2. DIAGRAM 2 also shows the needle carried up, slipped *under* the first Straight Stitch on the right, *over* the outside loop, *under* both legs of the small loop in the center, *over* the outside loop again, and *under* the Straight Stitch on the left side. It is pulled on through and inserted down below, then brought out to the left-hand side for starting the Straight Stitches again.

FIGURE 1 shows a group of these stitches worked. A look at the completed stitch will show that the interlacing raises the first chain and depresses the second one.

The left-hander uses the same directions, passing the needle under the threads from left to right for ease of working.

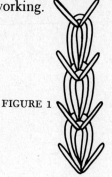

FIGURE 1

309 · WING STITCH

This is a decorative little stitch which makes a nice border or a detached stitch on its own. If you are working a scene with birds, it can be used for a small bird in flight, far in the background. The stitches are worked from left to right and so is the border.

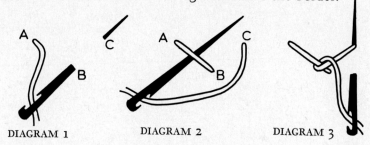

DIAGRAM 1   DIAGRAM 2   DIAGRAM 3

DIAGRAM 1 shows the thread brought out at A. The needle is inserted at B to the right and down, emerging at C, slanting up again to the same level as A. The distance BC is not as long as the distance AB. DIAGRAM 2 shows the thread coming out at C and the needle slipped under the first stitch (AB), from the bottom toward the top, without entering the fabric. After this has been pulled through, the needle is brought out and inserted directly below C, on the same level as B. It emerges at C as in DIAGRAM 3. FIGURE 1 shows a row of these stitches completed.

The left-hander turns the diagrams upside down.

FIGURE 1

The method of working a Striped Woven Band is exactly the same as a Diagonal Woven Band (151), but the arrangement of the colors is different. The foundation is made of laid threads, as shown in DIAGRAM 1.

DIAGRAM 2 shows the working thread of two contrasting colors emerging from the fabric in almost the same spot, just above the first bar on the left-hand side. This entire band is worked with two blunt needles, used alternately but kept threaded all the time. DIAGRAM 2 also shows the lighter shade already slipped under the top bar and over, out of the way, while the dark shade is in the process of going over bar 1, with the needle passed under the second bar to complete that movement. On the next action, the light thread is brought around to the top and laid over the second bar and the needle passed under the third bar.

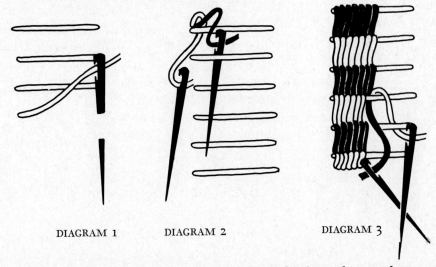

DIAGRAM 1   DIAGRAM 2   DIAGRAM 3

These two colors are passed over and under bars alternately, on down to the end, and finished off. The work is started again at the top as close as possible to the last row, and the needle and thread are worked in rows alternately down the lines of laid threads, all the dark ones going over the same bar and all the light ones over another bar. As can be seen from DIAGRAM 3, the completed band presents alternate stripes of light and dark which lie horizontally across the band.

The left-hander might want to start the working from the right-hand side, but there are no special instructions.

This stitch is not used a good deal, but it does come in handy occasionally for border or band fillings. It is worked in two complete journeys and with some overstitching which the diagrams help to make clearer.

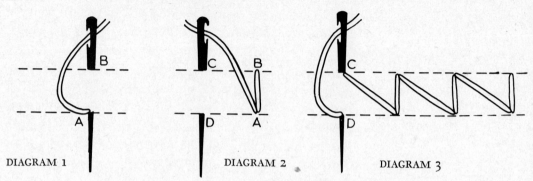

DIAGRAM 1   DIAGRAM 2   DIAGRAM 3

The work is begun at the right-hand end between two parallel lines. After the thread has emerged at A, the needle is inserted at B directly above and brought right out again below at A. Next the needle is carried to the left and inserted on the upper line at C and comes out directly below at D, forming a diagonal stitch between the parallel lines. The thread is then carried up to the top of the line, inserted at C, and brought out again at D, as shown in DIAGRAM 3. DIAGRAM 3 also shows several stitches worked on this first journey between the parallel lines. When the end of the border has been reached, the process is exactly reversed. Again take diagonal stitches, with the needle going in and out twice at the bottom of the upright stitches.

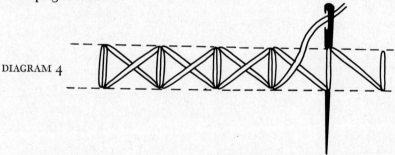

DIAGRAM 4

DIAGRAM 4 shows some of these stitches completed, ending up with oblong crosses and double upright stitches between. It is really a prettier stitch than it appears in the diagram.

The left-hander will probably find the directions easier to follow if he turns the diagram upside down, but the actual working of the stitches has nothing complicated about it.

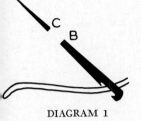

DIAGRAM 1

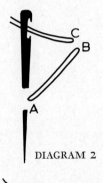

DIAGRAM 2

DIAGRAM 3

I discovered this stitch in a Victorian embroidery magazine and have not seen it elsewhere. It is a sort of fussy little busy work, popular during that period, but in trying it out, I find it does work up into an interesting zigzag border, particularly with fairly heavy thread.

The diagrams pretty much explain the action of the needle and thread, which is worked from the top down. Diagram 1 shows the first of two slanting stitches being formed and the needle emerging, to be in position to start the second slanting stitch. Diagram 2 shows the second stitch being formed parallel to the first one and the needle emerging down a short way below A. The needle is then slipped under the upper straight stitch, not going through the fabric, and pulled on through, but not too tightly.

Diagram 4 shows the needle again passed under the same stitch and also under the loop of the working thread. This is again pulled up, but this time a little tighter. The needle is then inserted just below the base of that stitch. These five actions complete the first section of this stitch.

The needle just inserted goes down below and emerges slanting downward, to be in position to work the same process in reverse on the opposite end of the Straight Stitches. Diagram 6 shows the needle slipped up under the base of the stitch above, to complete the first of the two Straight Stitches. It is pulled on through without entering any fabric. Diagram 4 shows the needle inserted to make the second bar for this stitch. From there on you would go back to steps 3 to 5, to work from where the needle emerges at 7. If it helps, you might turn the diagram over.

Since these two stitches are worked alternately, the left-hander should need no special instructions, but you might want to turn the diagram upside down.

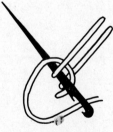

DIAGRAM 4

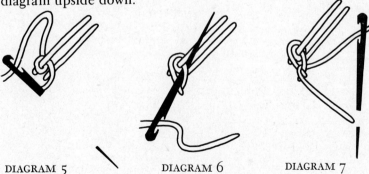

DIAGRAM 5   DIAGRAM 6   DIAGRAM 7

PLATE 5: These eighteenth-century children make enchanting
decorative subjects for pictures, pillows, bedspreads.
Work is basically crewel, but for fine outlines,
some threads are embroidery floss.

PLATE 7: This traditional Jacobean pattern contains 35 embroidery stitches. Changing the colors of threads can change completely the appearance of the design; it can even be stitched in only two colors.

PLATE 6: In this abstract design, rendered entirely in cotton threads, ordinary embroidery stitches are distorted for interesting effects.

PLATE 8: A collection of embroidered pieces that make perfect gifts. "Peace symbol" pillow is completed quickly with heavy yarn and only four stitches. Traditional pillow is worked fast, too, since the design is not continuous but scattered, thus can be expanded or contracted at will. The doorstop, a covered brick, also makes a handsome bookend. Abstract design on satin handbag is worked in silk threads, while traditional designs are applied to modern envelope purses.

Appendix A: Terms Used in Embroidery

A number of terms are used in this and other embroidery books which might be unfamiliar to American needlewomen. Some terms might define a different application than is in common use. Many expressions used or items referred to in British publications, the origin of much of our stitch heritage, go under different titles here.

So to clarify the various types of embroidery without going into an entire how-to section, I have added this glossary of embroidery terms for the reader's assistance.

APPLIED WORK OR APPLIQUÉ

Applied Work or Appliqué, as it is usually called, is an ancient type of decorative work that is still very much in use today. As with most classifications of embroidery, the name is descriptive. It is a method of applying one piece of fabric to another, usually with decorative stitchery. There are two types—onlay and inlay. The names again are descriptive. Onlay work is most common and is simply the placing of one piece of material on top of another and attaching it with stitchery. Much of this is done today by machine, but almost any method of embroidery can be used, incorporating every conceivable type of material from delicate nets or silks to heavy fabric for large hangings. Felt and the new bonded fabrics are popular because they don't fray. Appliqué work gives a maximum effect with a minimum of effort.

Inlay appliqué has been rarely used, except by certain groups such as the San Blas Indians of Panama, until a recent revival. This method requires two or more layers of fabric, worked by cutting away the surface material to expose the color desired. The upper layers must be carefully stitched to anchor, the stitches as near to invisible as possible. The pieces are sometimes further enriched with surface embroidery.

ASSISI EMBROIDERY

Assisi Embroidery is a combination of Cross Stitch and the Holbein Stitch worked in the usual manner, but the principle of design is reversed. Areas of Cross Stitch are worked and edged with Holbein Stitch; however, this is background. The design is left unworked, giving a rather formal appearance to the piece. By using the Two-Sided Cross Stitch, Assisi Work will be the same on both sides.

BATISTE

Batiste was originally a fine linen cambric or lawn. Now it is usually cotton of the same texture and is used in fine embroidery such as White Work.

BLACK WORK

Black Work was originally done by combining various geometric designs, made up of Straight Stitches worked with black silk on white, evenweave linen. It became fashionable during the reign of Henry VIII and continued throughout the sixteenth century. It was thought to have been introduced into England by Catherine of Aragon, and for this reason, it is often referred to as Spanish Work. Authorities have found evidence of earlier use, and many of Holbein's paintings show Black Work in detail. Very few examples have survived, because of the effects of the dye on the silk. It was often worked with the addition of metallic threads and is still done today in Spain with black wool.

Black Work is again in favor, but is usually worked on fabric of loose weave and with cotton embroidery thread. This present interpretation is not as restricted. Earlier work had all the motifs outlined with Holbein Stitch or metal threads. It lends itself very nicely to the present ideas of dress and decorating.

BLUNT NEEDLE

A blunt needle is any needle without a sharp point. It is sold under a variety of names—tapestry needle, yarn needle, and rug needle being a few. When used in the text of this book, the term covers all of these, depending on the size of thread being worked.

BRITISH SATIN

British Satin is a rich-looking cotton fabric. It is of upholstery quality, but has the appearance of satin so it is useful for furnishings of delicate design that will have wear.

BRODERIE ANGLAISE

This delightful, open type of embroidery consists of open spaces of various shapes and sizes. The openings are cut or punched with a stiletto and then overcast. Work is finished off with an edge of scallops. It is also termed Ayrshire, English, Eyelet, Madeira, or Swiss Work.

BULLION

Bullion is metal coil, used in Ecclesiastical Embroidery. It is similar to rough purl but of a larger diameter.

CANDLEWICK

Candlewick is a method of tufting with a heavy, soft cotton thread. The thread is called Candlewick thread and is usually worked on a coarse muslin. It is also referred to in the United States as chenille.

CANVAS

Canvas, when used in connection with embroidery, is a background fabric for Canvas Embroidery. It is not the tightly woven fabric used for tents, sails, and deck chairs. Instead, it is a special background material woven to form regular meshes and falls into two broad classifications: Mono or Single Mesh, and Penelope or Double Mesh. Single Mesh is easier to work, but when you are working two sizes of the same stitch, Penelope weave is needed.

Both types come in a variety of sizes, determined by the number of threads per inch. In this country, the finest to be found is No. 28 (twenty-eight threads per inch), and ranges on up to No. 3. As a rule, any canvas with five or fewer threads per inch is classified as Rug or Quick Point.

CANVAS EMBROIDERY

Canvas Embroidery or Canvas Work is embroidery done on canvas. (See above.) The stitchery originally covered the entire surface, which was woven on linen, flax, or even silk. Today a wide range of meshes (threads per inch) is available, but most of the canvas is woven of hemp or cotton.

This type of work has several misnomers, the most common being "needlepoint." True needlepoint is an embroidery stitch or a type of needle-made lace. "Gros point" is another misused term; it is in fact a type of raised work called Venetian Point and distinguished by the large stitch. "Tapestry work" has also been applied to Canvas Embroidery; the term resulted from the early canvas work done to imitate woven tapestries.

"Needlepoint" and "gros point" are done in a diagonal stitch that covers one intersection of the canvas. "Tapestry work" is done in an upright stitch over horizontal threads. All three of these mistaken identities are worked entirely in one stitch, whereas Canvas Embroidery covers some two hundred stitches.

CHAINED STITCHES

Chained Stitches is a classification often used in needlework schools and textbooks, covering all types of chain stitch. This comprehensive group begins with the simple looped chain and develops through various stages of complexity, finally arriving at ones like the Plaited Braid, which is probably the most intricate of all Chain Stitches.

COMPOSITE STITCHES

Composite Stitches are a large group of stitches whose common classification lies in the fact that they each require two or more stitches for their construction. Usually one forms the foundation, and the other is worked or interlaced upon it. These stitches are beautiful in themselves and create a rich texture without the need of color.

COUNTED THREADWORK

Counted Threadwork is exactly that and must be done on material with an even weave. It is commonly done with Cross Stitch, but is used in other methods of embroidery, including some with geometric patterns such as Black Work. Other types include Hardanger Embroidery, Drawn Fabric, Drawn Thread, Assisi Work, and Canvas Embroidery.

CREWEL EMBROIDERY

Crewel has been mistakenly classed as a type of embroidery when actually it is a type of thread. Crewel thread is a very fine two-ply wool, which has not so far been successfully produced in the United States. It can be used effectively with other thread, but then it becomes embroidery or stitchery. A number of companies sell kits called "Crewel," but they contain Persian wool which is made up of threads containing three strands of two-ply wool which isn't as fine or smooth as true Crewel wool. True Crewel wool comes from England and France.

CUTWORK

Cutwork is the name given to forms of embroidery where portions of the background fabric are cut away in various motifs to form the design. Numerous Edging and Insertion Stitches are used to give this work a distinct air of grandeur. The term includes Simple Cutwork, Renaissance, Richelieu, and Italian Cutwork.

DETACHED STITCHES

This group of stitches consists of those worked, as the name implies, without entering the background except for edge anchoring. Usually worked into the previous row, these stitches sometimes require a bit of practice to maintain an even tension. Many of these stitches were adapted from Needle Lace and are not as difficult as the final effect makes them appear.

DRAWN FABRIC WORK

Drawn Fabric Work is not to be confused with Drawn Thread Work. No threads are removed in the execution of Drawn Fabric Work. It is easiest to work on a frame on a coarse evenweave, preferably linen or scrim.

A blunt needle is used with a working thread of approximately the same weight, color, and texture as the background material. Various patterns are formed by pulling groups of threads together, resulting in some delightful, lacy appearances. This work has enjoyed a revival recently, with the patterns done on a large scale. With the new fabrics, Drawn Fabric Work can result in dramatic curtain or wall hangings, especially if there is subtle plaid involved.

DRAWN THREAD WORK

Drawn Thread Work is just that. Several distinctive types, known by their individual names, come under this heading: Needleweaving, Hardanger, and Hedebo. A fabric with a distinct weave is needed, and threads are carefully cut and drawn. The various methods of working are described under the individual headings.

The original work was of a delicate lacelike nature, but when employed with the bolder fabrics of today, it can have quite exciting results.

ECCLESIASTICAL EMBROIDERY

Ecclesiastical Embroidery, stitchery done for churches, includes Gold Work, Canvas Embroidery, White Work, and regular embroidery. The type of work would depend on the use of the article, just as in the home or on wearing apparel.

EDGING

Edging usually refers to a type of stitch that gives a finished edge to a project. Some of these, such as the Buttonhole Stitch, include the hemming process also, and others are purely decorative on a hem that has been completed in some other manner.

EMBROIDERY

According to Merriam-Webster, Second Edition, embroidery is "The art or process of embroidering or ornamenting cloths, leather, etc., with needlework." This includes all the many types of surface enrichment worked on numerous background materials.

EVENWEAVE

Evenweave is a fabric, originally linen, which has threads of equal size and number in both directions. When sold, it is classified by the threads per inch, which means the number of threads woven in each direction. Evenweave is used for Counted Thread Work, and the number of threads per inch regulates the size of the stitches.

FILLING

Filling is another descriptive term, meaning the filling of an area, either background or design, with some method of embroidery. Some stitches are classified as Filling Stitches, while others, such as a Detached Stitch, can serve the same purpose when worked in groups.

FLAT STITCHES

The Flat Stitches are the simplest of all stitches to form. From a single Straight Stitch, you can develop all the others in this classification. This holds true whether they are placed side by side (Satin Stitch), along a line (Running or Back Stitch), or Overlap (various Cross Stitches).

FOUNDATION THREADS

Foundation Threads refer to embroidery threads, not those of the background. These are really Straight Stitches used to form a foundation layer for some type of pattern or raised stitch.

FRAME

Frames are fully covered in the Introduction. The term is used throughout the book, unless otherwise specified, to cover all types of round or square frames.

GOLD WORK

This rich type of embroidery includes all metalwork—silver, copper, aluminum, and their substitutes. In the books or chapters that describe this type of work, the handling of silk, sequins, and jewels (real or not) is usually covered. This method of embroidery requires a special technique for the handling of threads and should be carefully studied before attempted.

HARDANGER EMBROIDERY

This Drawn Thread Work is world-known and was developed by the people of a district in Norway called Hardanger. It is characterized by little groups of Satin Stitch known as Kloster blocks, which are arranged to form geometric patterns and designs.

HEDEBO EMBROIDERY

Hedebo Emboidery is a Danish type of Drawn Thread Work originating among peasants in an area known as Heden ("the heath"), near Copenhagen. *Bo* means to live—hence Hedebo is the work of the people who live on the heath. It has been somewhat refined or stylized over the years so that some of the peasant qualities were lost, but in recent years, there has been a movement toward reviving the work in its older and purer form.

HEMSTITCHING

Hemstitching is a Drawn Thread method of working borders. It is very effective in itself, but is often used with other Drawn Thread Embroidery. It not only secures the hem and strengthens the edges, but ties together the loose threads in convenient little groups which facilitate the later working of decorative stitches.

HESSIAN

Hessian is the English name for burlap, a rough textured fabric with a fairly loose weave, which is an effective background. It has very poor wearing qualities so it should be reserved for pictures and wall hangings.

HOOP

Hoops are circular frames and covered under that description.

HUCK WEAVING

Huck Weaving is actually Darning patterns worked on a certain type of fabric called huck or huck toweling. This type of work is not being used much at the present time.

INSERTION

Insertion is commonly used in connection with Insertion Stitches. These stitches form decorative methods of holding two separate pieces of material together.

ISOLATED STITCHES

Isolated Stitches are lumped together by the final result rather than by method. Each stitch is completely finished when the steps in the diagram are completed. They can be used as a single stitch, combined with more of the same, or with other stitches. The

French Knot is a good example. It is used singly, in lines, and as a solid filling, and blends beautifully with many other stitches.

JACOBEAN EMBROIDERY

Jacobean Emboidery is characterized by designs rather than method, although it has been often classed with the misnomer "Crewel Embroidery" in recent years. In seventeenth-century England, embroidery with Crewel wool and "grotesque, exotic" motifs from the Orient, coupled with birds, beasts, butterflies, and plants, gained wide popularity. The dominant motif was the Tree of Life theme, combined with symbols of the Stuart and Tudor families (carnation and rose) along with new discoveries—the strawberry and potato flower.

Jacobean Embroidery was carried over to America by immigrants, although lack of wool and dyes made it difficult to do well. The motifs were less standardized than in England, local nature being drawn upon for designs—a deer was used in place of the stag, for instance.

In England, every type of stitch was used, as well as silk thread, but in America, the stitches were limited to those that showed on the surface and were not wasted on the under side. It was traditionally worked on strong linen twill in bright colors without regard to nature.

KNOTTED STITCHES

Knotted Stitches form an interesting group. They add texture and dimension in contrast to the smoother stitches. They may be used singly, in lines, and as fillings both open and closed, giving a rich irregular surface.

LINEN TWILL

Linen Twill is a tightly woven fabric, usually natural in color, that is very durable. It is used, as a rule, in traditional Crewel and Jacobean Embroidery.

LOOP STITCHES

Loop Stitches, as a group, bridge the gap between Flat Stitches and Chained Stitches, and they consist mainly of Buttonhole variations. There is no evidence of their use in medieval work, probably because all work was then done in a frame. Loop Stitches are by nature hand stitches, and the use of the thumb in the working is indispensable.

MOUNTMELLICK EMBROIDERY

Contrary to other forms of White Work, Mountmellick Embroidery is of a bold, coarse effect with no cutwork or drawnwork. It's really stitchery in relief and more realistic than stylized in design. Both background material and working thread are coarse.

NEEDLE LACE

Needle Lace, as the name suggests, is work with a needle and a single thread. It can be considered as a derivative of openwork or cutwork, and its stitches are made up of those as well as Insertion Stitches and many of the detached stitches used in surface embroidery. It is usually worked on a foundation of parchment which is later removed.

NEEDLE WEAVING

Needle Weaving is a form of Drawn Thread Work, and the name describes the method. The process is the same as that diagrammed in the Needle Weaving Stitch (No. 244), but various designs can be achieved by voiding areas or changing the color of the working thread.

It makes a strong border and is an ancient method of decoration. Examples have been found in Egyptian tombs, dating back over three thousand years.

OPEN FILLING

Open Filling is a term used to describe the covering of an area in which the background material is a part of the overall effect. This should not be confused with Powdered Filling. Open Filling is a continuous stitch worked in a manner that allows the background to show.

OPUS ANGLICANUM

The Ecclesiastical Embroidery of thirteenth-century England was renowned throughout the civilized world. The Medieval or Underside Couching of gold threads was largely responsible. The few examples remaining today are regarded with respect when it is remembered that this work was all done without the aid of steel needles.

PEARL COTTON

Pearl Cotton thread is mercerized and tightly twisted. This produces a nice gloss and a firm working thread. It comes in a variety of colors and several sizes.

PICKING

Picking describes very aptly the process for removing unwanted stitchery. Thread is seldom reusable after having been worked, so that the fastest method is to clip carefully with scissors and pick out. I find a pair of tweezers with scissorlike handles an asset if the area is of any size.

PICOT

Picot is a little loop ornamentation, usually buttonholed, used on Edging Stitches and in Open Work Embroidery.

PLAITING

Plaiting is an old-fashioned word for braiding, which can mean the intertwining of threads by hand to form an individual strip with a woven texture, or can be used to describe a stitch done with a needle and single thread to produce a braidlike effect on background fabric.

POWDERED FILLING

Powdered Filling is the technique of filling a space with Isolated Stitches scattered around, usually to form a pattern. However, the Seed Stitch and French Knots often go from closely spaced to more open to give dimension to an area.

PURL

When used in surface stitchery, this term refers not to the knitting stitch but to a smooth metal coil. These coils come in long strips, tightly coiled up like a spring. They are cut into smaller sections and couched down in gold work. Purls come in different sizes and textures. Other types have special names such as Check Purl, Pearl Purl, and Rough Purl.

RENAISSANCE EMBROIDERY

This type of cutwork goes a bit beyond simple cutwork in that bars are introduced. Open spaces are left between the motifs on the design, and these are filled with bars of thread which are worked over with the Buttonhole Stitch and sometimes the Spider Web. The whole appearance is more open and lacy than simple cutwork.

RICHELIEU EMBROIDERY

Richelieu Embroidery is really Renaissance Embroidery with Picots added to the bars to give a richer result. The two are sometimes confused.

RYA WORK

Rya Work is done on a special Rya canvas using the Turkey Knot Stitch. There are usually several strands of wool in the needle, and it can be worked with or without a gauge. This produces a shaggy pile, which can be trimmed to various lengths for sculptured effects. Rya wool has a high luster, and when it is used with three threads in the needle at once, unique shadings can be achieved. Rya Work is in wide use at the present time in pillows, rugs, and wall hangings.

SCRIM

Scrim is a fabric that was originally of a gauzelike quality. The term is applied to many loosely woven fabrics at present, but in general, refers to linen scrim, similar to evenweave.

SHADOW WORK

Shadow Work, as the name would imply, is done on fine fabric such as lawn or organdy, which allows the stitching on the underside to show through. Closed Herringbone is generally used in this work, and it is sometimes combined with delicate appliqué.

SMOCKING

Smock is derived from the Anglo-Saxon word meaning "shift," "chemise," or "shirt." It was originally peasant work, as these loose tunics were worn by the men who worked in the fields and villages. Several types of Stem and Chevron Stitches make up the various patterns used in Smocking.

SPANISH WORK—see BLACK WORK

STILETTO

The embroidery stiletto is an implement used when working with metal threads. Originally, it was a handle with a screw on the end so a needle could be inserted and made firm. Today stilettos have wooden or plastic handles with metal points already attached. The stiletto resembles a small ice pick and is used for piercing holes in the background fabric so that the metal threads can be inserted.

STUFF

Stuff is a term found in very old embroidery books or periodicals and covers any kind of background material.

TAMBOUR WORK

Tambour work, or Tambour Crochet, is a combination of techniques done on a frame. Tambour is French for "drum," later for "hoop," and our round frames were originally called that. Tambour Work is a technique developed in China, as were round hoops, and introduced into Europe about the middle of the nineteenth century.

The fabric must be tightly stretched on a frame. The implement used looks like a very fine rug hook; it has a wooden handle with a metal tip shaped like a crochet hook. A thimble of unusual shape is often worn to accelerate the action. The thread is held underneath in the left hand, and the hook above in the right. The hook pierces the fabric, and the thread is pulled to the surface, forming a Chain Stitch which can be worked continuously.

Originally, this work was done on a fine white fabric with a firm white thread. It is widely used in India now for "crewel" work, sold by the yard, on a coarse cotton fabric and colored wool threads.

The same method is also used for beading. The underside is the right side in this case, and the beads are strung on the working thread, pushed up one at a time with the left thumb as each stitch is made.

TAPESTRY—*see* CANVAS EMBROIDERY

TIE-DOWN STITCHES

Tie-Down Stitches are just that; usually small stitches at the end of a series of stitches to carry the thread to the back of the work so it can be finished off.

VENETIAN EMBROIDERY

Venetian Embroidery is a form of cutwork that has more padding under the embroidery and is therefore a more ornate version of Richelieu Embroidery.

VOIDING

Voiding in embroidery is employed in areas to achieve certain effects. The Chinese use it with great artistry in their silk work. Very fine lines of fabric are left between areas of Satin Stitching to produce a remarkable appearance.

WHITE WORK

White Work originally referred to delicate embroidery on fine white fabric, usually with some cutwork included. Now the name covers any white-on-white method of embroidery.

WAX

Wax refers to Beeswax which is used on silk thread. The thread is pulled across a cake of wax to strengthen it so that it won't fray or break when working on metal threads.

Appendix B: Cross-Reference of Stitch Names

The stitches have been placed in alphabetical order throughout, in text and index, under the name that is in most common use at the present time. In some cases this might mean a sacrifice of a title that is more technically correct, but then our nomenclature changes as time passes. I believe the term "plait" is still used in England but many Americans don't even know the term and would refer to such a technique as "braid."

Some stitches have a number of different names. In other instances the same name has been applied to two or more different stitches. It was felt that, for this book to be of practical use, a person should be able to look up the title he is familiar with as quickly as possible.

The cross-reference lists every alternate stitch known, in alphabetical order, with the title used in this book following.

Antique Stitch	ROMANIAN STITCH
Anundsjö	SPLIT STITCH—SWEDISH
Arrowhead Cross Stitch	CROSS STITCH—ITALIAN
Beaded Stitch	CORAL STITCH
Block Shading Stitch	SATIN STITCH—ENCROACHING
Brier Stitch	THORN STITCH
Bullion Bar Stitch	INSERTION STITCH—BAR
Catch Stitch	HERRINGBONE STITCH
Caterpillar Stitch	BULLION STITCH
Chained Feather Stitch	FEATHER STITCH—KNOTTED
Checkered Stitch	CHAIN STITCH—CHECKERED
Chinese Stitch	CROSS STITCH—ORIENTAL
Coil Stitch	BULLION STITCH
Coral Knot	CORAL STITCH
Cordonnet Stitch	RUNNING STITCH—WHIPPED
Crewel Stitch	STEM STITCH
Crossed Fly Stitch	FLY STITCH—FILLING
Darning Stitch	BURDEN STITCH—TRADITIONAL
Double Back Stitch	HERRINGBONE STITCH—CLOSED
Double Pekinese Stitch	CRETAN STITCH—LACED
Double Running Stitch	HOLBEIN STITCH
Dot Stitch	SEED STITCH
Embroidery Stitch	LONG AND SHORT STITCH
Faggot Filling Stitch	SHEAF FILLING STITCH

Faggoting	INSERTION STITCH—CRETAN
Feather Stitch	LONG AND SHORT STITCH
Figure Stitch	COUCHING—ROMANIAN
French Dot	FRENCH KNOT
German Interlacing Stitch	HERRINGBONE STITCH—LACED
German Knot Stitch	CORAL STITCH
Ghiordes Knot Stitch	TURKEY KNOT STITCH
God's Eye	SPIDER WEB—LOZENGE
Gordian Knot Stitch	BRAID STITCH
Herringbone Stitch—Raised	HERRINGBONE STITCH—PLAITED
Holy Point	HOLLIE STITCH
Holy Stitch	HOLLIE STITCH
Indian Filling Stitch	ROMANIAN STITCH
Interlaced Band Stitch	CRETAN STITCH—LACED OR HERRINGBONE STITCH—LADDER FILLING
Italian Couching	FRILLED COUCHING
Kensington Outline Stitch	SPLIT STITCH
Knot Stitch	BULLION STITCH OR EDGING STITCH—ANTWERP
Knotted Stitch	CORAL STITCH OR FRENCH KNOT
Knotted Blanket Stitch	EDGING STITCH—ANTWERP
Ladder Stitch	CHAIN STITCH—OPEN
Laid Stitch	COUCHING—ROMANIAN
Lazy Daisy Stitch	CHAIN STITCH—DETACHED
Leviathan Stitch	CROSS STITCH—DOUBLE
Line Square	HOLBEIN STITCH
Link Stitch	CHAIN STITCH—KNOTTED
Long Armed Feather Stitch	CRETAN STITCH OR FEATHER STITCH—SPINE
Looped Shading Stitch	WAVE STITCH—CLOSED
Looped and Tied Stitch	CRETAN STITCH—LACED
Magic Stitch	CHAIN STITCH—CHECKERED
Medieval Couching	COUCHING—UNDERSIDE
Mexican Stitch	CLOUD FILLING STITCH
Mussul Stitch	HERRINGBONE STITCH
New England Laid Stitch	NEW ENGLAND STITCH
Old English Knot Stitch	DOUBLE KNOT STITCH
Open Loop Stitch	FLY STITCH
Oriental Stitch	COUCHING—ROMANIAN OR ROMANIAN STITCH
Outline Stitch	STEM STITCH
Overlaid Stitch	COUCHING—ROMANIAN
Overlapping Herringbone Stitch	FISHBONE STITCH—RAISED
Palestrina Stitch	DOUBLE KNOT STITCH

Persian Stitch	CRETAN STITCH
Pessante Stitch	DARNING STITCH—DOUBLE
Plaited Slav Stitch	CROSS STITCH—LONG ARMED
Plumage Stitch	LONG AND SHORT STITCH
Puerto Rico Stitch	BULLION STITCH
Post Stitch	BULLION STITCH
Roll Stitch	BULLION STITCH
Roman Stitch	COUCHING—ROMANIAN
Russian Cross Stitch	HERRINGBONE STITCH
Russian Stitch	HERRINGBONE STITCH
Sampler Stitch	CROSS STITCH
Scroll Stitch	CORAL STITCH
Seed Filling Stitch	SEED STITCH
Shading	LONG AND SHORT STITCH OR STEM STITCH—FILLING, SOLID
Single Coral Stitch	FEATHER STITCH
Single Knot Line Stitch	SCROLL STITCH
Slanted Feather Stitch	FEATHER STITCH
Smyrna Stitch	CROSS STITCH—DOUBLE OR DOUBLE KNOT STITCH
Snail Trail	CORAL STITCH
Spanish Coral Stitch	CHAIN STITCH—CRESTED
Speckling Stitch	SEED STITCH
Spider Web—Ribbed	SPIDER WEB—WHIPPED
Spine Stitch	CRETAN STITCH—LONG ARMED
Stalk Stitch	STEM STITCH
Stroke Stitch	STRAIGHT STITCH OR HOLBEIN STITCH
Surface Darning	WEAVING STITCH
Square Boss Stitch	RAISED KNOT STITCH
Square Stitch	CHAIN STITCH—OPEN
Tapestry Shading Stitch	LONG AND SHORT STITCH
Tied Coral Stitch	DOUBLE KNOT STITCH
Tied Stitch	FLY STITCH
Trailing Stitch	COUCHING—SATIN
Turkey Work	TURKEY KNOT STITCH
Twisted Knot Stitch	FRENCH KNOT
Two-sided Line Stitch	HOLBEIN STITCH
Two-sided Stroke Stitch	HOLBEIN STITCH
Van Dyke Chain Stitch	CHAIN STITCH—ZIGZAG
Wheel Stitch	BUTTONHOLE STITCH—WHEEL
Worm Stitch	BULLION STITCH
Y Stitch	FLY STITCH

Appendix C: Suggested Uses of Embroidery Stitches

This classification of the stitches is merely a guideline. Many of the border stitches can be used as a line. The outline stitches are generally worked as a single outline but can be combined with other stitches to form borders or to fill motifs. Rows of various line stitches, when worked side by side, form a solid filling. An isolated stitch can be used to fill an area and thus becomes an open or solid filling.

Don't limit yourself. If the stitch is listed under only one category, prove it can be used in other ways. Then record this either on your sampler or by notations in your book.

In a few cases a whole group of stitches is lumped together under one heading, such as Insertion or Couching.

BROAD LINE AND BORDER STITCHES

Arrowhead Stitch
Back Stitch—Threaded
Back Stitch—Threaded, Double
Back Stitch—Triple
Back Stitch—Triple, Closed
Basket Stitch
Basque Stitch
Bosnia Stitch
Braid Stitch
Braid Stitch—Plaited
Breton Stitch
Blanket Stitch
Buttonhole Stitch
Buttonhole Stitch—Alternating
Buttonhole Stitch—Closed
Buttonhole Stitch—Crossed
Buttonhole Stitch—Double
Buttonhole Stitch—Knotted
Buttonhole Stitch—Raised Band
Buttonhole Stitch—Raised Edge
Buttonhole Stitch—Spiral
Buttonhole Stitch—Tailor's
Buttonhole Stitch—Threaded
Buttonhole Stitch—Whipped
Buttonhole Stitch—Zigzag
Chain Stitch—Cable, Double
Chain Stitch—Cable, Zigzag
Chain Stitch—Crested
Chain Stitch—Crested, Zigzag
Chain Stitch—Crossed
Chain Stitch—Double

Chain Stitch—Double, Alternating
Chain Stitch—Double, Crested
Chain Stitch—Double, Linked
Chain Stitch—Double, Tied
Chain Stitch—Double, Whipped
Chain Stitch—Feathered
Chain Stitch—Heavy
Chain Stitch—Hungarian Braid
Chain Stitch—Interlaced
Chain Stitch—Ornate
Chain Stitch—Raised Band
Chain Stitch—Raised Band, Linked
Chain Stitch—Raised Band, Twisted
Chain Stitch—Raised Band, Variations
Chain Stitch—Rick-Rack
Chain Stitch—Rosette
Chain Stitch—Shell
Chain Stitch—Singhalese
Chain Stitch—Spine
Chain Stitch—Threaded
Chain Stitch—Triple
Chain Stitch—Twisted, Alternating
Chain Stitch—Twisted, Barred
Chain Stitch—Twisted, Lace Border
Chain Stitch—Twisted, Open
Chain Stitch—Twisted, Tied Ladder
Chain Stitch—Twisted, Zigzag
Chevron Stitch
Chevron Stitch—Double
Chevron Stitch—Pagoda
Chevron Stitch—Raised
Coral Stitch—Zigzag

Couching—Fancy
Couching—Frilled
Couching—Loop
Couching—Pendant
Couching—Raised Band
Cretan Stitch
Cretan Stitch—Catch
Cretan Stitch—Chained
Cretan Stitch—Closed
Cretan Stitch—Crossed
Cretan Stitch—French
Cretan Stitch—Irish
Cretan Stitch—Laced
Cretan Stitch—Long-Armed
Cretan Stitch—Open
Cretan Stitch—Reversed
Cretan Stitch—Scotch
Cretan Stitch—Splayed
Cretan Stitch—Triple
Cross Stitch—Enriched
Cross Stitch—Italian
Cross Stitch—Knotted
Cross Stitch—Long Armed
Cross Stitch—Montenegrin
Cross Stitch—Oriental
Cross Stitch—Two Sided
Cross Stitch—Two-trip
Diagonal Woven Band
Diamond Stitch
Diamond Stitch—Knotted
Feather Stitch
Feather Stitch—Closed
Feather Stitch—Double
Feather Stitch—Egyptian

Feather Stitch—Floral
Feather Stitch—Inverted
Feather Stitch—Knotted
Feather Stitch—Plaited
Feather Stitch—Raised Band
Feather Stitch—Single
Feather Stitch—Spanish Knotted
Feather Stitch—Spine
Feather Stitch—Straight
Feather Stitch—Swinging
Feather Stitch—Triple
Feather Stitch—Zigzag
Fern Stitch
Fishbone Stitch
Fishbone Stitch—Open
Fishbone Stitch—Raised
Flat Stitch
Fly Stitch
Fly Stitch—Broad Double
Fly Stitch—Chained
Fly Stitch—Closed
Fly Stitch—Double
Fly Stitch—Interlaced
Fly Stitch—Plaited
Fly Stitch—Reversed
Fly Stitch—Whipped
Four Sided Stitch
Four Sided Stitch—Italian
French Knot—Border Stitch
French Knot—Buttonhole
Guilloche Stitch
Herringbone Stitch
Herringbone Stitch—Closed
Herringbone Stitch—Crisscross
Herringbone Stitch—Double
Herringbone Stitch—Laced
Herringbone Stitch—Ladder
         Filling
Herringbone Stitch—Plaited
Herringbone Stitch—Square
Herringbone Stitch—Threaded
Herringbone Stitch—Tied
Herringbone Stitch—Triple
High Pyramid Chain Stitch
Laced Knot Stitch
Ladder Stitch
Lattice Band Stitch
Leaf Stitch
Loop Stitch
Needle Weaving Stitch
Overlap Stitch
Pearl Stitch
Pekinese Stitch
Petal Stitch
Portuguese Border Stitch

Rope Stitch
Romanian Stitch
Running Stitch—Threaded
Satin Stitch—Twisted
Sheaf Stitch
Sheaf Stitch—Italian
Sorbello Stitch
Stem Stitch—Alternating
Step Stitch
Surprise Chain Stitch
Thorn Stitch
Triangle Stitch
Van Dyke Stitch
Wheat Ear Stitch
Wheat Ear Stitch—Plaited
Winged Stitch
Woven Band—Striped
Zigzag Stitch
Zigzag Stitch—Spanish Knotted

OUTLINE STITCHES

Back Stitch
Back Stitch—Threaded
Back Stitch—Whipped
Basque Knot Stitch
Blanket Stitch
Buttonhole Stitch
Buttonhole Stitch—Closed
Buttonhole Stitch—Crossed
Buttonhole Stitch—Spiral
Buttonhole Stitch—Tailor's
Buttonhole Stitch—Whipped
Chain Stitch
Chain Stitch—Back Stitched
Chain Stitch—Broken
Chain Stitch—Broad
Chain Stitch—Cable
Chain Stitch—Cable, Knotted
Chain Stitch—Cable, Knotted,
         Variation
Chain Stitch—Cable, Open Round
Chain Stitch—Cable, Portuguese
Chain Stitch—Cable, Slipped
Chain Stitch—Cable, Slip Up
Chain Stitch—Checkered
Chain Stitch—Knotted
Chain Stitch—Open
Chain Stitch—Twisted
Chain Stitch—Whipped
Chinese Knot
Coral Stitch
Couching
Couching—Satin
Double Knot

Holbein Stitch
Overcast Stitch
Overcast Stitch—Detached
Palestrina Knot Stitch—Reversed
Pearl Stitch
Pekinese Stitch
Running Stitch
Running Stitch—Whipped
Scroll Stitch
Split Stitch
Stem Stitch
Stem Stitch—Alternating
Stem Stitch—Long
Stem Stitch—Portuguese
Stem Stitch—Whipped

EDGING STITCHES

Blanket Stitch
Buttonhole Stitch
Buttonhole Stitch—Closed
Buttonhole Stitch—Crossed
Buttonhole Stitch—Knotted
Buttonhole Stitch—Raised Edge
Buttonhole Stitch—Tailor's
Buttonhole Stitch—Whipped
Edging Stitch—Antwerp
Edging Stitch—Armenian
Edging Stitch—Braid
Edging Stitch—Looped
Edging Stitch—Plaited
Edging Stitch—Picot, a, b, c, d, and e

INSERTION STITCHES

Insertion Stitch—Bar
Insertion Stitch—Buttonhole
Insertion Stitch—Cretan
Insertion Stitch—Italian Buttonhole
Insertion Stitch—Knotted
Insertion Stitch—Laid
Insertion Stitch—Plaited
Insertion Stitch—Twisted
Interlacing Stitch
Laced Edge Stitch

ISOLATED STITCHES

Algerian Eye
Bullion Stitch
Buttonhole Stitch—Wheel
Chain Stitch—Detached
Chain Stitch—Detached, Long-Armed
Chain Stitch—Detached, Slipped
Chain Stitch—Russian
Chain Stitch—Twisted, Detached

Chinese Knot
Cross Stitch—Double
Crow's Foot Stitch
Ermine Filling Stitch
Fly Stitch
Four Legged Knot Stitch
French Knot
Maltese Cross Stitch
Overlap Stitch
Raised Knot Stitch
Renaissance Stitch
Satin Stitch—Twisted
Seed Stitch
Sheaf Stitch
Sheaf Stitch—Italian
Spider Web—Lozenge
Spider Web—Raised
Spider Web—Ringed
Spider Web—Whipped
Spider Web—Woven
Split Stitch
Star Stitch
Straight Stitch
Wheat Ear Stitch
Wing Stitch

DETACHED FILLING STITCHES

Buttonhole Stitch—Detached
Buttonhole Stitch—Filling, Fancy
Buttonhole Stitch—Filling, Knotted
Buttonhole Stitch—Filling, Open·
Ceylon Stitch
Cretan Stitch—Open Filling
Hollie Stitch
Honeycomb Filling Stitch
Insertion Stitches
Lace Filling Stitch
Lattice Stitch—Twisted
Maltese Cross Stitch
Portuguese Border Stitch
Trellis Stitch

OPEN FILLING

Arrowhead Stitch
Back Stitch—Trellis
Burden Stitch (spaced)
Buttonhole Stitch—Egyptian
Buttonhole Stitch—Filling (spaced)
Chain Stitch—Detached, Filling
Chain Stitch—Russian
Chain Stitch—Twisted, Detached
Cloud Filling
Couching—No. 113 a, e, and f

Cretan Stitch
Cross Stitch
Cross Stitch—Moorish Diagonal
Cross Stitch—Oriental
Crown Stitch
Darning Stitch
Darning Stitch—Japanese
Diamond Stitch—Filling
Diamond Stitch—Knotted
Ermine Filling Stitch
Feather Stitch
Fishbone Stitch—Open
Fly Stitch
Fly Stitch—Filling
Fly Stitch—Plaited
Herringbone Stitch—Double
Holbein Stitch
Japanese Stitch
Ladder Stitch
Laid Work—Couched
Laid Work—Open Filling
Leaf Stitch
Link Filling
Loop Stitch
Seed Stitch
Sheaf Stitch—Filling
Star Stitch
Stem Stitch—French Filling
Straight Stitch
Sword Edging Stitch
Tête-de-Boeuf Stitch
Wave Stitch—Open
Wheat Ear Stitch—Detached

SOLID FILLING

Algerian Eye Stitch
Brick Stitch
Burden Stitch—Recent and
    Traditional
Chain Stitch (solid rows)
Chinese Knot
Coral Stitch (solid rows)
Couching—Bokhara
Couching—Loop
Couching—Pendant
Couching—Romanian
Couching—Underside
Cretan Stitch—Closed
Cross Stitch
Cross Stitch—Italian
Cross Stitch—Two Sided
Cross Stitch—Two Trip
Darning

Darning Stitch—Double
Darning Stitch—Pattern
Double Knot Stitch(solid rows)
Eyelet Stitch
Fishbone Stitch
Fishbone Stitch—Raised
Flat Stitch
Fly Stitch—Closed
Four Sided Stitch
Four Sided Stitch—Italian
Herringbone Stitch
Herringbone Stitch—Closed
Herringbone Stitch—Plaited
Japanese Stitch
Laid Work
Laid Work—Triangle
Long and Short Stitch
New England Stitch
Pekinese Stitch (solid rows)
Rope Stitch
Satin Stitch
Satin Stitch—Counted
Satin Stitch—Padded
Satin Stitch—Surface
Satin Stitch—Whipped
Split Stitch (solid rows)
Stem Stitch—Filling, Solid
Turkey Knot Stitch
Wave Stitch—Closed
Weaving Stitch
Woven Band Stitch

SHADING STITCHES

Brick Stitch
Burden Stitch—Recent and
    Traditional
Buttonhole Stitch—Shading
Chain Stitch (in rows shaded)
Chinese Knot
Cloud Filling
Coral Stitch (rows shaded)
Couching
Cretan Stitch (interlocking rows)
Darning Stitch (in rows shaded)
Double Knot Stitch (in rows shaded)
Laid Work—Shaded
Long and Short Stitch
Romanian Stitch
Satin Stitch—Encroaching
Split Stitch (in rows shaded)
Stem Stitch—Filling, Shaded
Turkey Knot Stitch
Wave Stitch—Closed

Appendix D: List of Suppliers

American Crewel Studio
Box 553
Westfield, N. J.
    Transfers and complete line
    of fabrics and threads.
    Catalog sent on request.

The Embroiderer's Guild
National Headquarters
30 East 60th Street, Room 1505
New York, N. Y. 10022
    Members can receive information
    about Guild branches, teachers,
    and supplies in the United States.

DMC Corporation
Elizabeth, N. J.
    Will furnish name of supplier in
    your area for DMC threads and frames.

Paternayan Bros., Inc.
312 East 95th Street
New York, N. Y. 10028
    Distributor of imported wool
    threads and canvas. Will give
    name of nearest retail store.

Joan Toggitt Ltd.
1170 Broadway
New York, N. Y.
    Threads and backgrounds. Can
    supply name of your local retailer.

Stitch Witchery
Route 10
Denville, N. J. 07084
    Classes and retailer for all
    supplies. No mail order.

Bibliography

To my knowledge this first group of books is no longer being published.

Alford, Lady Marion, *Handbook of Embroidery*. London: 1880.

Brained and Armstrong, *Embroidery*. 1910.

Butterick Publishing Co., *Embroideries and Their Stitches*. New York: 1905.

Christie, Mrs. Archibald, *Samplers and Stitches*. London: Batsford, 1959.

Church, Ella Rodman, *Artistic Embroidery*. 1880.

Day, Lewis F., *Art in Needlework*. London: Batsford, 1900.

Higgin, B. L., *Handbook of Embroidery*. London: Royal School of Art Needlework, 1880.

Huish, Marcus B., LL. B., *Samplers and Tapestry Embroideries*. London: Fine Art Society, Longmans Green and Co., 1900.

James Pearsall Co., *Embroidery*. 1909.

Marshall, Francis and Hugh, *Old English Embroidery*. London: Horace Cox, Windsor House, 1894.

Pesel, Louisa F., *Portfolios*. London: Lund Humphries Co. Ltd., n.d.

Townsend, Paulson, *Embroidery or the Craft of the Needle*. London: Design Master of Royal School of Needlework, 1899.

The following books are books in print.

Anchor Manual of Needlework. Newton Centre, Mass.: Branford, 1958.

Butler, Anne, *Embroidery Stitches*. New York: Frederick A. Praeger, 1968.

Davis, Mildred, *The Art of Crewel Embroidery*. New York: Crown Publishers, 1962.

Ethoven, Jacqueline, *The Stitches of Creative Embroidery*. New York: Reinhold Pub. Co., 1964.

Fry, Gladys Windsor, *Embroidery and Needlework*, 5th ed. London: Sir Isaac Pitman & Sons Ltd., 1959.

Howard, Constance, *Inspiration for Embroidery*. London: Batsford, 1966.

John, Edith, *Creative Stitches*. London: Batsford, 1967.

Filling Stitches. London: Batsford, 1967.

Karasz, Mariska, *Adventures in Stitches*. New York: Funk & Wagnalls, 1949.

Liley, Alison, *The Craft of Embroidery*. London: Mills & Boon Ltd., 1961.

Snook, Barbara, *Needlework Stitches*. New York: Crown Publishers, 1963.

Thomas, Mary, *Dictionary of Stitches*, 16th ed. London: Hodder & Staughton Ltd., 1965.

Mary Thomas's Embroidery Book. 12th ed. London: Hodder & Staughton Ltd., 1964.

Wilson, Erica, *Crewel Embroidery*. New York: Charles Scribner's Sons, 1962.

Index of Embroidery Stitches